THE HOP BROWN-LADY COMETS STORY

By:
Francis Nash

"K.J."
GO Radio

The Hop Brown-Lady Comets Story . . . published by Temoca Press

Copyright © 2003, Francis Nash

Library of Congress Control Number: 2003112878

ISBN: 0-9746145-0-5

TABLE OF CONTENTS

ACKNOWLEDGMENTS

We gratefully acknowledge the cooperation of many in writing this history.

Our *Thanks* to all the folks associated with West Carter High School sports, the Brown family, and all those interviewed in writing this book.

Special Thanks to
Chris Perry for Research Assistance
Ruthie Back for Photographic Design and Pictures (Pictures in text courtesy of Back Photography unless otherwise noted.)
To- Carter Co. Broadcasting Co. (WGOH-WUGO)
for sponsorship
Cover–Tim Harris print, John Flavell photo (The Independent)
Ruthie Back photo

All profits from the sale of this book, are being donated to the Hop Brown Scholarship Fund

About the Author

Francis Nash is general manager of WGOH-WUGO, TV–31 Grayson, Ky, having worked at the station since 1966, where among his duties were play-by-play sports. He received his Bachelors degree at Kentucky Christian College and holds three post-graduate degrees from Morehead State University.

He has also served as minister of Sugar Grove Christian Church in Owingsville, Ky. for 35 years and is Director of Workers for Mexico Christian Mission. He and his wife Pam, have two daughters and five grandchildren.

He is author of the book *Towers over Kentucky, a History of Radio-TV in the Bluegrass State,* and many other journal and magazine articles.

INTRODUCTION

In 1966, WGOH- known as GO Radio, Grayson-Olive Hill, received authority from the government to operate on the FM band and broadcast at night. Immediately plans were made to enable the station, for the first time, to carry local basketball games live for the fans of Carter County.

I was fresh out of high school, attending college, and learning the radio ropes part-time. When it came District tournament time, we prepared to broadcast a game and I was elected to do play-by-play. As a youth, I loved and played all sports and the opportunity to tell about them now on the radio was quite exciting.

As a rock 'n roll disc jockey, I had taken a name that would sound both palatable as a cool jock and a sports announcer. I became Ken Jackson, or K. J. and that stage name remains to this day.

Those broadcasts in March of 1967 marked the beginning of my calling games on the radio for the next 37 years. I have been thankful to be a part of those seasons and each year of West Carter girls basketball and Hop Brown's career.

I first encountered Hop Brown, as a player, while doing the Olive Hill games in 1969 and never knew then where he obtained the nickname, but reasoned in my mind it might have been that great first step, like hopping, as he drove around the opponents.

When he came back to coach the girls, he was attempting to bring some degree of excitement to what was a dull game. He worked hard at it and had the character and virtues to make a difference, as well as the determination to build a winner.

There is no question that Hop Brown helped change the game, and alter the attitude of many a rigid male sports fans, who would have declared then, that girls playing basketball was not worth watching.

When girls basketball arrived on the scene, it was largely ignored by everyone, including the radio, as we had established a pretty intense schedule of carrying the boys games for East and West Carter and really didn't have time or sponsors for the girls. We relented in the first few years and did carry each District girls championship game.

Naturally, trying to follow both county teams, East and West, was tricky with the rival fans accusing us of favoring the other. Every time, as you'd expect, it was the losing school always thinking the radio was favoring the winner. We carried both in equal numbers every year and the temperature of that rivalry measured pretty hot at times.

The competition is still strong, but thankfully a lot of the rancor and bitterness has mellowed and folks try to applaud good efforts on the part of both schools, their players and coaches.

By the mid-80s, Hop Brown was succeeding in changing attitudes and the improvement in the girls basketball skills was becoming obvious. Our FM station had become WUGO and we had decided to do all District and Region tournament games for the girls and also the East and West games during regular season.

The championship play of the Lady Comets soon caused us to add some other regular season games as well, and we have increased the number of live broadcasts through the years, to where it is fairly comparable to the boys. Our station has received many state and national honors for community service, but nothing has been more satisfying than following the Lady Comets and bringing the games to 16th Region fans.

They have taken us to eight Sweet Sixteen tourneys and who could dream of any greater thrill as a sportscaster than announcing . . . "it's over, West Carter is the State Champion!" That joy was especially intense since I had been there since the beginning and witnessed the transformation of the game and the development of the team through the years. The unique format in Kentucky that puts all schools together, regardless of size, to play for the title, made the victory by our small-town school even more dramatic.

Sports thrills have not been mine alone, as other announcers have assisted through the years. My partner, Tom Gemeinhart, has done all the statistics for the games since 1971 and became the best numbers-cruncher in the business. Tim Carper joined the team to help in play-by-play and color in the summer of 2000. Several have filled in play-by-play and done game commentary over the years including Paul Williams, Jeff Cline, Willard Knipp, Terry Kidd, Mike Phillips, Dick Damron, Ron Arnett and Doc Murphy.

At each game, the pre-game and post-game comments from the coaches were a regular feature, and I have to admit the first ones with

Coach Brown created some anxious moments as you never knew what he was going to say, to agree or disagree with you, or come out with a line that would just leave you without a follow-up.

Over the years, though, we came to know one another well and it was an enjoyable experience to talk with the man who loved to coach and loved his girls. Without a doubt, he was the most colorful and cooperative coach one could have the pleasure of working with in a broadcast career.

We often shared good quotes, sports stories, and talked about Cleveland's football prospects, since I had grown up an ardent Browns fan, as was Hop.

While his career was cut short by cancer, Hop cherished and lived every moment he had to the fullest and would be the first to tell you that he was able to see wonderful dreams come true and be blessed in so many ways. To use one of his favorite phrases, his life was "so special."

John Hop Brown left his mark on girls basketball and built a winning tradition at West Carter, including bringing an unlikely State championship to a small town in northeastern Kentucky.

Hop Brown loved his hometown, his school and everything about sports, especially winning. But more importantly, he loved people.

When we watched in 2000, as Kandi Brown hit the final free throws and then jumped into her father's arms to celebrate a State championship, we made reference on the radio to "quite a storybook finish."

Well the time for the -story book- has come.

It is right that his life and the 25 years he spent guiding the West Carter girls be chronicled in this history . . . so what follows in these pages is the **Hop Brown-Lady Comets Story.**

CHAPTER I
THE ANNOUNCEMENT

It was a relatively routine evening at the Brown household in Olive Hill, May 9,1978. Hop was in the downstairs den watching television and listening to the Reds on WGOH radio. Sharon was upstairs attending to some chores but also keeping an ear on the baseball game, when a news bulletin interrupted the play-by-play.

"The Carter Co. Board of Education, meeting tonight, voted 3–2 to employ Jim Webb as head boys basketball coach at West Carter High School, employ Grady Lowe as assistant coach, and to hire John "Hop" Brown as girls basketball coach and head baseball coach at West Carter High for the coming 1978–79 school year," the announcer reported.

"Did you hear that, Hoppy" Sharon yelled. "Yes," was the reply, "But I didn't apply for any girls coaching job. I can't coach girls basketball."

Hop Brown had always dreamed of coaching basketball, and wanted to be the one to direct his beloved "Comets." What were they trying to do, making him coach of the "Lady Comets?"

Hop's first coaching experience had actually come as a seventh-grader at Clark Hill Elementary School. The principal, charged with also coaching the basketball team, that year, often had little time for that duty and left the chore to him. He said the fellow students liked him and he wasn't hard on them. He just tried to keep things organized so they could play ball.

Hop Brown was a sports fanatic and loved to play ball, as far back as he can remember, growing up in a two-bedroom home in the Clark Hill section of Olive Hill, Ky. John Carl Brown was born August 15, 1950, the tenth of eleven children of Bill and Betty Brown. John was born at Stovall Hospital in Grayson, and his mother said the nursery was so crowded they had no beds, and little Johnny spent his first days in a make shift crib—a dresser drawer.

His father passed away of a heart attack when John was just six years old. With little space and money, he had to share the bedroom with his brothers David and Gary during his growing-up years. The other siblings were older—Glen Arnold, George, Janie, Olive, Clell, Maxine, and Nancy Sue, so Hop spent most of his time with his two brothers. Another brother, Jack, died in infancy.

His mother was a very conservative and religious person and wanted her kids to do right, study the Bible and go to church. The family didn't travel much since his mom couldn't afford a car and didn't know how to drive, anyway, and except for an occasional trip to Olive Hill for a ball-game, Hop seldom left Clark Hill. He remembered it as a friendly place, where everyone cared for each other, and kids were cherished.

His older brother David said, "Clark Hill was a great place to grow up, since everyone was pretty equal. All the fathers earned about the same at the brickyard and there were no jealousies and divisions, just a great neighborhood." David, who played baseball himself, believed Hop and Gary developed into good players because they played with older boys all the time.

It was his older sister, Janie, though, who gave John the nickname "Hop" that would endure and identify and endear him in the hearts and minds of folks throughout his life.

While the standard story-line was that he loved Hopalong Cassidy and often mimicked the popular TV cowboy, that wasn't the real reason he first received the name. His sister, one day, watched him drag home after a day of play, looking pretty dirty and ragged, and exclaimed. "Johnny, get in here and clean up, you're looking like Hoppy," referring to a particular fellow known in Olive Hill as seldom cleaning up real well! The "Hoppy" name stuck, but all his life, Janie, was his only relative who actually still called him Johnny.

Hop remembered his father as a truly hard worker, a foreman at the Brickyard in Olive Hill, and not real fond of his boys substituting summer baseball for working in the garden. Some of his harshest scoldings came as a result of playing instead of working. He recalled all-day baseball games in the vacant lot near the house, sometimes with final scores in the hundreds.

His sister, Nancy Sue, the youngest of the Brown girls, was closest in age to Hop and remembered him as a boy who was wonderful at all sports. "He dribbled that basketball from morning til late night, it would take three of us to drag him in after dark, kicking and screaming," she said. Nancy was a cheerleader at Olive Hill, loved sports, and enjoyed watching Hop play until she moved away to Chicago. She called the three younger Brown brothers, "squeaky clean guys, just the best." She remembers her father as being such an outgoing person and sincerely believes that Hop's personality is his dad shining through.

Hop developed a deep love for all sports, especially baseball and basketball, but also followed football. The school system did not have football teams in that day. He became a dedicated fan of Cincinnati Reds baseball and of the Cleveland Browns football team. Those two sports franchises dominated the interest of folks in eastern Kentucky in those days, since the television featured them every weekend. He remembered watching Jim Brown and the Cleveland team every Sunday, and his fondness for them would become an important part of his life, made especially grand since they shared the same name.

His basketball talent was recognized as early as five years old, but his career started as a Clark Hill Elementary School "Hawk." Johnny Parsons had coached Hop at Clark Hill in the 5th and 6th grades, left to go to Erie school for a year, but returned and coached the Hawks to the county championship the next year, when Hop starred as an eighth-grader and led the team in scoring. Parsons said he was one of the most dedicated players he had ever seen, constantly practicing hoops, but at the same time not neglecting his studies. Parsons commented, "Johnny was just a unique kid, one-hundred percent cooperative and one of the best." Hop also played volleyball for Clark Hill and loved that, too, Parsons said. Volleyball, for many years, was a popular county sport for elementary schools until abandoned in the mid-60s.

After grade school, Hop went on to play basketball for the Olive Hill High School Comets of legendary coach Jack Fultz. Andrew Jack Fultz had been a star for Olive Hill in the 1940s and played on the regional championship team in 1944. That year the Comets lost in the semi-finals of the State tournament to Harlan.

Fultz came back as a teacher in 1950 and the next year took over the basketball coaching duties, and developed the Comets into one of the most feared and respected basketball teams in eastern Kentucky. They won the 16th Region championship in 1955,1956, and in 1959. The '59 Comets lost in the Kentucky Sweet Sixteen semi-finals to North Marshall by 2 points, when two starters were hurt early in the second half, denying the Comets a golden opportunity to move on to a state title, a goal the boys would never achieve.

Jack Fultz remembered seeing John Brown as an eighth grader and knowing he was a fine ball player. "What impressed me most, was his confidence," Fultz said. "He wanted the ball and he was the kind of player you wanted to have the ball in those final seconds, because he was going to find a way to get it done. He knew he could do it."

While Hop Brown enjoyed winning seasons under Coach Fultz for three years and then in his senior year of 1968–69 under Coach Bert Greene, he never made it to a regional championship game as a player.

He scored over 1350 points for Olive Hill, and in his senior year, averaged 24.5 points per game, the highest season average of any player in Olive Hill history, surpassing Comet luminaries, Wade Eden and Coach Greene. Besides his ability to score, fans admired his hustle, tenacity, and sheer dedication to winning.

Coach Fultz retired in 1968, after 17 seasons, and later would chronicle the entire history of Olive Hill High School sports through 1971, the last year of the school before consolidation as West Carter. This 800–page volume entitled *"The Comets Tale"* is a sports publication of epic proportions. In that book, Fultz describes Brown's senior year as "phenomenal." "Playing his natural position, guard, he really put on an offensive show, game after game. After a few lessons, administered by Brown, teams started setting their defense to stop him. Most of the time it was of no avail. He simply had the knack of being able to outmaneuver the defense, either getting an open shot or drawing the foul. He earned a position among the all-time greats at guard at OHHS." (page 621)

In a game against Maysville that year, Hop scored 44 points, the third highest single-game mark. Fultz described that game in the book—"His performance was one of the greatest individual shows in Comet history, if not the greatest, considering the caliber of the opposition. It was unbelievable how he ripped through the tough Bulldog defense." (page 617)

Maysville won the game, though, 64–62, and oddly enough, it was the first game Betty Brown, Hop's mother, ever attended. She wasn't much on sports and after the game didn't realize Hop had even scored let alone put on the performance of a lifetime. Hop remembered that she was upset that she saw him rolling on the floor so much. She never attended another game, but Hop played his heart out for her that night. Hop became the object of affection and adoration from the girls and fans after the performance. As for him, he felt angry, because they had lost a game they should have won.

Hop cherished his time playing for Jack Fultz and Bert Greene, saying he had the best of both worlds, with one of the greatest coaches of all time and one of the Comets best players guiding his high school career.

Bert Greene always admired Hop's ability to slash to the basket for the score and his tremendous love and knowledge of the game." Nobody was better than Hop in taking the ball to the basket." He figured Hop for a great coach someday. In later years, Coach Greene said he never thought his accomplishments would be with girls basketball, but he was proud of Hop's hard work for the girls game.

Hop, as an Olive Hill Comet, eyes a free throw, a skill he emphasized to his girls

Hop's younger brother, Gary, would follow him as a prolific scorer for Coach Greene and the Comets, playing two years at Olive Hill and two at West Carter. He produced 1266 points in his junior and senior years at West. Gary and Hop were very close growing up, and Gary has said, "Hop was my idol, I wanted to be like him. He was the best basketball player I'd ever seen."

Hop Brown also satisfied his desire for baseball action as a Comet, playing shortstop, catcher and pitching. It was his ability to hit the long ball that attracted attention, though, as in one game, he hit three homers and narrowly missed a fourth. That prowess as a batsman would later be demonstrated for years in the local softball leagues.

Upon graduation, Hop had hoped to play basketball at Morehead State University, but the school never took an interest in offering a scholarship. Coach Fultz would say years later that he was the "best kept secret" and should have received a scholarship from MSU, because he was better than anyone they had at guard at the time. Some experts may have thought him, a step too slow for a 6'1 guard, to compete on a major college level. He became a freshman at Morehead in the fall of 1969 but decided not to try-out as a walk-on. The University of Cincinnati and Kansas made overtures to Hop about a basketball scholarship, but he never responded, not relishing to travel that far from home.

It was at Olive Hill High School that Hop Brown began dating an attractive blond cheerleader, Sharon James. Their first date, they recalled, was at the Dixie Theatre, where they could take in a show for fifteen cents. They would continue their relationship in college and the high-school sweethearts married on Sept 26, 1970 in a ceremony at the First Christian Church in Olive Hill performed by Dick Damron, the minister, a man who would later play an additional role in their spiritual lives. Damron's church had built a strong youth program that attracted sometimes 60–70 Olive Hill youth to meetings.

Hop and Sharon married as he was about to ship out to the army and training at Fort Knox, Ky. He had been drafted away from his college studies in the newly-enacted lottery system that brought up his number.

Sharon was the only daughter of Clyde and Eunice James, owners of the popular Olive Hill eatery and hang-out, James Drive-In. She had two older brothers, Gary and Larry, but her father had passed away when she was twelve.

By the next Spring, Hop was off to Gelnhausen, Germany. In the summer of 1971, Sharon joined him and brought along their first born child, Kimberly Ann. Hop had been very apprehensive about entering the service and was shocked and disappointed at being drafted. Since, other than a short stint at a summer job near Chicago, he had not been away from Carter County for any length of time, he wasn't positive he could really handle it. But like sports, he was determined to put his heart into the situation and actually learned to like the army and seriously considered a career with the military after his two-year obligation. He remembered entering basic training weighing about 150 pounds, but by the time he received his orders for overseas, tipping the scale at a more muscular 195 pounds.

He also remembered his most upsetting moment at Fort Knox, when a whole troop of recruits began cussing and hollering at him as he jerked them around a truck en route to maneuvers. Hop had been told to take a truckload of men up to a training site on base. The only problem was he had never driven a standard-shift vehicle and although he advised his superior officer of his lack of knowledge, he was told to do it anyway. The tongue-lashings ceased when Hop, applying a combination of coaching and parenting, stopped the vehicle, went back into the truck and told the men, to shut their foul mouths, that he was doing the best he could.

While in Germany, Hop and Sharon lived with Joe Hunter, his tank commander, and later platoon sergeant and a strong friendship developed. They played together on the base softball team and were division champions, going 80–1 on the season. Hunter said although Hop was a draftee, he quickly made sergeant and had "leader written all over his presence." People back then would seek his advice and the two friends often talked for hours about their plans. Hop's dream was to coach boys basketball in Olive Hill.

One day his first sergeant, whom he really liked and respected, placed a one-hundred dollar bill in his hand and assured him there would be a $10,000 bonus coming if he signed-up for a five-year tour of duty. The prospect of that kind of cash enthralled the young Kentucky boy and he decided that would be his best course of action. "The army needed him and he could be rich overnight," he thought. He enjoyed the military and his sergeant status meant he had a great deal of freedom.

However, Sharon and his mother-in-law intervened arguing against it, convincing Hop to come home and return to college. He realized he could resume his studies at Morehead with the help of the GI bill and receive $300 a month in addition. His second thoughts told him that the military life might not be the best for his family, now that they had a little girl to think about.

The Brown family returned to the States in November of 1972 to settle down in the home of Eunice James, Sharon's mother, in Olive Hill and Hop enrolled again at MSU. Sharon put her education on hold for awhile and took a job with the Counts-Duvall Law office in Olive Hill. Another addition to the family came along in May of 1975, when a second daughter, Karla, was born.

Hop completed his degree work at Morehead State and did his student teaching at Rowan Co. High School under Warren Cooper, a Morehead basketball star and former coach. He was thankful that Cooper seemed to back up everything he did. Hop admired Cooper and enjoyed his time at Rowan Co. which included coaching the boys freshman basketball team for

John Brown made sergeant in the army and enjoyed the service.

Coach Ted Trent. The team had a great season and he might have stepped into coaching there, but no teaching positions were open in the Rowan school system at the time.

He remembered one of his duties at Rowan each day was filling the pop machines in the hallway. It may sound like a rather mundane task, but Hop credited it with helping him getting to know lots of students and in fact, inspired him, to really want to help kids.

Hop was working part-time in the summers for Northeast Area Development Corporation, headquartered in Olive Hill, with programs that helped the needy, and upon finishing his degree, went to that job full-time in 1975. A few months later, he was offered a position at the federal prison near Ashland, Ky. with a salary of $16,000 a year, more than double what he was earning and he quickly changed occupations. The money was good, but the work was not enjoyable.

Hop determined that he needed to be teaching, and accepted a position at Upper Tygart Elementary for the 1977 school year. A year later he was moved to West Carter High School and began a career in the classroom there, teaching Physical Education, Math and later, Drivers Education. The first year at the high school was difficult and he pondered whether he was really cut out to be a teacher. A study hall with problem students was particularly trying. His friend, Jim Webb, counseled him to stay with it because the first year is always the toughest.

West Carter High had been formed by the Carter County School System in 1971–72 with a consolidation plan that brought together students from Carter High School and Olive Hill High. East Carter was formed in Grayson merging Prichard and Hitchins High Schools. While East Carter opted to select a new team name, choosing "Raiders" as a compromise between the Hitchins Tigers and Prichard Yellowjackets, the folks on the west end of the county wanted to keep their tradition alive and the new school retained the "Comets" nickname that had made Olive Hill sports famous. Former Comet coach, Jack Fultz, who had become principal at Olive Hill after his retirement from basketball, was the principal at the newly-merged school and believed it was the right thing to do.

Bert Greene had been chosen to continue coaching the new school's basketball team, as he had done when he replaced Fultz at Olive Hill. By 1978, although he had won two District championships, Greene had suffered through seven straight losing seasons with the West Carter basketball program, something hard to endure with the Olive Hill fans accustomed to winning, and he decided to step down at the end of that year. The call for applications for the head coaching position went out in the early Spring of 1978.

The School Board received applications from Jim Webb, Grady Lowe, and John Brown. Webb was a 1966 graduate of Carter High School where he had a productive basketball career for the Wildcats. He had been coaching at Lawton Elementary. Lowe was a basketball star for Olive Hill High, having also graduated in 1966.

Three applications coming from three very good friends. Jim, Grady and Hop were all local basketball stars, all military veterans, and even teammates on an independent softball team that had obtained a measure of fame in eastern Kentucky for its winning ways. Who would get the coveted job?

When Hop Brown returned to Morehead after the army to pursue his degree, his vision was to go back and coach the West Carter Comets and bring them a regional championship, something that had eluded him as a player. His dreams were of Comet trips to the Sweet Sixteen. A dream that would come true, of course, just not in the way his mind's eye had seen it back then.

Grady Lowe, as Bert Greene's assistant for two years, seemed to have the inside track for the head job when the school board began its deliberations.

The girls basketball program was now in the mix in the Carter County school system, often known for its politically-charged atmosphere when it came to hiring school personnel. The West Carter girls position had been difficult to fill. The Lady Comets had three coaches in four years of play.

It was none other than Jack Fultz as principal of West Carter in early 1970s, that had wanted girls to have the opportunity to play basketball. His recommendation, as a KHSAA board member, to mandate girls play had once died for a lack of a second at a state meeting, but the pressure eventually mounted and the state instituted girls basketball with the 74–75 school year and a State tournament was held at the end of that season.

Girls state tournaments had been played in the Bluegrass yearly between 1920 and 1932, under the old girls game rules. The Olive Hill team in those years was sporadic and records are unclear how many years a team actually played other schools, as few schools had competing teams. They weren't called the "Lady Comets" back then, though, but the "Shooting Stars."

The teams from Ashland High School, under coach W. B. Jackson, won five State championships during that early era.

On May 10, 1978, Hop Brown made his way to the offices of the Superintendent of Schools to determine what was behind the unexpected announcement he had heard the evening before. He was sure he couldn't coach girls. His only association with girls basketball had been refereeing several West Carter games. That experience was not pleasant, as girls play was quite ragged in those days. He recalled in his mind, four quarters of jump balls, scraps on the floor, fouls, turnovers and poor shooting. It was not the kind of basketball Hop Brown was used to playing or watching, let alone trying to coach.

He had been told his chances for the boys head coaching job were probably not good, but some had hinted he might become the assistant, and be in a position eventually to fulfill his dream. Three friends, former outstanding players, vying for the bench job they had always desired. Each would come away that day with a coaching job, but not necessarily the one they anticipated.

History would take some strange twists for these three. All would enjoy the opportunity to see their offspring move to stardom on the basketball court at West.

Jim Webb and Grady Lowe, their respective sons, Jeremy and Casey, and Hop Brown, his daughters, Kim, Karla and Kandi. Hop and Grady would coach their kids. Jim Webb went on to be head coach for eleven years for the West Carter Comets, with Lowe as his assistant. Grady would later get his chance and directed the Comets for 13 years, from 1989–2002, until his contract was not renewed as coach after the 2002 season. Ironically Jim Webb, was the high school principal at the time.

And as fate would have it, the one who received the least desirable coaching job in West Carter sports that day would be the only one to bring home what the school had long coveted—a State Championship!

It almost didn't happen, though, as when Hop Brown walked into Supt. Harold Holbrook's office that day, he was determined to inform him that coaching the girls would not work. "I can't coach girls, Mr. Holbrook, they won't like me." he recalled saying. "Why, you won't use profanity on them, will you?" Holbrook queried. Hop replied, "Oh no, I won't do that," a pledge that he would indeed keep through his entire career. "It's just I'll probably work them too hard, and they'll quit, I'm sure," he stated.

Holbrook, a former basketball coach at Prichard High, recalled that he had sorted out in his mind that with three good applications for the boys job, he needed to find someone to get the girls program at West on the right track with some discipline and organization. He knew of Hop's knowledge of the game, his work ethic, and dedication. He knew he would do a good job, he now just had to convince him to accept the challenge, if just on a trial basis. Years later, he admitted he never in his wildest dreams thought it would turn out the way it did.

"Just give it a try, Hop," he urged. "Take it for three years, and see where it leads."

John Brown had never backed down from any daunting task in the past, but this one was not in his dreams, not a part of his plan.

He walked out of Harold Holbrook's office at the courthouse in Grayson that day, though, agreeing to make an effort at coaching the West Carter girls. He couldn't have imagined that the greatest thrills of his basketball life and the most memorable moments in the county's sports history would later come at the soon-to-be-built, *Holbrook Complex,* West Carter.

CHAPTER 2

THE STRUGGLE

When West Carter principal, Jack Fultz, contemplated the beginning of girls basketball, he called upon teacher and one of his former players, Mike Barker, to get a team together in 1974 realizing the full schedule and official start would come in the fall of that year.

West and East High had new schools at the time, but neither had gym facilities. The West boys program played games at the National Guard Armory and practice for all the teams was difficult utilizing the old Olive Hill gym, which was now an elementary school, as well as the Armory floor. The girls were relegated to finding anywhere they could, and Barker often took them to Clark Hill Elementary, a much smaller gym floor. There was really no money allocated for the program so it was a matter of having the team members buy everything they needed or beg, borrow or fundraise to obtain the necessities.

Barker arranged for four games that first year, two each against Rowan Co. and University Breckenridge School, both of whom had played some girls basketball on the intramural and club level since back in the 1960s. The Lady Comets won two and lost two. He remembered that the girls were just so eager to play and wanted to learn, but most didn't even know the rules of the game. He was surprised that the girls would really mix it up and fight hard on the floor, but their fundamentals were lacking.

A few had some experience and two seniors that year, Janet Sparks and Carla Rice, possessed real size and ability. Sparks scored 25 points in one game and upon graduation, played basketball for a traveling Armed Forces team. Barker believed both girls could have made quite an impact had they not been graduating that year, without having played in an official game.

The Lady Comets first full year of basketball was the 1974–75 season and it was still a non-funded program with very little fan interest. Games were attended mostly by parents, and the play was marred by fouls, jump balls, and erratic shooting. Some games were played in the afternoon

The first West girls team to take the floor in '74 for a shortened season
J. Burchett, S. Rice, S. Wilburn, P. Viars, F. Clark, Coach Mike Barker, C. Rice, B.
Gearhart, S. Burchett, T. Vanlandingham, C. King, J. Sparks
photo-courtesy Mike Barker

with few people watching or even caring. Barker's wife, Charlotte, helped him with the team and they wound up with just one victory and twelve losses, that premier season.

The Comets beat Louisa 50–39 for the first-ever girls varsity win. County rival East Carter beat the Comets twice and they lost to Rowan Co. three times. Ashland, the traditional basketball powerhouse in the region, handed them their worst loss, 79–27. Garnet "Von" Messer, who would later become Hop Brown's highly-regarded assistant coach, was the leading scorer that first season. Other top scorers were Sue Ann Burchett and Tammy Vanlandingham.

The first 62nd District girls basketball tournament was played in March of 1975 at the Hitchins Elementary gym, hosted by East Carter and the Lady Raiders (actually known as the "Raiderettes" in those days) won it. Lewis Co. beat West 52–41. There were only three schools participating, as Elliott Co. would not develop their girls team until the following year.

Coach Barker said he had a good time coaching the girls. It was difficult, though, in those early days and he decided not to continue as coach after that season, desiring instead to devote more time to his church work.

It was a chore finding anyone who actually wanted to coach the girls, but teacher Kathleen Lewis Mullins, agreed to lead the program in the fall of 1975.

The Lady Comets record was 6–15 for that 1975–76 season and they won their first post-season game, beating Elliott Co. in the District Tournament, 29–20. They lost to East Carter in the championship game, but made their first trip to a 16th Region tournament, losing to Ashland at Paul Blazer gym, 57–26. Ashland, during the season, had administered a 105–25 trouncing at the Armory, in one of the most disheartening moments in the Lady Comets' short history.

Von Messer again led the team in scoring for the year, with Ellen Hicks, Marcella Logan, Brenda Reynolds, and Julia Sparks, Janet's younger sister, making big contributions. One of Messer's big games was 27 points against Lawrence Co. Her younger sister, Angie now was also on the team, and they would be joined by their two other sisters, Annette and Lisa the following year.

Coach Mullins elected not to take the team the next year and Bette Greenhill was enlisted to head up the Lady Comets. Neither woman had much previous basketball experience beyond the physical education introduction in college. Greenhill, realizing her shortcomings, asked family friend, Marvin Gearhart, to be her assistant and teach the girls. Gearhart was a former Olive Hill star, and his three daughters would all later be an integral part of Comet history.

The Lady Comets finished 7–11 in the 1976–77 season with the highlight being their first victory over cross-county rival, East Carter, February 8th at Olive Hill Elementary gym. They took the win, 39–34 with balanced scoring, lead by Annette Messer's 10 points, Julia Sparks, nine and Von Messer and Brenda Reynolds adding eight apiece.

East Carter coach, Vicky Young, says she'll never forget the broad smile on the normally stoic Coach Gearhart's face after that upset. East came back two days later in a game played at Kentucky Christian College in Grayson and beat West 43–38. East also defeated them in the District championship game 51–40. West then lost in the Regional first round to Russell.

Prior to tournament time, however, Gearhart had left the volunteer assistant position, after some dissension arose on the squad. Greenhill said many of the girls complained to her that he was too hard on them and expected too much of them. "A lot of the girls just thought he took everything too seriously, I guess," she would say years later, "but he was teaching them about defenses and offenses, but many of them just weren't ready for that style and intensity of play."

The four Messer sisters, who had grown up playing basketball with boys, disagreed with their teammates and were excited about learning plays and working hard, but the majority vote prevailed and Greenhill coached the remainder of the season solo. Then, citing lack of time because of family commitments, didn't take the job for the following year.

Kathleen Mullins agreed to return as coach of the Lady Comets in 1977–78 so they could field a team and finished with the same record as her earlier stint, 6–15. The Messer sisters- Angie, Von, and Annette, along with Julia Sparks, Brenda Reynolds and Charla Bauers made for a pretty solid six, and the Lady Comets almost pulled off their first district championship, falling to East Carter in overtime 61–57 in the title game. They were beaten by Rowan Co. 57–40 in the first round of the Region.

John Hop Brown attended the 62nd District championship game in Grayson, with friend Tex English, and commented after the heart-breaking loss, "You know, those girls have some talent." Well, little did he know that he would be taking those same girls, minus Von Perry, to their first winning season and District championship, one year later.

Kathleen Mullins resigned as coach after the season but continued to teach business and serve as senior sponsor at West Carter. She earned her Masters degree and served as guidance counselor at West Carter until stricken with colon cancer. She passed away August 29, 1991, with over a thousand former students and co-workers attending her funeral. She was a passionate teacher who instilled a spirit of pride in her students, players, and her two children, Michelle and Justin, and was a loyal Comet fan.

Bette Greenhill taught elementary school at Clark Hill, Lawton, and Olive Hill until her retirement in 1999. All her four children, Falissa, Janena, Johnny, and Scot played some sports at West.

Mike Barker continued his teaching positions and became principal at West Carter Middle School in 1989.

Hop Brown reported for duty as head coach of the West Carter Lady Comets in October of 1978 and put the girls through the hardest practice they had ever experienced in a hot, steamy Olive Hill Elementary gymnasium. Many of the girls didn't come back the next day and by the time the season started, no cuts had to be made. The twelve girls who endured it all, including the runs to and from the Olive Hill gym to the National Guard Armory and back up the steps to the school, suited up as Brown's first team.

The girls who joked with him as "Hop" that first day, learned they would call him "Coach Brown" and soon understand that discipline and a lot of hard work were about to become the hallmark of girls basketball at West Carter High.

Hop would later look back on that first year and realize that he had really put those girls through quite a difficult regimen in preparing them for the season and the rigor of the routine was indelibly etched into the memory of all the players on those first Brown teams. But Hop was impressed with the desire of many of the girls to learn the game of basketball.

Brenda Reynolds had played for Coach Greenhill and Coach Mullins and thought they were both great people, but did not have much basketball experience. She played that first year under Coach Brown and figured her reputation had followed her when during one of the first practices he asked who is "Brenda." She raised her hand and he proceeded to tell her that he heard she had several technical fouls the year before and that there would be none of that or she would be sitting next to him the whole game.

She remembers all that running and said, "we definitely were in shape." She appreciated learning the fundamentals from Coach Brown and has followed the Lady Comets closely through the years.

Hop had no assistant coach during the first four years, and even became bus driver for away games because there was no money for that either. That did change, though, when he realized after one away loss, that he was so angry, it was not safe for him to drive the girls home in such a condition. Principal Bill Calhoun, finally found some money to provide the girls a driver. Sharon Brown accompanied him to games and helped in various ways with the girls, including making sure it was safe to enter the dressing room.

The first few years of coaching were a struggle for Hop Brown, trying to bring some respect and popularity to the game, while teaching the fundamentals to the girls. Besides spending time teaching them to dribble, pass, and shoot, he emphasized good defense and of course, being in top condition. All the girls reported they began to see how the game was to be played through Hop's example and the excitement about winning started to grow.

All the while, Hop was fine-tuning his practices, his coaching philosophy, and dealing with team situations. He admitted later, his first years were filled with a lot of angry and frustrating episodes from his intense personality and more than a few technical fouls from the officials.

He also realized early on, he would have to alter the way he had envisioned handling players. He confided once in his old coach, Jack Fultz, that you sure couldn't treat girls the same way you would coach boys. In general, they were just more sensitive and realizing that was a big step toward success.

Hop has said that his early scouting and expectations were skewed by a lack of experience with girls basketball. For instance, after some victories in that first year, he would scout other teams and declare them easy to beat, only later to be whipped badly by them.

Another adjustment was in bench coaching and game strategy. While struggling to teach the girls fundamentals of the game and make them a sound team, he had spent less time on the development of plays and the skill of adjusting to other defenses and game situations, which would cost the Lady Comets some games, he felt.

The first team of the Hop Brown era consisted of Seniors-Julia Sparks, Brenda Reynolds and Angie Messer; Juniors- Charla Bauers, Elizabeth Dalenberg; Sophomores-Lori James, Larae Kiser, Annette Messer, Kathy Kitchen; Freshmen-Kim Stafford, Nici Raybourn, Lisa Messer.

They won their first game, 54–40, over Elliott and then rolled over Fleming Co. and Menifee Co. before losing to Raceland 63–45. They won two games in the Eastern Kentucky Conference tournament before losing in the title game to Rowan Co., 56–42.

The games with East Carter in January and February 1979 saw Hop's girls beat East Carter back-to-back by a shocking 25 points and then 18 points and the fans on the west end of the county began to take notice, as there was nothing like beating East in any sport.

The 62nd District Tournament at Lewis Co. that year would see East Carter's string of four straight championships come to an end as the Lady Raiders were beaten in the first game by Lewis Co. 57–52. West beat Elliott Co. and then defeated Lewis Co. 60–44 to bring West Carter girls basketball the first of many District championship trophies. It was quite an unexpected accomplishment for Hop's first year at the helm.

Buoyed by a strong finish to the season, and twice the victories of any other West team, Hop was confident the team could actually win the Region. Those hopes were dashed in the first game at Russell gym, though, as Greenup Co. eliminated West 56–49 in a game that haunted Hop for years because he knew the Lady Comets were a better team. He blamed himself for the loss but resolved to be better prepared for in-game adjustments in the future. His first year came to an end with a record of 13–7.

The Lady Comets placed four of their five starters- Angie and Annette Messer, Julia Sparks and Brenda Reynolds on the *Ashland Daily Independent's* All-Area team, which was one more than the Region champion, Boyd Co.! Area coaches voted on the team and apparently had taken a liking to Hop and his hustling girls.

Julia Sparks and Annette Messer led the team in scoring that first year averaging 13 per game, but Sparks was a senior along with starters Brenda Reynolds and Angie Messer. Annette Messer also became a strong rebounder averaging over 13 per game, and Hop described her as the type of player who could even mix it up well with the boys. Annette would say years later that Coach Brown often had to yell at her to motivate her to do her best and she would stare at him, but then take it to heart.

Angie became the second of the Messer sisters to graduate from West Carter basketball. She was the defensive specialist on the Lady Comet teams, most always getting assigned to guard the opponent's best player. Hop quickly learned that, unlike Annette, the best way to motivate Angie was with a soft-spoken word or two.

The season was truly a great start for Hop Brown in his task of building a winner at West Carter. The team had scored an average of 52 points per game for the season.

Despite losing three starters, the 1979–80 Lady Comets would be just as successful with the emergence of freshmen Pam Biggs and Brenda Carpenter and the improvement of Elizabeth Dalenberg and Charla Bauers to complement the play of star Annette Messer.

The season didn't begin well though, as the Lady Comets were only 2–3 at the Christmas break with a loss to Lewis Co. and two against Rowan Co. Later in the season, a powerful East Carter team would hang two lopsided losses on them, but the excitement was to come in March at the brand new gym at West Carter.

Finally, with the construction of the Holbrook Complex gym facility, the Lady Comets had a place to call home and the first game played in the new facility was one of the most memorable in Comet history.

East Carter had several bona-fide college prospects, including Kelli Cromer, who went to play at Marshall University. They had been ranked among the state's top ten teams that year. The Raiderettes were 19–4 and ready to challenge for a Kentucky Sweet Sixteen bid. Without a doubt, East and West girls were the best in the district but by the traditional blind draw format they had to play each other in the opening game.

There was a good crowd for the first-round match-up. East Carter led at half by six and by three going into the fourth quarter in a real battle. The ending, though, was sweet for the Lady Comets—a dramatic 69–67 upset, on the buzzer-beating shot by Lisa "Pee Wee" Messer, the youngest of the Messer sisters who described it as " absolutely the greatest thrill" she has ever had. It was made even sweeter by the fact that she had cousins playing for the Lady Raiders, in what had become sort of a friendly family grudge match. For East Carter, it was a night of tears and disappointment, losing a game they felt sure would be theirs.

Hop Brown had scored, for the faithful Olive Hill fans, an elimination win over the cross-county rivals, properly christening the new gym. The celebration would continue the next night, as the Lady Comets clobbered Lewis Co. to take their second straight District championship.

A further indication of the improvement in the West Carter girls program came the next week, at Summit Junior High gym, when the Lady Comets won the school's first regional tournament game, as Annette Messer put on a 20–point show to pull off a 41–40 victory over the Ashland Kittens, a team that had often beaten the Lady Comets, without mercy, in earlier years. Two incredible wins for the program in the span of one week, and the girls were starting to see the work ethic and philosophy of Coach Brown pay off.

In the semi-finals, the bubble burst, however, against the Lady Vikings of Rowan Co. who, led by Karla May and Tammy Collins, beat West, 54–36. Rowan lost to Boyd Co. in the finals, but the following year won the Region, the first of four for Coach Claudia Hicks in the 1980s.

Coach Hicks later noted that Hop Brown had truly changed the face of West Carter basketball. The girls, she said, "were disciplined, fundamentally sound, and without a doubt, he was starting to build a program that would compete with anyone."

Hop's second year, ended with an overall record of 15–7 and some truly exhilarating moments with his gals. Annette Messer led the squad in offensive categories, with Dalenberg and Biggs also averaging close to double figures in scoring for the season.. Charla Bauers received several awards for her play-making and defense, and Messer and Bauers, made the All-Conference team in the EKC.

Ashland, Boyd Co. Russell and Rowan Co. had dominated the first six years of the girls basketball in the 16th Region. Was West Carter ready to compete now with that elite group? The answer, coming in the next few years was, -no- at least——not yet.

The next three years of girls basketball at West Carter saw records broken for wins during a season, however, the Lady Comets lost control of the District title and would not regain it until 1984, which oddly enough was Hop Brown's first losing season after five straight winning records.

West recorded 16 victories against eight losses in 1980–81; went 14–10 in 1981–82 and then put up a record 18 victories with eight losses in the 1982–83 season.

The 1981 season would be Annette Messer's senior year and she became the first Lady Comet to score 1,000 career points, and make honorable mention, All-State. Other starters that year, were Pam Biggs, Kathy Kitchen, Brenda Carpenter and Lisa Messer. Messer and Biggs received All-Conference, District and Region honors for the season.

The Lady Comets played well at times during the year, but couldn't beat East Carter, Rowan Co. or Ashland. They lost in the District title game to East Carter 58–53 at East's gym in a payback for West's inhospitable defeat of the Lady Raiders the year before. West was edged by Ashland in the Region first-round 64–57.

Following the 1981 season, Alice Kidwell, wife of boys coach Gary Kidwell, stepped down as Lewis Co. coach after seven years, and Don Gaunce took over.

With Annette Messer gone, West fell to 14–10 the next year (1981–82) and once again had trouble competing against the likes of Russell, Ashland and Rowan Co. East Carter also handed the Lady Comets two regular season losses, including a disheartening 65–45 loss in the first round of the District at West Carter.

Pam Biggs and Brenda Carpenter were the offensive leaders and took All-EKC honors, both averaging 14 points a game.

The last of the four Messer sisters, Lisa, graduated that year. There was optimism in the camp for the next fall, with two taller girls, Lenore Sparks and Dana Smith, poised to make a difference in the lineup. Smith would also make a difference for years to come in the coaching ranks for West, as well.

Two events of the Spring semester of 1982 were to have long-range repercussions in the history of West Carter girls basketball. A third child, Kandi, was born to Hop and Sharon Brown, in January. The birth was made possible only after surgical procedures at Mayo Clinic reversing Sharon's early tubal ligation, following Karla's birth. She and Hop had decided that they indeed wanted to have more children and maybe a boy this time. But it was not to be . . . not yet, that is. Instead a girl, who would become one of the greatest players in Lady Comet history, graced the Brown household and it wouldn't be long before she was knocking down long shots in the gym.

Meanwhile, older sister, Kim, was starting to show interest in basketball and a grade school program had been started up at Olive Hill Elementary under the direction of former Lady Comet, Angie Messer Johnson with help from her husband, Jerome. She was beginning to mold what would become the first regional championship team.

Another significant event of that Spring was the college graduation of the oldest Messer sister, Von, and her stated desire to return and help with basketball at her alma mater. While there was no funding yet for an assistant coach, Hop Brown would get his first bench help, that fall, as Perry volunteered her time. The following year, she became the first paid assistant coach.

Meanwhile, Hop had given up his baseball coaching duties at West. While he loved the game immensely, even more than basketball, and felt he could teach the boys, he cited a total frustration in playing all games on the road, since the school had yet to develop a good home field. He couldn't run the baseball team by his standards, so he decided to give full attention to "girls roundball," as he called it.

In many ways, 1982–83 became the best season yet for the girls program, with 18 victories including their first Eastern Kentucky Conference championship and wins over Boyd Co. and Rowan Co. They captured the championship of the Greenup Co. Invitational Tournament. Hop Brown received his first post-season honor, as EKC Coach of the Year.

The season might have been even bigger had it not been for a blow from the KHSAA, declaring that Brenda Carpenter was ineligible to play her senior year because she had reached the age limit of 19. The school decided to appeal the decision but while on the way to Louisville, Von Perry and Brenda were involved in an accident on icy roads and never arrived for the appointment. They dropped the issue and Brenda settled for helping out on the bench her final year.

The Lady Comets broke their losing streak against East that year, by taking them to photo finishes twice, winning 47–44 and 58–57. But the post-season would prove disappointing, just barely escaping an upset by Lewis Co. in the first round of the District, 55–52, the Comets lost the District championship to East Carter, 42–37, the Lady Raiders third straight title. It was a tough night for Coaches Brown and Perry, feeling that they had missed a golden opportunity to capture the District trophy.

West advanced to the regional tournament as a runner-up and played better, losing to the eventual champion, the Ashland Kittens, 60–53, after going into the fourth quarter, all tied at 38 apiece.

Senior Pam Biggs scored over 400 points during the year and became the Lady Comets all-time leading scorer. Biggs remembers the night she surpassed 1,000 at the Boyd Co. Christmas tournament, and they

Hop loved coaching baseball, but couldn't get the facilities he wanted

stopped the game. She didn't have a clue she was doing something special with her fifth point of the night. Biggs was selected honorable-mention All-State at the end of the year.

Biggs remembered, "Coach Brown was hard. When you played for him, he wanted your best." Biggs had wanted to play while in the 8th grade, and was certainly good enough, but the rules had changed at that time, and Hop had to break the news to her that she would have to wait a year. Biggs had known Coach Brown all her life and grew up just four doors down from his family. She even remembers Hop lifting her up to shoot at the old hoop on her tree, when she was a pre-schooler.

Lenore Sparks also received several honors, including All-EKC, after averaging 10 per game, and she and Dana Smith finally gave the team some rebounding strength. Seniors Cheri Nolen and Connie Baker also provided scoring punch that year, and Nolen developed a free throw touch, shooting 75% on the season. Smith and Sparks would be back for the next season.

Celebrating their first ever District Tournament championship, 1979, Coach Brown
with Charla Bauers and Angie Messer.

The next three years, though, proved to be the most trying times for Coach Brown, as his winning tradition was shat-
tered with disappointing records and the loss of players.

It would become a time of reflection for Hop Brown, as
he began to wonder if building a regional championship team was really in
the cards, or if he even needed to be coaching the girls. Visions of getting
a boys head coaching position began to flash around in his head again. Several factors helped him stay the course. His competitive spirit—that force
within him that would not let him give up, and then the interest his oldest
daughter, Kim, and their neighbor, Brenda English, were showing in playing basketball. The two were spending a lot of time shooting hoops on the
neighborhood goal and beginning to develop into quality elementary players. Hop was sustained by the desire to coach his own daughter and the
determination to bring Olive Hill a winner.

While the 1983–84 Comets scored only eight wins in the season, they
did regain the District championship trophy from East Carter by beating the
Lady Raiders 57–50 with Lenore Sparks and Dana Smith scoring 20 points
apiece. The Lady Comets had been down by six points at the half, but came
back to break the three-year hold that East had on the District trophy.

The two teams had played only once during the season, a thrilling
overtime win for the Raiderettes, 70–64. West suffered 40–point losses to

Ashland, Rowan, and Russell that season, but drew the Lady Devils in the first round of the Region and played them strong before falling 48–38. Russell lost to Rowan Co. in the Region championship.

The two seniors, Sparks and Smith, led the Lady Comets in rebounding and scoring for the season. Smith posted a double-double, averaging 14 points and 11 rebounds on the year and both made All-EKC.

The fall of '84 started badly for Coach Brown, when he realized he would have no starter returning. Graduating his top two scorers was compounded by the decision of the Greenhill sisters and Rena Bond not to play basketball. The two daughters of former coach, Bette Greenhill, had been on the starting five, the previous year. Falissa would have been a senior, but had some off-season surgery and decided not to play and when her older sister quit, Janea Greenhill, a real good sophomore, opted to concentrate on studies and left the team as well. Annie Douglas, a promising freshmen, also elected not to play.

The loss of all those players, troubled Hop Brown all year, as if he was lacking in motivational power to inspire the girls to want to play or had been too hard on them. Von Perry remembers that it was just a few years when they had a "dry spell" of strong athletes. The task of rebuilding was ahead but some superstars were waiting in the wings.

One of those youngsters, freshman Sheila Kay Porter, emerged as the team's leading scorer and rebounder, averaging ten points a game in the 1984–85 season.

The lone senior, Cindy Piper, averaged eight points per game. It was a strange schedule, with three games vs. Menifee Co. resulting in one win and two losses. West lost to Lewis Co. by 11 points and never came close to beating anyone besides Menifee, suffering lop-sided defeats all year. The Lady Comets were embarrassed by East Carter 73–37, the worst loss against the arch-rival in the school's history.

West entered the post-season with an uncharacteristic record of 1–13. They drew a bye in the three-team district as Elliott Co. did not have a girls team that year. East beat Lewis and then Lewis had to face West. West avenged the early loss by taking the Lady Lions 53–48 and prepared to defend their District title against East Carter, who was heavily favored and playing on their home court, just the sort of thing to get Hop Brown and his girls pumped up to rectify the miseries of the season.

The Lady Comets rose to the occasion and jumped out to a lead and were on top by 11 points at halftime. But the Lady Raiders came roaring back to take the victory 60–51, behind Rebecca Bush's 25 points, and spoiled the upset bid. West, as runner-up, lost to Russell in the Region Tournament, 54–30 to close out the year at 2–15, the low point of Hop Brown's coaching career. The struggle to build the program seemed to hit a deep valley.

While the previous years were marred by some talented girls quitting the team, the 1985–86 season found two girls return to don the Lady Comet uniform for their senior year. Carolyn Reynolds, who had quit after her freshman year, and Rena Bond came out for the team and joined a crew of the younger players that were developing their skills. It was a year of promise with a return to some respectability, but not a winning record as the Comets finished 7–15 overall, and failed to reach the Regional tournament, as it turned out the last time Coach Hop Brown and his girls ever stayed home from the Region.

The Lady Comets had split with East Carter in the regular season games, but lost twice to district foe, Lewis Co. In addition, the Lady Comets suffered the embarrassment of losing two games in the District on their home court, in the three-team tourney. They fell to East Carter 65–48, after losing the opening game to Lewis Co. 64–60. However, that would be the last win the Lady Lions were to get over a Hop Brown team, as the District dynasty was poised to begin. Tammy Hall, in her first year as coach of Lewis Co., had three wins over the Lady Comets.

Sophomore Sheila Kay Porter led the team in scoring and rebounding again that season with 11 points and 10 rebounds per game, while Reynolds and Bond both started and averaged nine points per game. Candie Baker and Rachel Henderson rounded out the starting five. Freshmen Kim Brown, Brenda English and Gina Taylor started logging some playing time a precursor of great things to come.

That '86 season found girls play on the court speeded up considerably as the Kentucky High School Athletic Association adopted the alternating-possession rule, eliminating those troublesome and time-consuming jump balls. In addition, girls teams were allowed to use the slightly smaller basketball, resulting in better ball-handling and shooting. The smaller "girls" ball became mandatory in the 1988–89 season.

The West Carter faithful fans were rewarded the following season as 1986–87 saw some hard work pay off and the blossoming of young talent helped the Lady Comets post a 19–9 record, the most wins in their history, and capture the first of an incredible ten straight District championships.

By tournament time that year, a solid five had developed with Sheila Kay Porter, Jana Jones and Gina Taylor up front, and Suzi Layne and Rachel Henderson, playmaking in the backcourt.

The Lady Comets were invited back to Greenup that December and won the tournament again. They continued steady improvement as the season progressed. They split regular season play with East Carter, losing 43–31 and then winning a nail-biter 44–42 at home, but were still unable to chalk up any victories over the regional powerhouses.

The blind draw for the District Tournament at Elliott Co. gym pitted East against West in the first round, and a loss would mean elimination. It was a real duel with the Lady Comets leading by nine points going into the final period. Coach Brian Buck's East team came back in the fourth quarter, led by Kristy Cromer and Aimee Arnett, as the team hit 11 out of 14 free throws, but fell short and West Carter advanced with a 62–59 victory and a trip to the Region. They whipped Lewis Co. 69–45 in the title game with 11 players getting into the scoring column. East's Cromer went on to play college ball at Eastern and Arnett starred for Kentucky Christian. Porter, Jones, and Taylor were named All-Distirct for West.

The Lady Comets picked up their second Region tournament win in history with a 71–48 triumph over Fairview at Morehead State University, and then met the Ashland Kittens for the chance to advance to the championship game. Ashland was the defending 16th Region champions and looking toward another title match-up with Rowan Co.

The two teams played even through the first quarter and West trailed by five at halftime. But Angie Johnson of Ashland proved too much to handle and the Kittens, of Coach Connie Greene, pulled away for a 62–46 win and went on to take another Region tourney crown, her second in a row, and the school's fifth, overall.

Sheila Kay Porter, received several post-season honors including All-EKC and again led the Lady Comets in scoring and rebounding with sophomores Gina Taylor and Brenda English putting up strong numbers along with Suzi Layne and Amy Mays. Senior Guard Rachel Henderson set the school record for assists.

Coach Brown received *Ashland Daily Independent* area Coach of the Year honors in a poll of his peers, a honor he called rather "embarrassing" since his team had lost to Ashland in the Region semi-final. But the team had improved immensely. Their 37% shooting percentage was a team record, one that would later be broken many times over. For the first time, all twelve girls scored double figure totals for the year, and the team put more points on the scoreboard than any Lady Comet team. The numbers were pretty encouraging and it was a "turning point" season in the mind of Hop Brown, and one that brought increased interest and support from the school and community. But it was only a small taste of the excitement that lay just ahead.

CHAPTER 3

THE VICTORY

Hop Brown once said that he wished he had seen the 3–point play in his high school basketball days, because he loved to shoot it as soon as he crossed that mid-court line.

That was exactly the sentiment he conveyed to his team as they gathered to start practice for the 1987–88 season, and the beginning of the 3–point shot in Kentucky high school basketball. He told the girls that they were going to shoot it often and fifteen minutes have been devoted to that shot alone every practice since that time. Hop Brown had always believed in shooting, and the quickest way to get yanked from a game was to pass up a shot. His philosophy that "100% of shots not taken, don't go in" would guide the team's offense for years to come. The Lady Comets willingness to shoot from behind the arc brought criticism, even from some of Hop Brown's friends during the year. They warned about living and dying by the "3." In the end, it brought new life to the offense not only that year, but in the years to come.

They would not be afraid to throw up the long-distance bomb and gain an advantage on the opponents, who were usually taller than his Lady Comets, and his own daughter, Kim, had been working hard to develop the potent weapon. She had put in a lot of time that summer, because Dad had told her if she wanted more playing time she would have to work harder. She and neighbor, Brenda English, marked the 3–spot on their blacktop court and began firing away.

There was certainly no favoritism when it came to coaching Kim as she often remembers many pretty good tongue-lashings from the coach that brought her to the point of tears and wondering why he was always picking on his own daughter. It caused her some hurt, but her dad always explained he was trying to make her a better player.

Hop Brown joked with the media in pre-season that Kim probably would see more playing time because, he quipped, "her mother says she's good." Sharon indicated she had been Kim's advocate with the coach, for more playing time.

Kim Brown, Brenda English, Gina Taylor and Missy Greenhill were now juniors on the West Carter team that was anchored by Sheila Kay Porter, senior center, as they started that monumental season. The Lady Comets graduated guards Henderson and Layne, so the backcourt positions were open, and then came a shock, when forward, Jana Jones, decided to pass up her senior year of basketball.

Hop Brown and Von Perry had never set long-term goals with their teams and visions of a region championship were certainly not dancing in their heads when they tipped the first ball up for the new season, because they knew that Rowan Co. and Ashland would be tough to beat again. No other team in the 16th Region had been able to capture a championship except Ashland, Rowan, Russell and Boyd Co. and there was no reason to believe that would change, although most observers that year felt the region was probably more wide open than it had been in the past.

The season started with a loss to Rowan Co. 51–45 and the Lady Comets failed to hit a three-pointer. The first "trey" in Lady Comet history was swished by Missy Greenhill in the second game victory over Paintsville.

The Lady Comets lost again to Rowan Co. by 14 points in the Boyd Co. Holiday Tournament, and after Christmas prepared to take the first real road trip in the team's history. Hop Brown had been lobbying with other coaches to invite his team to some of the big tournaments. He wanted to test them against out-of-region competition and Whitesburg coach, John High, obliged with an invitation to their Holiday classic.

Everyone agreed the trip proved to be quite an eye-opener. The girls received their "baptism of fire" against 15th Region opponents, losing all three games. They dropped the opener to Whitesburg, played better but still lost to M.C. Napier and Dilce Combs. It seemed every girl returned home with some minor injury, bruise, bloody nose, or scratches and scrapes. Sheila Kay Porter said it was a "learning experience" for sure. Brenda English felt the team had been taught a lesson in rough play and they would take away from it a determination to be more physical themselves in the future. The Comets turned the calendar to 1988 with a record of 4–5, but Hop Brown knew the trip to Whitesburg would make a difference in his team and gave them the attitude of playing "more agressively."

The girls then reeled off nine straight victories before running into Rowan Co. in February and being tripped up 68–61. During the streak, the Lady Comets beat the two-time defending region champs, Ashland Kittens, on the road, 72–53 and they began to believe they might have something special going.

Prior to the Ashland win, the Lady Comets had beaten a good Morgan Co. team in West Liberty, with Porter scoring 33 points. That game, though, ended with a bench-clearing fight on the floor, proving that girls action could turn ugly. During the January win streak, though, the Lady Comets suffered a loss, when their fifth leading scorer, Amy Mays, went down with a knee injury and would be unable to play much the rest of the way. She had been a good quick, play-making guard for the Comets.

The team hit a peak after the Ashland victory, beating excellent Montgomery and Menifee

Brenda English on '88 and '89 State Tourney teams, the first Lady Comet to receive a big college scholarship

teams and then gaining revenge with a victory over Whitesburg 64–59. The 91 points scored in the Lewis Co. victory right after that, was the most in the school's history.

The District tournament began in Vanceburg with the Lady Comets sporting a record of 21–6 with the only team in the Region able to beat them being their old nemesis, Claudia Hicks and the Rowan Co. Lady Vikings.

West took the District opener with an easy win over Lewis, but then there was a narrow escape against arch-rival East Carter. The Comets led by 11 going into the fourth quarter of the title game, but just like the year before, a Raiderette rally trimmed the margin of victory to three, 61–58 to throw a scare into the favored Comets. Sheila Kay Porter hit the free throws with 16 seconds left that nailed down the win. The victory allowed the Lady Comets to advance as the champion and go back to their home court, where for the first time, West Carter and Olive Hill would play host to the 16th Region girls basketball tournament.

The first game of the 16th Region tournament belonged to the Lady Comets as English and Porter led the way to a 67–52 win over Russell, putting West in the semi-finals against Menifee Co.

The Lady Cats had a good team that year, and had played West tough in the regular season. But West could see what was shaping up for Tuesday

night, a possible showdown with Rowan Co. The experienced Lady
Vikings had been in the Region championship game seven out of the previous eight years, had won four titles and been runner-up three times,
including the two previous years, losing to Ashland. They were tough, hungry to get back to the Sweet Sixteen and had whipped the Lady Comets
three times in the season.

With a home court encounter in mind, Hop Brown initiated a couple
of things he had never done before. He closed practice that weekend and
began to look ahead to the Lady Vikings, even though he knew he must
beat Menifee in the Monday game.

A defensive plan was put in place, kept under wraps and the Lady Comets
took the court Monday, eager to get at Rowan. It almost didn't happen.

Menifee Co. jumped out to an early lead and was on top by two at
the intermission. Then came the second half, and the long hours of Kim
Brown's outside shooting practice truly paid off. She was able to give her
dad, the team, and the community their first Region title game opportunity, hitting four three-pointers in the third and fourth quarters including
the one with time running out to pull off the dramatic 45–44 semi-final
win. A collective sigh of relief went up from the stands and bench when
that shot flew through the nets, and then Menifee Co. failed to counter
with a long three at the buzzer. The big game with Rowan Co. was 24
hours away.

West had not really played well in the earlier meetings with the Lady
Vikings and Hop Brown felt his girls were capable of winning, and had a
better, more versatile team.

The problem was 6'1 All-State center for Rowan, Julie Magrane. The
solution, he felt, was a hybrid triangle and two defense with someone in
front of and behind Magrane all the time, and a third shading toward her to
keep her from getting the ball.

West Carter's post players, Porter, English, and Taylor alternated
sticking to Magrane like glue and she quickly became frustrated. Coach
Claudia Hicks said that was the key to the game, as it was impossible to get
Magrane the ball and the other girls didn't rise to the challenge to take up
the slack. Magrane was held to 14 points, with 10 of those coming early,
before she eventually got into foul trouble in the second quarter.

Besides carrying out the defensive game plan brilliantly, West had
great balance in scoring from their five, along with excellent ball-handling
and claimed the greatest victory in the school's girls basketball history and

Kim Brown goes after the long bomb

their first trip to the Sweet Sixteen. It was an emotional night for the fans of Olive Hill, to get their first 16th Region championship on their own floor and to do it against the favored Lady Vikings, the thorn in their side for a decade, made the night extra special.

At the final horn, with the scoreboard reading West 60 Rowan Co. 47, the biggest, wildest celebration the gym had ever experience erupted. Principal George Steele said it was a crowd in excess of 1,300. He was especially glad to see the victory for Coach Brown, who had gone through a difficult three years, when he had first become principal at West. For Coach Hop Brown, it was a "picture-perfect victory" and the goal of taking West to the State was fulfilled. He was carried around the floor and hailed as the conquering hero.

Brenda English said it was a real team effort. "All year, we just tried to improve and we wanted to win. We had different high scorers every game." Having grown up next to Hop and Sharon, it was an especially exhilarating time for Brenda. "We were on cloud nine for days."

The girls were pretty speechless on the post-game radio show, but words like "awesome" "great" "unbelievable" were common and the banners that had read "State-bound" were no longer pep tools, but a testimony of the great game played, as the words were now chanted in harmony by a happy group of cheerleaders with a thousand fans chiming in and making plans for a trip to Frankfort.

No West Carter team had ever participated in a state basketball tournament, although the old Olive Hill Comets boys team had been there on four occasions, the latest being in 1959.

West Carter starters, Porter, Taylor, Brown and English made the All-Region team, but all later would say the individual honors of that special season meant little compared to the wonderful feeling of winning as a team and capturing what they thought was the ultimate prize, the trip to the State.

Just getting to go to the "Greatest Show in Hoops" was the dream come true. Thoughts of winning such a tournament were beyond their imagination. They were just glad to be there and hoping to make a decent showing was the main goal now.

Hop, the Conquering hero, gets a ride—Headed to the Sweet Sixteen for the first time

Principal George Steele remembers the occasion as "one of the greatest thrills I have had. It was a dream come true and quite an honor to drive Hop through Olive Hill, as the Region champion."

West Carter was to play the final first round game of the Sweet Sixteen, on Thursday March 24th 9 p.m. at the Farnham Dudgeon Civic Center in Frankfort. The caravan, leaving Olive Hill around 11 A.M. was enormous, with live radio broadcasts, banners, pep rally, cameras, horns, and seemingly half the county lining the road to send off the new Queens of 16th Region basketball. As the girls looked at their adoring throng from the Greyhound bus loaned by Morehead State University, tears filled their eyes, while a small sense of pride filled the heart of Coach Hop Brown and his staff, proud of the work the girls had done and the joy they had brought to the fans of Olive Hill.

Exactly ten years earlier, John Hop Brown had been preparing to apply for the job of coaching the boys at West Carter, and now he was heading west on I-64 to the State tournament, with "his girls", and five busloads of fans and dozens of cars following.

The Clark County Cardinals, the opponents for the opening round game in Frankfort, were champions of Region 10 with a record of 27–4 and four senior starters led by All-Stater Jennifer Berryman. One of their three losses was to top-ranked Louisville Southern, the eventual champion that year.

West Carter was the little underdog from eastern Kentucky facing the 6–foot front line of a powerhouse team, and Clark Co. jumped out to a 20 point early lead and were on top 33–15 at the half, with the Comets ice cold from the field. It looked like the Lady Cards might just blow the West girls out of the gym in the second half, but it didn't happen, thanks to the long-range heroics of the daughter, Coach Brown, fondly called, "Kimbo."

She scored six three-pointers in the second half and the team knew she had the hot hand. They continued to feed her and the Lady Comets pulled to within 5 points with 50 seconds remaining. But Clark Co. prevailed 56–47 as Berryman was unstoppable with 26 points. Kim Brown had 23 for the Lady Comets with seven three-pointers, a state tournament single-game record that stands to this day. Despite the performance, she failed to make the All-Tournament team, an oversight that irritated Dad-Coach Brown, and puzzled those in attendance.

The West Carter rally had been sparked in part, it seemed, by the injury to forward Gina Taylor, who had to be carried off the floor after a collision with Berryman.

Coach Brown's staff had adopted the motto during the season, "Winning isn't everything, but wanting to is." He had heard the quote on the radio, originally attributed to Bobby Knight. That night, the Lady Comets proved they wanted to win and gave it 100 percent. As Hop told one reporter after the game, "we're small from our nose to our toes, but we're big inside."

The Lady Comets had made a good showing on behalf of the region and went home feeling satisfied about the season. It was a monumental year in the history of West Carter sports. The team would be remembered for years to come as the group "that started it all." No longer would the perennial powers of Ashland, Russell, Boyd and Rowan be the only teams to contend. The West Carter girls had arrived to finally take their place among the region's best.

Four of the five West Carter starters would return for another season, but the Lady Comets graduated the greatest player in their history to that date. Sheila Kay Porter had lead the team in scoring and rebounding every year since she suited up for varsity including a 15 per-game average her final year. She had become the all-time leading scorer and rebounder with 1250 points and 850 rebounds.

She recalled feeling somewhat of an outsider, coming from Lawton to play with the West Carter "town kids" that first year. She had always worn number–40– but was told that was Pam Biggs' number and would be a mighty difficult jersey to fill. She said she thought she could and indeed went out and proved it with an outstanding career. She participated in the Ky-Ohio All-Star game, which Hop Brown was chosen to coach for the first time and also named EKC and All Area Coach of the Year. Porter, Kim Brown and Brenda English were All-EKC and All-Area selections.

City sends off their Regional Champs to the State '88

Kim Brown shot 38% from three-point land and averaged 10 points per game. Point-guard Missy Greenhill averaged three per game, Gina Taylor 10, and Brenda English 14 per game. Karla McDowell and Samantha Layne were the other seniors on the State Tournament team, that finished 26–7, the best record in history and the tenth season of coaching for Hop Brown.

Brown had now compiled a record in his first decade of 138–102, with a region championship, five district titles and an EKC championship.

The season of 1988–89 started quite differently than the previous ones of the Hop Brown era. The Lady Comets were defending region champions. The cover story on the *Daily Independent* season preview was about them and the four returning starters. The consensus of coaches, sportswriters and broadcasters was that West would repeat as champs. Filling Porter's shoes would not be possible, but West had their quarterback Missy Greenhill, their three-point shooter, Kim Brown, and their versatile forwards, Brenda English and Gina Taylor returning. The team had worked in the off-season at summer camps and looked forward to the new season.

Would there be pressure to win? Hop Brown responded to that question in early season by saying, "When we went 2–15, that's pressure . . . this year- no way." The Lady Comets appeared to be ready to assume the new role of region favorites. Amy Mays or Carolee Barker looked ready to step into that fifth starting role, but Mays soon went down again with that bad knee and was unable to compete the rest of the season. Teammates would call it a great loss but Barker stepped in to start at forward.

West opened the season with six straight wins including the EKC tournament championship and a victory over Lexington Lafayette in their first appearance in the Bryan Station Classic. The streak was stopped in the Boyd Co. tournament by Rowan Co. 45–43, a loss the Lady Comets would avenge by 21 points in February.

Hop Brown finally got his invitation to a Louisville classic and participated in the Male Holiday event, beating Henry Clay but losing to Iroquois.

West handed their rival East Carter and Hop's good friend, Coach Brian Buck, one of their worst defeats, 86–46 in mid-season in a game where Kim Brown hit seven 3–pointers to tie her own record. The next game, however, West suffered their third loss, a 67–65 heartbreaker at Ashland. West entered post-season with a record of 24–4 after a loss to Coach John High's Whitesburg team at home and then seven straight victories.

The District tournament draw found the Lady Comets playing East in Grayson and it wasn't near as easy as the regular season. Coach Buck had his team primed and poised for an upset. West didn't play well, but pulled it out 43–34 and went on to breeze past Lewis Co. 70–37 to win their third straight District crown and move on to defend that Region title. West had been promised a two-year stint at hosting the Girls Region, but after their championship the previous year, the KHSAA moved the tournament to Summitt Jr. High in Boyd Co.

With Brenda English and Gina Taylor leading the way, West won their region opener 58–50 over Greenup Co. but barely got by Ashland in the semi-finals 68–65 when Brown scored just one three-pointer, but English poured in 27, and Barker had 14, to put them in the championship game against Russell.

Again the three-pointers weren't falling in the key game and Russell jumped out to an 8–0 lead before Hop called a time-out to settle the team down. The Lady Comets also trailed at the half but Gina Taylor sparked a third quarter rally as they roared back to claim the win. Taylor finished with 18 points. The team uttered a sigh of relief and suddenly felt the pressure of the season leave them with the victory that everyone expected but had to be gained out on the court, in order to relax.

Taylor said, "Everybody was for us last year, when we were underdogs, but this year they were gunning for us." The nervousness of those expectations may have been felt in the poorer than usual shooting in the tournament by the Lady Comets, but they had pulled it out and were headed back to Frankfort. Taylor, English, Brown and Barker received All-Tournament honors, with English selected as MVP.

For the girls the thrill was wonderful, but not quite the same as the year before, they would say. Coach Brown knew that the girls had not enjoyed the season victories as much, given the pressure of being the favorite to win it all. But now that it had been accomplished, it was a sense of relief and time for joy.

For Coach Brown and Coach Perry, every victory was sweet and back-to-back region titles, they knew, was a feat rarely accomplished. It would, however, pale in comparison to the achievements that lay ahead for West girls basketball.

Many media folk, who had developed a fondness for Hop Brown's friendly style and quick wit, alluded to his "fish" tie and tiepin as a possible source of good luck for the Lady Comets during tournament time the past two years. But Lady Luck nor Fish Luck would shine on the 16th Region for the 1989 State Tournament as they drew Region Six, and the defending State champions, Louisville Southern. Southern had dominated their region for years, and had won six out of the last seven region championships and their first state title the year before.

The game between West Carter and Louisville Southern at the Frankfort Civic Center was basically over within minutes. The Lady Trojans scored the first nine points, smothered the Lady Comets completely with their full-court pressure and coasted to an 83–38 first round win, the widest margin of victory (45) in State Tournament history.

Hop Brown acknowledged after the game that it could have been even worse, as Southern called off the press in the second quarter. The Lady Comets were no match for such an athletic team that would have four of their starters eventually go on to play major college basketball, including All-American, Lisa Harrison.

The Lady Comet players told the media after the game, that "they were the best we've ever seen." Coach Brown admitted that "we were pounded tonight for sure, but I'm proud as I can be of these girls."

The loss didn't dim the senior season of four stellar players of West Carter, who took the game in stride and realized that they had accomplished so much more than they ever imagined possible and enjoyed it all. The team was just one shy of 30 wins, at 29–5 and won the EKC season championship with a perfect record.

Brenda English set the single-season scoring record, Kim Brown had several three-point records, Missy Greenhill claimed a new free throw percentage record with 81%. Gina Taylor and English set records for steals and had raised the standard for defense at West. English averaged 16 points, Brown 12, Taylor 11 and Greenhill six for the season and all four were named to the All-Conference team, with English the MVP of the Eastern Kentucky Conference, while Brown and Taylor were chosen the Offensive and Defensive Players of the Year respectively. Best friends, English and Brown, were selected All-State honorable mention. English and Taylor had joined the 1,000 point club during the year, becoming the fourth and fifth players under Hop Brown to hit that milestone.

All four seniors joined Coach Brown and Von Perry on the 16th Region Mountain Shoot-Out All-Star team in the game against the 15th Region stars. The lone junior starter, Carolee Barker, had a good year, also, averaging eight points and six rebounds per game.

   Hop Brown received another Coach-of-the-Year award and presided over an emotional basketball banquet that saw the best class in West girls basketball history, that included his own daughter, take their final bows.

   Brenda English, became the first Lady Comet to win a scholarship to a Division I college, signing on to play at Morehead State. The back-to-back championships brought about a big change in girls basketball in Carter County and the region. English was speaking for the whole team when she would say, "We were certainly proud to be a part of that change."

   Two regional championship trophies now graced the case in the lobby of West Carter High, and many pictures and memorabilia began to fill the office of the girls basketball coach. The years ahead, though, for Hop Brown would mean finding additional space in both of those places—because there would be much more to come.

CHAPTER 4

THE STREAKS

The decade of the nineties began with the Lady Comet basketball program of Coach Hop Brown riding the crest of a wave of enthusiasm for girls basketball in Carter County and two straight Sweet 16 appearances. In addition, the girls were beginning to dominate the Eastern Kentucky Conference and the 62nd District. The next few years meant incredible win streaks for the Lady Comets in the district and conference, and by the time the decade ended and the new millenium began, an even more impressive streak would develop as West Carter would put together an unprecedented five straight regional championships and gain the ultimate prize in the year 2000.

The graduation in 1989 of the big four- Brown, English, Taylor and Greenhill left the cupboard a little bare for the start of the next season. However, a strong feeder system was beginning to sparkle in Olive Hill, with elementary and junior high girls, excited about moving up to a successful state tournament team. There was talent being developed under the tutelage of assistant Von Perry with her junior varsity team as well as Dana Smith, who was now working with the team and would begin the program of West Junior High School when it was established in 1990. In addition, girls were beginning to play year-round with basketball camps and amateur leagues.

Carolee Barker was the lone returning starter for Coach Brown when practiced opened in the fall of 1989. The Lady Comets won the EKC Tournament in December, beating Rowan Co. in the opening round. Rowan would stick them twice, though, in regular season play, and Ashland proved tough, dropping the Lady Comets two times in the season.

West won their fourth straight District Tournament title, beating East Carter 58–45 in the first round and then topped Lewis Co. 82–74 for the championship, in a wild game at West gym.

The Lady Comets advanced to the final four in the Region with a first round victory over Morgan Co. 83–70, but fell to the Ashland Kittens

72–55 ending any hopes of a three-peat. Ashland went on to beat Rowan Co in the championship game.

West went 19–11 for the season and Barker, Stephanie Rayburn and Madonna Tackett, who had developed a deadly 3–point shot, all finished the year averaging in double figures. Tammie McGlone and Nancy Birchfield averaged just shy of double digits, providing the Lady Comets with a solid and balanced offensive unit. Amy Mays was able to come back and play with sister, Lori, and contribute some in her senior year, despite heavy knee braces.

Barker, Rayburn, and Tackett all made All-EKC for the year with Rayburn named the top defensive player. Tackett's 84 three-pointers put her second on the all-time list. Her 85% free-throw shooting was a new season record, and her 73% charity line performance for her career was the best for a Lady Comet.

Once again, Coach Brown saw four starters graduate off his team, and the 1990–91 squad would have only starting center, Nancy Birchfield, returning.

The team started in November with a win over Fairview, but then suffered a 40–point loss to Ashland. They were beaten out in the first round of the conference tourney by Morgan Co, played East Carter four times during the year, losing twice to the Raiders, but then came back to beat them in the District championship 50–39, to keep that streak alive at five district trophies in a row.

West drew Menifee Co. for the Region and hosted the Lady Cats for the first round of the tournament. That year's tourney began a schedule of playing first round games at the four sites of the district winners, then moving the final four to the neutral court. West disposed of Menifee, 66–41, but then suffered one of their worst region tourney defeats, a 73–43 thrashing at the hands of the Lady Devils of Russell. Rowan Co. returned to the regional tourney winner's circle that year, beating Russell for the championship. West finished at 11–17 for the 1990–91 season marking the Lady Comets first losing record since 1986 and would be the last time Hop Brown finished below .500 during his coaching career.

Nancy Birchfield led the team in scoring for the season, with 439 points, the fourth best season total in Lady Comet history to that point. At 5'9, she had developed into a good, pure post player, with size and agility. A freshman, Michelle Tabor, came on strong playing JV and varsity and averaged 13 points for the Lady Comets, the most ever by a first-year player. Coach Brown called Tabor "the best pure shooter that had ever come into the gym." Hop and Sharon's middle daughter, Karla, a sophomore, scored 156 points off the bench, the most by a non-starter at West Carter and youngest daughter, Kandi, served as manager and number one fan. Birchfield and Tabor received several post-season honors and senior awards were given to Birchfield, Charity Brown, Chelle Gilliam, and Sonya Cook.

Birchfield said she learned a lot from Coach Brown, "patting me on the back when I needed it, and adjusting my attitude when that was called for. He was always willing to teach by showing you physically what he wanted you to do."

Michelle Tabor would return for the next season and her leadership continued, as she sparked the Lady Comets to a winning season in 1991–'92, finishing 16–14, back on the positive side of .500 and taking their sixth straight district championship.

Opening up the year, West

Michelle Tabor, one of West's best shooters, never got to the State tournament, but made her mark at Rio Grande College as a top scorer.

lost the EKC championship to Bath Co. in December and suffered a 40–point loss to Bath in January. The Lady Comets struggled against the likes of Ashland, Boyd Co, Russell and Rowan Co., but won all their district games and beat East Carter three times including the first round of the post-season 82–57, then crushed Lewis Co. 86–59 for the District tournament championship. West was no match for Boyd Co. in the first round of the 16th Region tournament, though, falling, 76–48. The Ashland Kittens, under Connie Greene, won their seventh region crown that year, defeating Russell in the finals.

That season saw the debut of Marla Gearhart, and the beginning of a new era in Lady Comet basketball. For the next dozen years, Hop Brown would always be able to write in one of Marvin and Judy Gearhart's talented daughters for his starting lineup. Marla impressed the crowds with her basketball savvy and ball-handling ability, even as an 8th grader that year, and averaged eight points per game in a starting role. Michelle Tabor led the team, totaling an even 500 points on the year, the second highest by a Lady Comet for a season. She hit 35% of her three-pointers, placing her second on the all-time Comet list and was named All-EKC. Gearhart's play as a junior high student marked a change in policy as heretofore the coaching staff had been reluctant to allow much playing time to the non-high school students, if there were enough upper class players to fill the roster. Coach Brown liked to carry only twelve on the roster, figuring any more than that made it difficult to get players in the game.

Gearhart had seen only limited junior varsity action as a 7th grader, and now was thrust into a position of point guard for the varsity. She called it a big responsibility but one the other players quickly accepted, despite her youth.

West graduated three of their first seven players that May—Laurie Sparks, Missy Taylor and Lori Mays, but the staff knew an exciting nucleus was returning for the following year and hopes were high.

 The season of 1992–'93 opened strong for the Lady Comets with three straight lop-sided victories including one over Rowan Co. in the EKC tourney semi-finals at Bath Co. in Owingsville. But in the championship game against the home team, the Lady Comets suffered a blow that would somewhat dampen their spirits for the year, but may have deepened their resolve to play harder. Michelle Tabor went down with a torn ACL in her knee and was out for the season. Their leading scorer, now in her junior year, faced some grueling months of rehabilitation after surgery. Bath Co. won the game 58–57.

Tabor called the injury a painful disappointment but resolved to make her recovery as quick as possible and said Coach Brown and all the team were so supportive of her in her rehabilitation. Intensely dedicated to the game and to hard work, Tabor was the ideal patient.

The coaching staff quickly made adjustments and the continued development of Marla Gearhart as well as some excellent three-point shooting by Karla Brown and rebounding and inside scoring strength from Stefanie Rose and Amy Tackett kept the Lady Comets on the winning track and a 20–8 record for the season.

The team returned to the Whitesburg holiday tournament where they went 1–2, recorded two wins over East by margins of 35 and 24 points, split with Ashland, and beat Rowan Co. in regular season play.

Tammy Mullins had taken over as head coach at cross-county East Carter, and West did not have to play them in the 62nd District Tournament for only the second time in history. The Comets easily won their seventh straight title without competition from either Elliott Co in the first round or Lewis in the championship game, which they won by 36 points.

West went to the regional with mixed feelings. They figured to be competitive, but knew in the back of their mind, that with Michelle Tabor healthy, they would have been the genuine favorite. They lost to Boyd Co. in the semi-finals of the 16th Region, 77–65, and the Lady Lions of Coach "Slick" Rice went on to capture their first region title in twelve years.

West had actually beaten Boyd, the region favorite, on the road, in the final regular season game by 22 points, but the Lady Lions, led by the Lueken twins, Laura and Kari, and Jamie Holbrook, turned the tables on the Lady Comets at Summit gym and eliminated West. The defense failed the Lady Comets that night, and the team that lived and died by the "three" perished, going 0–14 from long-range, the only game of the season without a trey.

The Lady Comets starting lineup was Karla Brown, Marla Gearhart, Stefanie Rose, Amy Tackett and Michelle Garvin. Both Coach Brown and Coach Perry would later admit that there is no doubt that with Michelle Tabor healthy the team would have been on its way to the Sweet Sixteen that year.

Karla Brown's career ended without the Sweet Sixteen trips of her older sister, Kim. She was selected All-Conference and named to play in the Ky-Ohio All-Star game. Marla Gearhart led the team in scoring for the season with 17 per-game average and was selected honorable-mention All-State as a freshman and named top offensive and defensive player in the EKC. Stefanie Rose averaged over nine rebounds per game and was the team's best shooter on the year. Brown averaged nine points and hit 36% of her long-range shots.

And while Karla made a big impression on West Carter basketball and enjoyed playing for her father, she would later admit that she probably didn't have the talent or the consistent work ethic of sisters Kim and Kandi.

Five other players graduated with Karla that year-Betsy Bailey, Charissa Barker, Michele Garvin and sisters Tracy and Stacy Piper, but the Lady Comet fans had thrilled to the antics of Marla Gearhart and now waited for the fall and the return of Michelle Tabor.

 Before the start of the 1993–94 season, the Brown family received quite a surprise with the doctor's announcement that Sharon was pregnant. It was a real shock for the family, and the doctor's would keep a close eye on Sharon during the next nine months, because of her age. She gave birth to a healthy baby boy in the Spring, April 28th 1994. John Kyle Cleveland Brown became an immediate celebrity and center of attention for his three older sisters. The names came from Dad, his favorite UK player, Kyle Macy, and his favorite football team.

The birth received the attention of the Cleveland team and WUGO radio arranged for special gifts to be delivered to the Hop Brown household from the Browns football team. In addition, there were UK presents, and of course, dreams of Dad someday teaching son all about "roundball."

The 1993–94 Lady Comet season dawned with expectations high and it seemed Tabor was back full strength and ready to lead the Comets in her senior year. West lost in the first week to Whitesburg, but then won the EKC Tournament, defeating Morgan Co. 60–53 to start a string of conference tournament championship trophies that would not end during the Hop Brown era.

Hop congratulates daughter, Karla, at closing Lady Comet banquet.

West presented a solid line-up of Marla Gearhart, Stacey Carter, Stefanie Rose, Michelle Tabor, and Amy Tackett, with strong support off the bench from Kimber Rayburn, Jennifer Justice, Ginger Brown, and Tara Duncan, and put together a record of 19–6 going into the District. The Lady Comets had trouble with Ashland and Russell and knew one of those two teams would stand in their way of a Sweet Sixteen trip.

The Lady Comets suffered a 60–49 loss to Morgan Co. on the road, January 10, 1994. That game marked the last EKC loss by a West Carter girls team until Jan 9, 2003, a string of 76 consecutive victories. Ten years without a conference loss would create a remarkable conference dynasty unparalleled anywhere in girls hoops.

The East-West rivalry was slowly deflating in interest as the Lady Raiders had seen a series of losing seasons. The Lady Comets beat them by 42 points in each of the regular season games that year. For the second year in a row, the two teams did not meet in the District as East lost to Lewis Co. in the first round, and the Lady Comets breezed to their eighth straight district championship beating Lewis 85–38 in the finals.

West Carter hosted the first round of the regional tourney and beat Fairview by 48 points setting up a showdown with Ashland in the semi-finals at Summit Jr. High gym in Ashland.

West claimed the victory in a great game, 66–60 avenging two season losses to the Kittens and putting themselves in the championship game for the third time in history. Tabor with 18 and Gearhart with 17 points led the way for the Lady Comets with Carter adding 11.

The title match-up against Russell was certain to be a battle. The Lady Devils had been region runner-up seven times, and had not won the championship since the first two years of girls basketball in 1975 and '76 and had a new coach in Anna Chaffins. They were hungry, motivated and talented.

West went to the locker room at half with what seemed to be a comfortable 11-point lead in the big game and the Comet faithful were thinking state tourney thoughts.

Then came the bizarre third quarter, when Michelle Tabor picked up three fouls, one a technical after a block call by the official. Tabor let the ball fly toward another official, but the referee on the scene thought she was throwing it to the stands in anger. The official later told Coach Brown it was a mistake, not to be too hard on her and leave her in the game. But Tabor had to sit down with four minutes left in the quarter. She and Stacey Carter both had four fouls. In the meantime, the full-court press was swallowing up the

Lady Comets and Russell was pounding down inside with Allison Osborn and Holly Reed. They took the lead with a minute to go in the quarter and went on to post an eight-point victory and advanced to the Sweet Sixteen, denying senior star Michelle Tabor the opportunity to appear in a state tournament.

Senior Stefanie Rose remembered the disappointment of that night, when they had a nice lead, but said they just couldn't contain Osborn in the second half. It would be remembered as the West team that seemed to have glory in their grasp, but let it slip away.

Coach Brown, said after the game, that while the fouls were a factor, the team just panicked, had trouble getting the ball up the court, and allowed Russell to get too many shots inside. Allison Osborn finished the game with 33 points and was named the tournament's Most Valuable Player.

Tabor concluded her career as the Lady Comet all-time leading scorer with 1470 points despite missing most of her junior year. She and Marla Gearhart were named All- Region, and All-EKC. Stefanie Rose led the team again in rebounding, putting her second in career rebounds for the Lady Comets. Amy Tackett topped the Lady Comet record for career free-throw percentage finishing her four years at 80%. Tabor had set a new single sea-son free-throw percentage record, connecting on 88% of her charity tosses and set the state record for most three-pointers in a year, 115. A season record of 23–7 was posted, their best year since the regional championship teams.

The knee injury and the technical foul controversy are imprinted in the minds of the Tabor family as well as Comet fans, realizing that erase those bad breaks and West Carter has possibly two more region trophies and one of their most prolific scorers has a chance to market her skills at the State Tournament. It didn't happen, though, prompting thoughts of one of the more famous "Hopisms" of Coach Brown—"ifs, ands and buts . . . if they were candy and nuts, we'd all have a Merry Christmas."

Tabor felt a victory in the championship game would have meant a scholarship to Morehead State for her, a scholarship that went to Osborn of Russell. Tabor, however, went on to make her mark in the record books of Rio Grande College.

With the three seniors that graduated, Rose, Tabor and Tackett, the team lost its leading rebounders and faced a task of building an inside game for the following year to go with two of the top guards in the region. With Gearhart's ball handling skills and Carter's extreme quickness, the Lady Comets had one of the best backcourt duos they had ever enjoyed. During the previous year, Gearhart was joined on the team by her eighth grade sister, Mira who, as a left-hander, was developing an accurate three-point shot.

Juniors Jennifer Justice and Ginger Brown stepped up to fill those inside positions for the Lady Comets when the 1994–95 season tipped off. West's opening two weeks was a carbon copy of the year before, with a victory over Fairview, a loss to Whitesburg then sweeping to another EKC Tournament title, beating Rowan, Morgan and then Lawrence Co. handily.

West participated in the Clark County tournament, for the first time, over the holiday, and beat Corbin, while losing to host, Clark Co. 64–50. The Lady Comets lost to Ashland and Montgomery Co., mid-year, but came back to defeat Ashland in February. In fact, West finished the year with a ten-game winning streak that included wins over Boyd Co, Rowan, Russell, and Ashland. They appeared ready to be dubbed the favorite for March Madness. The streak also included a 103–36 victory over Elliott Co., breaking their record for most points scored in a game.

West blasted its way to their ninth straight district championship, beating Lewis Co. 89–46, and then East Carter 63–35. Morgan Co. was no match for the Lady Comets as they hosted the first round of the Region and crushed the Lady Cougars 65–32, to set-up the semi-final encounter with the Ashland Kittens and the rubber match of the season. Each team owned one victory over the other and the winner of this one would likely make the Sweet Sixteen trip. Marla Gearhart and company appeared ready to stretch that win streak to 14 games.

It didn't happen, however, as the Kittens won 69–56 in the semi-final game, with Stacy Coomer and Kim Marsh dominating inside and finishing with 22 and 17 points respectively. The game was tied at the half, and the Kittens held a one-point lead going into the final quarter after a 45–foot shot by Kimber Rayburn at the buzzer was on target. Ashland hit their free throws down the stretch in the fourth quarter to seal the win and the season ended for West without the Region title. Gearhart was held to 11 points while Carter had 15.

Ashland went on to take the championship, with a 67–54 win over Rowan Co. West's final season record was 24–5. Marla Gearhart led the stats for the team with 16 points and five assists per game. Stacey Carter averaged 13 points per game, and hit 70 three-pointers for the season. Jennifer Justice led rebounding totals, averaging seven per game. The Lady Comets had come close again to winning it all and with only Carter graduating from the starters, the cry of "wait til next year" seemed appropriate for the Comet fans.

Carter and Gearhart were named All-Region and All-EKC. Jennifer Justice was also All-Conference and Carter was voted top senior in the region by the KABC and selected for the Ky-Ohio All-Star game. Carter continued playing locally with Kentucky Christian College in Grayson and had an outstanding college career and national championship rings with the Lady Knights. Reserves Candy Boggs and Tara Duncan graduated that year, and Kandi Brown, Hop's youngest daughter, got into two games and scored four points, during the EKC Tournament, when she dressed in place of an ill player. She was the first 7th grader ever to be brought up.

Her talent, developed over her youthful years of hanging out in the gym, was evident to all the fans of the region watching her in junior varsity action, and it would be hard for Dad to keep her out of the starting lineup the following year.

The 1995–96 season represented the last chance for Marla Gearhart, now a senior, to lead the Lady Comets to the State Tournament. With her sister, Mira, shooting well and Kandi Brown, ready for serious playing time as an 8th grader, some pieces of the puzzle appeared to be in place, if the team could find themselves as a unit. A bitter taste of three straight years of disappointing finishes when regional championships seemed in their grasp, only to vanish, dogged the coaching staff, team and fans. There appeared to be determination to rectify the situation and add to those '88 and '89 Region banners in the gym.

Marla would reflect later that the team thought they could win each of those years in '93, '94 and '95 but it "just wasn't our night at the right time." All the teams in the region had improved and tournament time was very competitive even if you had a good team.

West tipped off the season, as the favorite to win the 16th Region as they were featured on the cover of the *Daily Independent* Girls Basketball preview. As in previous years they took a victory in the opener with Fairview as the crowd witnessed Kandi Brown score her first three-pointer. In fact, she canned four of them on the night, for 12 points, off the bench. Hop determined it might not be good diplomacy to start Kandi as a 8th grader, but would use her for the season as the super sub, to rally the team as needed. West lost to Whitesburg in the second game of the year, but then won their third straight EKC tourney championship, beating Menifee, Lewis and Fairview by wide margins.

The Lady Comets were invited to the Lexington Bryan Station Classic and drew Harrison Co in the one-day event in December and picked up the win 66–48. The revived Ashland Kitten Invitational tournament during the Christmas break, saw an invitation go out to West Carter. The Lady Comets won the opening game against Clay Co. and then with a 37–point performance from Marla Gearhart whipped Whitesburg in the semi-finals, setting up the championship game with Ashland.

The Gearhart sisters put on a show that night at Blazer gym, with Marla scoring 23 and Mira cashing in 21 as they took home the championship with a 72–55 victory over Ashland, the host team. West proved their strength again later in January with a 48–45 victory over a highly-regarded Montgomery Co. team. West's record stood at 20–1 the second week of February, when their near perfect season hit a bump in the road. Old rival, Rowan Co. handed the Lady Comets a 66–61 loss in overtime at Morehead. Coach Curt Cundiff had his Lady Vikings playing well heading into the home stretch. The loss did not mar the EKC winning streak since it was not counted as a conference game.

West then suffered their third loss of the season at home when Ashland battled them basket for basket all night and wound up with a 56–54 victory. The Lady Comets closed out the regular season on Senior night, with a 82–46 win over Boyd Co., as Marla Gearhart took her final walk for the fans. Senior center Ginger Brown, forward Jennifer Justice and guard, Kimber Rayburn, would receive the applause of the fans, who certainly hoped even greater things were in store for the young ladies.

West Carter rolled to their tenth straight 62nd District championship at Lewis Co. gym with easy wins- 57–31 over Elliott Co. and an 81–36 drubbing of East Carter in the title game. Marla and Mira Gearhart, Jennifer Justice and Kandi Brown, were named All-Distirct, the first of five straight All-District honors for Kandi.

The first round of the 16th Region tournament was a slow down affair and while Boyd Co. throttled Marla Gearhart all night, limiting her to ten points, Mira came through with 12 points, all on long bombs, to capture a 35–18 victory and move on to Summit gym and the final four.

The pairings would make it clear what was ahead for the Lady Comets. To advance to the Sweet Sixteen in Bowling Green, they would have to beat the only two region teams that had dealt them losses that year—Rowan Co. and Ashland.

The Lady Comets turned in a solid performance in the semi-final with Rowan, leading all the way, and claiming a 51–42 victory that would put them in the championship game for the fourth time in their history.

The March 11th battle at Summit Gym, between West and Ashland ranks as one of the greatest girls title games in region history. The defending champion Kittens, versus the determined Lady Comets. The team with the most region titles, taking on the team seeking to make its place in history.

Ever the motivator, Hop Brown took Marla Gearhart aside to tell her she had to provide whatever it took to lead the team to victory, and "go out and show 'em." Marla responded with an individual performance unparalleled before or since, in region history—boys or girls. She remembers her dad telling her, "this is your stage, go out and play."

She shot 15 of 20 from the field, including five out of seven, three-pointers, two for two at the free-throw line for 37 points and five rebounds, tying her own single-game mark. That night, she was in a world of her own. Coaches, fans, sportswriters were lacking in adjectives to aptly describe what she did on the court. She made 11 of her last 12 shots. Years later, she said she couldn't really remember what she was thinking about during the game. "It was just one of those nights when you are in the zone and it all works right." She credited her sister Mira for plenty of assists.

The victory almost slipped away from the Lady Comets, though. Ashland's Nikki Young had come off the bench to score 11 points and West was struggling against the pressure defense. The Kittens led with two minutes to play, 53–51 when Lady Comet Kimber Rayburn drove to the basket to tie it. Then, Ashland's last shot at the basket fell off as time expired with the scored knotted, 53 all.

West outscored Ashland 5–0 in the overtime, with a basket by Jessica Jones, and free throws from Mira Gearhart and Jennifer Justice to claim the tense but exciting 58–53 win.

Coach Brown declared to the radio audience. "How sweet it is" remembering again that feeling of heading to the State Tournament. Marla Gearhart won thunderous approval from the crowd, when named the MVP. She told reporters that the team had worked too hard to be denied the big prize and she was determined to make it happen. The senior had indeed come through in the clutch. Kimber Rayburn and Mira Gearhart were also named to the All-Region squad. A great Comet celebration began at Summit gym and carried all the way back to Olive Hill. The team was state-bound for Bowling Green and Diddle Arena.

Hop called Marla's performance "unbelievable" but what he had come to expect from his point guard for five years. "She is just the complete package, a competitor to the end."

Three years of disappointment in trying to make it back to the State, was now behind them. The Lady Comets had a week to prepare, as they were scheduled to open the tournament up on March 20 against 1st region champ and newcomer to the State Tournament, Fulton Co., who had a record of 25–5. It would be the western end of the state versus the eastern, and a chance for the 16th Region to redeem itself, after having lost out in the first round for 14 years in a row. The region had not won a Sweet Six-teen tournament game since Rowan Co. made it to the semi-finals in 1981.

While the draw in 1988 and '89 had not been kind to the Lady Comets, this year's opponent presented an opportunity for victory. The first two Comet state tourney teams were just happy to be there, but this team had visions of staying awhile and playing several games on the big floor.

The Lady Comets arrived a day early to get ready for the Wednesday afternoon tip-off, but Mother Nature made an unexpected Spring deposit of snow on Kentucky Tuesday night, causing the first-ever postponement of state tournament games.

Finally, on Thursday evening the Lady Comets took the floor at West-ern Kentucky University for the contest but their determination was not matched by their play that particular night, and Fulton Co. ended the Comets season, dealing them a 64–58 loss.

Fulton Co. dominated the boards with 22, second-chance shots, out-rebounding West 42–24. Samantha Smith and Rachel Hamrick scored 41 points between them. In addition, a gritty box and one defense and often a double-teaming trap on Marla Gearhart kept her frustrated all night, and she finished with a season low of eight points. Fulton jumped out to an early lead, but West had trimmed it to three points by halftime and trailed 47–44 going into the fourth period. They could never overtake Fulton and suffered the loss, disappointing the several hundred West Carter fans who had made the long trip.

An obviously downcast Coach Brown, after the game, said his team was just flat, and got whipped badly on the boards and couldn't seem to get into the rhythm of the game. They didn't realize the quickness with which the Lady Pilots were able to play defense to keep Gearhart from getting the ball. Marla said she and the team were just evidently not ready for what was thrown at them. Ginger Brown, Jessi Jones and Kimber Rayburn all fouled out in the fourth quarter. Mira Gearhart led the scoring with 15 points. Coach Von Perry, who was overseeing the girls at the motel, felt the two late nights away from home, got the girls out of their routine and affected their play. She said that it was certainly a game that should have been won, as the Lady Comets were the better team, but not in sync on that night.

It was not a memorable night for Marla at Diddle Arena, and while she would never have another chance at a state tourney victory, her career with Eastern Kentucky University would put her back in that very gym for many great games against Western Kentucky. She became the second Lady Comet to play for a Division I NCAA school, winning a scholarship to suit up for the Lady Colonels.

The 1995–96 season had been an exciting one for the fans, with a final record of 30–4, although the violations later identified in the Whitesburg girls program meant a forfeiture of their victories, and the official record has been changed to 31–3, their first 30–win season. The Comets' 1994–95 record was subsequently also amended to 25–4. The team scored 70 points per game on the year, and was second in the state in regular season scoring average and held opponents to 43 points, ninth in the state in defense. West shot 70.9% from the charity line for the season, surpassing all previous highs and finishing tops in the state in that category, in what would become an almost annual honor.

Marla Gearhart had scored her 2,000th career point in February, and her final numbers stood at 2,264, eight hundred more than Michelle Tabor, the previous record-holder.

She averaged 19 points per game her senior year, and also set a career assist record. She was selected third-team All-State, first team by some newspapers, and again collected EKC honors, and named the 16th Region Player of the Year, and participated with Jennifer Justice in the Ky-Ohio All-Star game.

Justice set a Comet record for best shooting percentage for single season and career. Gearhart was the *Daily Independent's* Area Player of the Year for the second straight year. Sister, Mira, was also selected All-EKC along with Justice. Mira averaged 13 points as a sophomore and hit 37% of her shots behind the arc. For the first time, seven players had 100 or more rebounds, lead by Ginger Brown's 188 boards.

The senior class of Gearhart, Rayburn, Brown, and Justice finished with an overall record of 97–24 and a region title. They had begun a domination of the EKC, and won a tenth consecutive district championship, something only a handful of Kentucky teams have ever done.

Fans did not see it as the end, however, despite knowing the leading scorer in their history was graduating. The program was developing more

Marla Gearhart dazzled fans with her play and took her game on the road as an Eastern Kentucky Lady Colonel star
photo courtesy Tim Webb/EKU Sports

and more talent, and the junior varsity team of Coach Perry and Coach Smith had just completed another perfect season extending their winning streak to 58 straight games. Mira Gearhart and Kandi Brown, who had averaged eight points per game as an eighth grader, were eager for the next season to begin.

West Carter's first regional championship in 1988 was followed by a repeat, and now with the '96 title, the team saw some possibilities of duplicating that feat as the 1996–97 season opened. There was no question that Gearhart and Brown could provide scoring punch, but the other positions were true question marks for the coaches as play commenced.

The *Daily Independent* poll in the pre-season saw Ashland as the favorite with West Carter ranked second. The paper quoted Hop Brown as saying, "Well, our team won't be prime rib this year, but we're not going to be chopped liver, either."

The Lady Comets took the floor against Fairview to open the year, with Kandi Brown, Mira Gearhart, Carrie Jones, Jessi Jones, and Amy Branham as the starters. Summer Whitton came back out for basketball her senior year and became the first substitute, and the staff decided to dress

5'11 7th-grader, Meghan Hillman, who would see action in that first game. Hillman was one of the tallest players ever in the program and developing strong inside talent was important for any team, since girls basketball was becoming more physical.

The Lady Comets jumped into the season with a 13–game winning streak, including their fourth consecutive EKC Tournament title. The EKC final game turned into a good battle with old-rival, East Carter. The Lady Raiders program was on its way back up, as long-time boys assistant coach, Hager Easterling, took over as head coach and had hopes of breaking a disturbing trend, of ten losing seasons out of the previous eleven. A promising group of girls donned the East jerseys for the season. They played hard against West in the EKC championship game before falling, 45–39.

West won three games at the Laurel Co. Tournament, but lost to Scott Co, 61–50 in the first round of the Ashland Invitational. Their record stood at 14–1 as they came to Holbrook Complex East for a regular season game against the Lady Raiders.

West pulled out a nail-biter 45–44 on their rivals' court, but East held Kandi Brown to 4 points, and signaled that this might be the year they had a shot at beating the Lady Comets. They, indeed, went on to prove they could overcome the Comets, with a victory on January 29th, at West, 61–42 behind a strong inside performance by Andrea Buck and Teccoa Gallion. West's leading scorer, Mira Gearhart, was shut out in the second half.

The Lady Comets record stood at 19–3 including a loss the previous week to Montgomery Co. The East contest was not a conference game so the EKC winning streak remained intact, but the Lady Raiders had topped their rival for the first time, since 1991, as six years of futility had ended for East Carter and there was real joy in the Raider camp, for sure. Coach Easterling was happy to finally "get the monkey off our back" about the East-West rivalry, with a victory.

West finished out the year, without a loss, and went to the District Tournament with a record of 25–3, including two strong season wins over Ashland, the team rated ahead of them in the pre-season. It now appeared it was not the Kittens but the Lady Raiders that might stand in the way of a region championship repeat.

The Lady Comets took care of Lewis Co. 72–37 to set up the showdown with East Carter in the District title game.

A capacity crowd gathered for the action at East gym, with the Grayson folks truly fired up to end the 10-year grip the Lady Comets had on the District trophy.

West took a 26–19 lead to the locker room at the half, and increased their advantage to 39–30 to start the final period. But in the fourth quarter, Kandi Brown fouled out of the game, and the Lady Raiders rallied strong, pressed hard, and with a 16–0 run, took a huge victory, 49–44 to capture the 62nd District championship. The Lady Raiders had a solid lineup of Buck and Gallion inside with Lauren Scott, Freedom Sexton and Nicole Perry outside. The East girls basketball had returned to compete with the best and Coach Easterling, staff, players and fans were ecstatic. After the game, the girls were happy, not just for finally beating West Carter in the District Tournament, but that winning felt so good after some years of frustration.

Senior Freedom Sexton called it a night she'll never forget because she had never won a district title, and now East had a regular season and tournament win over West. She credited, "the team concept with all five players contributing" in helping East pull it off. "West Carter was just always tough competition and always had a good team," Sexton said.

Coach Easterling complimented the huge resolve on the part of his girls in that fourth quarter, but also felt the fact that the girls had dedicated themselves to hard work when he took over the program that previous summer. The work was finally paying dividends.

The West girls, for the first time in a decade, now found themselves runner-up in the District, but still alive in the quest for a regional title, if they could put themselves back together, after watching a victory slip away in the fourth quarter.

Coach Brown admitted the East pressure in the final period was his girls undoing. "We threw too many good passes to East Carter. I think they threw to everybody but me in those final minutes." He congratulated East on the thrilling and well-deserved win.

The Lady Comets drew Ashland for the first round and came into Blazer gym, knowing a victory would put them back on the right track and a possible rematch with East Carter in the final.

West had beaten the Kittens twice, 62–35 and 61–54 in regular season action, but that March evening belonged to Ashland as Nikki Young scored 22 points to lead them to a 60–45 win and end the Lady Comets season. The Kittens took charge early and lead all the way as West's hopes of a repeat regional championship vanished with lackadaisical play that night.

Ashland went on to take the region title beating East Carter in the finals. East had defeated Morgan and Boyd Co. to earn their first-ever appearance in a regional championship game, then lost to the Kittens

60–44, settling for the runner-up trophy in the 16th Region, their best-ever finish and quite an accomplishment for Coach Easterling's first year.

Ashland's victory over Murray in the first round of the State Tournament that year broke the 15-year losing streak of 16th Region teams in the Sweet Sixteen. The Kittens lost to Elizabethtown in the quarter-finals. After the tournament, Ashland coach Rick Griffith accepted a position as assistant at the University of Kentucky.

The totals were impressive for the 1996–97 West Carter season, with a record of 26–5. Mira Gearhart, Jessi Jones and Kandi Brown received many post-season honors, including All-Conference and All-District. Gearhart was the EKC Player of the Year. Carrie Jones was also All-District. Gearhart averaged 16 and Brown 15 points per game on the season. Gearhart's 41% from the 3–point range tied her older sister Marla's record and the team, as a whole, set a new mark, hitting 37% for the season from long-range.

The senior class of Summer Whitton, Amy Branham, Becky Collingsworth, Carrie Jones, and Jessi Jones had recorded 105 wins against just 19 losses during their career. Only two starters, Brown and Gearhart, would return for the 1997–98 season.

West had been the most consistent winning girls team of the decade, but they would have to live with the realization, that once again they had actually beaten the eventual Region champ in the regular season, but couldn't produce the key victory at tournament time. That had been the case actually since 1993, but only in '96 could they put it together to win the big prize. Four other titles seemed possible but they couldn't make them a reality. Could they improve on that issue? Hop Brown's teams of the next five years would answer that question with a resounding YES!

CHAPTER 5
THE BANNER

When interviewed at the start of the 1997–98 season, Coach Hop Brown joked that they would definitely be young. "I have five girls who still believe in Santa Claus, the Easter Bunny and the Tooth Fairy." That was probably an exaggeration, it might have been actually only three, but youth was definitely the defining word for the roster heading into regular season play.

The Lady Comets would be dressing four middle-school students on the varsity for the first time in their history. 8th graders Meghan Hillman and Kayla Jones, and 7th grader, Megen Gearhart all figured to be in the plans that included the seniors, Mira Gearhart and Wanda Dean, and sophomore, Kandi Brown, as possible starters.

The pre-season consensus of 16th Region coaches was that East Carter, Boyd Co. and Ashland all would be ahead of the Comets, but they certainly knew to be on the lookout for Hop and company when tournament time rolled around, as the kids gained experience and improved.

West opened the season winning their first five games, adding to their string of EKC tournament championships. They recorded two wins each over Morgan Co. and Rowan Co. The girls took their lumps in the Lexington Bryan Station Classic, losing to the home team, 65–47. The Lady Defenders came back and beat them again in the inaugural Queen of the Bluegrass Tournament in Grayson a week later. The first year of the round-robin tournament at East Carter saw the Lady Comets go 4–1 and take third-place with another victory over Rowan Co. and wins against Hart Co., South Oldham, and Harrison Co., some pretty strong girls programs. Mira Gearhart and Kandi Brown, who had been leading the team in scoring, were selected to the All-Tourney team.

The Christmas season was pretty well covered up with basketball as the team headed for the Laurel Co. Tournament right after Santa Claus came ..(for those who still believed!)

The Lady Comets beat Phelps the first night, but then lost two games in a row, to Estill Co. and North Laurel, before heading back home. However, Mira Gearhart did not make the trip at all, as she was dealing with some back pain at the time, and rest was recommended by the doctor. Mira said she had never had any problems before but figured the holiday would be a good time to allow some healing.

Mira came back strong and joined Kandi Brown to lead the team to a 68–43 home win over Greenup on January 5th to give Hop Brown his 350th career victory and Kandi collected her 1,000th career point on a special night for father and daughter.

Three nights later, the duo of Gearhart and Brown netted 20 points apiece to beat East Carter 52–36. The other two region favorites, Ashland and Boyd Co. proved tough and the Lady Comets lost to the Kittens 62–50 and to Boyd 75–64 in January.

The rematch with East Carter was played before a large crowd in Grayson, and the fans got their money's worth with a battle that went into overtime before West prevailed 65–62, with Brown racking up 29 points.

The Montgomery Co. Lady Indians came to West Carter, ranked as the top team in the state, but without superstar Beth Vice, who was out with a knee injury. West fell 50–47, but did some growing up that night, and would not lose another basketball game until those same Lady Indians embarrassed them in the State Tournament in Richmond, six weeks later.

That six-week run was one of the most incredible stretches Hop Brown's charges had ever experienced. The Gearhart-Brown scoring machine was hitting on all cylinders and the youngsters were suddenly showing signs of maturity beyond their years. They soundly whipped the two teams that had bested them so easily earlier in the season, running past Ashland 74–43 and crushing Boyd Co. 65–38 to close out regular season play with a record of 21–7, but realized the success of the year was going to be measured in the way they played East, Boyd and Ashland during March Madness.

The 62nd District Tournament would be played on their home court, and by the luck of the draw, they pulled East Carter for the opening game, essentially making the third game of the season with the Lady Raiders, the championship game of the District.

You could cut the tension with a knife that night, as the fans realized that one of these good basketball teams would not go on to the Region, despite both having big seasons. East was 18–7, and had been ranked first in the region. But their determined effort that night came up short and the Lady Comets moved on, whipping the Lady Raiders before a delighted West Carter crowd. Brown scored 26 and Gearhart 20 in the impressive 60–44 win.

West took the championship the next night, 66–40 over Lewis Co. and headed for region play knowing that Ashland and Boyd Co. both lay in waiting for an ambush.

West hosted the first round region game and disposed of Rowan Co. 65–51, their fourth win of the year over their old rival. Under a new format, one that Coach Hop Brown publicly opposed, the 16th Region girls teams would hold semi-finals Tuesday and finals Wednesday at their traditional site at Summit Jr. High gym in Boyd Co., forcing them to play three nights in a row to win the title.

The Ashland Kittens came into the semi-final game with a record of 13–13 and although picked by many to win the region, they had fallen on hard times, and poor play in the second half of the season. The Lady Comets dominated and advanced to the title game with a 62–42 victory, thus eliminating the defending region champions.

Were the Lady Comets too young to handle the pressure of a 16th Region championship battle, especially against the strong inside game of Boyd Co.'s Latosha Negrete and Sarah Click? Could the deadly outside shooting of Gearhart and Brown come through against the Lady Lions? Would the new zone defenses the coaching staff had developed over the year work for the West girls in the clutch?

A huge delegation from Olive Hill gathered to watch for the answers in the Region final and cheered wildly the result- A 56–42 victory and a trip to Richmond and the Sweet Sixteen. Gearhart had 22 and Brown 15 points and between them, made 24 of 28 free throws in the game. Negrete and Click were held to six and nine points respectively as Boyd Co. shot poorly and couldn't avoid foul trouble with their aggressive, pressing defense. West capitalized at the line and held off a fourth quarter rally attempt to hoist the trophy, the fourth region title in the schools history.

Mira and Kandi were named Co-MVP's and both said they were glad to share it. They played together well, and both growing up with basketball dads, knew the real intricacies of the game besides being "pure shooters." They had provided the leadership for the entire year and now couldn't have been happier as they celebrated a great and truly unexpected region championship. Meghan Hillman joined them on the All-Tourney team.

Hop and staff had used a seven-player rotation with Gearhart, Brown, senior Wanda Dean, and 8th graders Hillman and Kayla Jones starting, with freshman Cathy Day, and 7th grader Megen Gearhart, the first reserves. Hop had dubbed his young team "the diaper dandies" and had quipped to reporters that he had underwear older than some of the girls!

Well, the "diaper dandies" were headed to the "The Big Dance," and no one could say they had backed into the title. They had beaten the top three teams in the 16th Region and won their five games of the post-season by an average margin of 18 points.

Observers have lauded the coaching staff with truly a great achievement molding that young group into a champion, but the staff credited the extremely hard work of all players in wanting to learn and, as a team, dedicating their summers to basketball and improving their skills. Hop Brown also many times cited the team's courage and relaxed style. They simply went out, with nothing to lose, and played freely. He often stated, "I guess they are too young to even know about pressure or what they are achieving." And Coach Brown enjoyed a supply of new underwear, thanks to concerned fans!

Meghan Hillman and Kayla Jones seemed to confirm all that, when they would remember years later, that the tournament championship game and the State Tournament didn't feel that much different to them, than the other wins.

Plenty of excitement surrounded the second trip to the Sweet Sixteen in three years, and a lot of media attention to what was one of the youngest teams ever to compete there. Their opponent, the Muhlehburg North Stars, of the third region, had a record of 20–10 and was making their debut in a Girls Sweet Sixteen. The match-up seemed perfect for West to take their first state tourney victory.

Both teams came out flat before a Wednesday night crowd at McBrayer Arena in Richmond and at the end of the first eight minutes it was 5–4 in favor of the Lady Comets. West took a six-point halftime lead to the locker room and continued to expand it in the second half to win 58–40, using their match-up and pressing zone defenses that had worked wonders down the stretch to stymie the Stars offense. West had erased a one-point deficit in the 2nd quarter, when Megen Gearhart came off the bench to hit a "trey" and was able to squeeze her little 5'4 frame through the defenders and down baseline for another bucket to ignite the Lady Comet crowd.

With Ashland's win the previous year, it was the second straight victory for the 16th Region at the State, after being the proverbial doormat of the State Tournament for so many years. It was an impressive victory for the young team and the ease of it also gave opportunity for senior reserves, Leigh Pendlum and Beth Baker, to get into a state tourney game.

Hop Brown commented to reporters in the post-game, that many people had mentioned before the year started, it might be a long season for him, what with five seniors graduating in '97. He declared, "I guess everyone was right, when they said it was going to be a long season . . . By-gosh, we're still playing."

So into the quarter-finals, now, the "diaper dandies" pranced and they had captured not only the hearts of the West Carter fans, but many others as well. A loud and festive crowd of Carter Countians had made the trip to Richmond and the girls responded to that adoration.

It was a well-rounded effort, with 8th graders Meghan Hillman and Kayla Jones, scoring 15 points and grabbing 13 rebounds between them. And as usual, Mira Gearhart and Kandi Brown led the scoring with 18 and 15 respectively. The victory was especially gratifying for the duo, since they had been a part of the '96 squad that lost to Fulton Co. in the State first round in Bowling Green. It was truly special for Mira, who had played in that losing game with older sister, Marla, but now could share the joy of a win with kid sister Megen, known as "Li'l Penny." She had acquired the nickname from the puppet of Penny Hardaway, as seen on a TV commercial. Hardaway was one of her favorite NBA players.

Mira said years later, that the '96 trip with Marla was really nice because she knew it was big sis's dream to play in a State Tournament and it had been seven years since West Carter had gone to the State. The '98 trip was great for her because it was also her senior year and she was there with Megen.

All the girls had a day to savor their big win over Muhlenberg, before meeting top-ranked Montgomery Co. in the quarter-finals Friday afternoon. The Lady Indians were the last team to defeat West and were riding high, despite losing their All-State player, Beth Vice, to a season-ending knee injury. West had lost to them by only three points earlier, though, and felt good about the upcoming game.

That day, however, the Lady Indians proved to be too much to handle for the Lady Comets as they fell behind 21–4 at the end of the first quarter and were never able to recover. The quickness and aggressive defense overwhelmed West, suffering a 62–27 beating and ending the season. The elation of the first round victory was dampened by the loss. It was the lowest scoring total ever for a Comet team since their early years and one of the lowest in state tourney history.

Montgomery had not lost to a Kentucky opponent all year, and advanced to the championship game before falling to Elizabethtown 45–37. It was wonderful yet sad season for Coach Hopey Newkirk's girls, playing the second half of the schedule without Beth Vice, who was named Miss Basketball, and then living with the realization with her in the lineup, they surely would have been taking the championship trophy back to Mt. Sterling.

For senior starters, Mira Gearhart and Wanda Dean, who were best friends, it was not the way they would have liked to end their careers, as Gearhart had just six points and Dean two. Meghan Hillman was shut down from the field, and Kandi Brown was held to ten points, while Kayla Jones failed to score. Megen Gearhart came off the bench to collect eight points. Mira had been hit hard early in the game and suffered a headache, and never seemed to recover to get into the flow of the game.

Hop Brown was disappointed with the teams' lackluster play, but still lauded the kids great effort for the year. "I'm as proud as I can be of these girls," he told the radio audience. They finished up 27–8 on the season and overachieved in the minds of most people. The molding of the '98 group, many see, as Brown's greatest coaching year.

The senior class had logged a record of 109–20 with two region championships, while being perfect in the EKC. Mira Gearhart had finished right behind her sister, Marla, on the all-time points list for West Carter, after averaging 18 per game her final year.

Kandi Brown averaged 16 points and nine rebounds per game and set a record for most rebounds, deflections and assists in a season. Both girls were among the best in the state in free-throw shooting finishing with identical 83.3% stats. As they had shared Region MVP honors, they shared Conference honors with Kandi named Offensive Player of the Year and Mira, the Player of the Year. Both were selected honorable-mention All-State and Kandi was named the *Daily Independent* Player of the Year while Mira was selected as top area senior player in the coaches poll.

While she had offers to play college ball, Mira decided to give sports a rest and pursue her studies at Morehead State, without basketball in the picture. She said she was just "burnt out," but remained excited about watching Megen play many more years for the Lady Comets.

Kandi and the "diaper dandies" seemed ready to get right back at summer ball quickly and fans couldn't resist dreaming about what exciting days might be ahead with Kandi's versatile talent and the continued improvement of Jones, Hillman, Gearhart and Cathy Day. In the back of

his mind, Hop Brown, figured that the next season could be pretty interesting to say the least.

The young girls worked hard in team AAU and summer
camps and by the time the 1998–99 season prepared to tip-off,
Coach Brown pronounced his "dandies" a little more mature. He
knew his daughter, Kandi, was indeed an All-State candidate and
capable of taking the team to the top. But he also made known to the *Daily
Independent* in the pre-season interview that "she's not the only bird in the
flock." Gearhart, while only an 8th grader, appeared ready to step in for older
sister, Mira. Cathy Day, a sophomore, and Jones, and Hillman, now at the
high school as freshmen, would present a solid lineup that earned them the
favorite role in the 16th Region and even a spot in the top ten in state-wide
polls, respect a Carter County girls team had never received in pre-season.

Meghan Hillman was now 6'1 and along with Kayla Jones, West now
had strong inside weapons to go with their reputation of a great outside shooting team. Jones was so tough and determined on the floor, she was nicknamed,
"Bulldog." Brown, Gearhart and Day figured to be able to fill it up from behind
the arc when needed. It would be, overall, a younger team than the previous
year and without a senior starter their future truly appeared very bright.

The 16th Region seemed more balanced than in recent years, and Coach
Hop Brown predicted that at least six teams had to be considered contenders.

Both Fairview and Morgan Co. gave West all they wanted to start the
season, just getting by the Lady Eagles 61–56 and beating Morgan Co by
nine. Morgan Co. came even closer the next week in the first round of the
EKC as West squeezed out a 54–49 win to advance. They defeated East
Carter 55–39 to win their sixth straight conference tourney title.

West came into the Queen of the Bluegrass Tournament with an 8–0
record and beat Wayne Co. in the opener. The second game against Boyd
Co, though, saw the Lady Lions take a big 15–point halftime lead. The
Lady Comets battled back, but Kandi Brown went down with an ankle
injury in the fourth quarter and had to be taken out of the game. Boyd went
on to win, 84–78. West, without Kandi, was whipped badly the next day by
North Hardin 86–50, one of the widest loss margins in their history as the
girls seemed completely disinterested in the game.

Kandi was back in shape and ready for the Ashland Kitten Invitational in January at Blazer gym and led the team in scoring all three nights
as West took the title with wins over Bryan Station, East Carter and then

Ashland in the final 48–46. They avenged the earlier loss to Boyd Co. by beating the Lady Lions at West gym, 58–45 in mid-January.

Once again, it was Montgomery Co. that handed the Comets their last regular season loss before tournament time, as the Lady Indians had returned the same five from their State runner-up team. This time the game was much closer before West succumbed 57–47 at Mt. Sterling. The Lady Comets finished up season play with eight consecutive victories including wins again over Ashland, Boyd, and East Carter.

The picture for March Madness was a copy of the year before. The Lady Comets knew they would find themselves playing those three teams for the right to advance to the State and hoped they could replay their success.

The first showdown came against East Carter in the District championship when the two rivals met for the fifth time in the season. Hop had to convince his girls not to believe the old adage that you can't beat a good team three times in one year, because they were now faced with the challenge to win for the fifth time, over what was a strong Lady Raider lineup. East featured Lauren Scott and Teccoa Gallion, both college prospects. Gallion would go on to enjoy an outstanding career at Pikeville College and Scott played for Transylvania, before sidelined by illness.

The margin of victory for West over their county rival had been just seven points on two occasions that year, and East was fired up coming into Elliott Co. gym for the championship tilt.

When the buzzer had sounded that evening, Kandi Brown, for the first time in two years, had not one field goal in the scorebook, only five free throws. But while the Lady Raiders had concentrated on stopping West's star, she was helping the supporting cast come through in a big way, and the Comets crushed the Raiders dreams of an upset, 58–31. Gallion had been held to just two points by the Comet defense. West was advancing to the Region as the District champ, with the possibility of seeing East for an incredible sixth time if they both played well at Morehead.

West hosted the Russell Lady Devils for the first round of the Region and knew Coach Anna Chaffin's team was dangerous, having improved through the year. Kayla Jones had a big night with 19 points and West moved on with a 55–41 victory and in the meantime, Morgan Co. had beaten East Carter. West would play Boyd Co. next and then in all likelihood take on Ashland for the title, if they could handle the Lady Lions.

Kandi was truly ready for this one and electrified the crowd with a 31–point performance as the Comets controlled it from the outset and captured a 52–36 win to assure their sixth appearance in a region championship game.

West had beaten Ashland by two in the AKIT, but whipped them soundly 70–45 in February. Once again it appeared the Kittens were self-destructing in the second half of the year and came into the post-season with a losing record.

In the title game, West Carter was up on the Kittens 21–16, three minutes into the third quarter, when it happened. Sophomore Cathy Day, who had not scored in the game, but was being left open by an Ashland defense shaded toward Brown, popped in the first of five consecutive three-pointers and the game was over. West went on to bury Ashland 58–32 with Day the hero and everyone glad for her.

Since the tournament officials had the unfortunate policy of voting for the All-Tournament selections at halftime, Day was the only Lady Comet starter who was not named to the team, despite a 23–point performance in the championship game. Megen Gearhart finished with 13 points. It was Day and Gearhart who had come off the bench for the previous year's championship team and now they were playing the role of leading this year's edition back to the Sweet Sixteen.

Kandi Brown won her second straight tourney MVP trophy and the nets came down at Morehead State for the second consecutive year for the maroon and white. Kandi told reporters after the game, that the win truly demonstrated that West was team-oriented, not caring about individual honors, but just wanting to win.

Coach Brown called it a great thrill, a "magical run" with a group of young ladies who played together so well and developed a feel of how to win. For the second time in Lady Comet history, Hop Brown had seen back-to-back region titles. He noted the big difference though was the age. The '88 and '89 teams were led by juniors and seniors. This team had no senior and he knew that the intelligence and courage these girls had displayed meant there would be many more thrilling roads to travel in the "magical run."

Hop Brown became the first region coach to win five titles, including three of the last four. In typical fashion, he denied he actually had won any, giving full credit to the girls. The trophy cases at West Carter were full, but certainly more room would be found, as needed, for laurels that might loom ahead for this young team.

Mandy Sterling was the leading scorer for Ashland that March night, with 18 points, and little did Hop and the team realize that the guard who had given them fits for several years was soon to become one of them.

The Lady Comets rolled into Bowling Green with the fourth best record among the sixteen contenders and had been ranked among the top ten in the state, all-season long. Montgomery was the top pick again, without a loss to any Kentucky team. They played in the lower bracket with another favorite, Louisville Assumption.

West Carter and Lexington Catholic were the best teams of the upper bracket. As luck would have it, the Lady Comets and Lady Knights had to face each other in the first round, Wednesday night. Catholic was making their first tourney trip and it figured to be a real war. With three appearances in the past four years, Hop and West were becoming well known among the KHSAA folks and gaining lots of state-wide fans.

Lexington came out in a press to test the composure of 8th grader, Megen Gearhart, at point guard and "Penny" responded with repeated drives, slipping through and under the defenders and Kandi Brown took charge early. West was up after the first quarter and took a 27–23 lead to the locker room at half, with Brown's 16 points topping the Knight's Kelli Stamper, another All-State candidate, who had been held to four points.

Then came the third quarter and Catholic went back to man-to-man half-court defense and put the clamps on West's shooting, holding them to a mere three points in the period and taking a 39–30 advantage into the fourth stanza. West quickly rallied, though, and heading into the final two minutes had tied up the game and had possession with just 1:20 left on the game clock. The Lady Comets ran the clock down to 17 seconds preparing to set up the shot to win it, when a pass from Brown sailed over the head of Gearhart and out of bounds.

Stamper went down and hit a jumper in the lane with 12 seconds remaining, to put Catholic in front, but a three-pointer could still win it for West. Then, Coach Bob Tripure, realizing his team had three fouls to give before the bonus, told his girls to foul after the in-bounds pass, disrupting the play and using up time. Finally with just two seconds left, Kandi Brown fired a shot that rattled off at the buzzer and the Lady Knights had snatched the victory, 46–44. The West bench and fans felt Kandi had been fouled again on the shot, but officials aren't known for calling those incidences on a last second attempt with the game on the line.

It was a heart-breaking loss for the Lady Comets and one that would be replayed in their mind during the months ahead.

West was the top free-throw shooting team in the state for the season at 73.3% with Brown's 87% the second individual best. But they didn't get a chance to show their stuff at the line, with only three free throws all night. Only 13 fouls were called in the game by the officials. But Coach Brown said the third quarter, though, had proven to be the downfall of the Comets' victory hopes.

A tough draw and a tough loss. The "diaper dandies" were growing up and had been one shot away from beating the team that then went on to claim the State championship that year. Louisville Assumption beat Montgomery Co, in the semi-finals, denying the Lady Indians the big prize again. Lexington Catholic defeated Assumption 57–42 to take the state title in their first trip to a Sweet 16. Kelli Stamper was the Most Valuable Player.

While he didn't reveal his thoughts until years later, Coach Hop Brown felt going into the tournament that his team could win a state championship that year, something inconceivable for West or any 16th Region team a few years earlier. Hop knew the girls were a special bunch. He told the media in Bowling Green, after the Catholic loss, that they were going to go home, work harder over the summer, and they would be back and will be "pretty darned good" next year, privately thinking, we definitely are going to win it all in 2000.

Kandi Brown had demonstrated that she was, not only a legitimate All-Stater, but a top candidate for Miss Basketball, her senior year. Dad certainly agreed but refused to mount any personal publicity campaign others might be tempted to do, feeling it would detract from the team spirit. The staff and the school, however, sent out mailings through the state to tout Kandi's worthiness as a Miss Basketball in 2000. Kandi made the All-Tourney team for the '99 Sweet Sixteen and was named 3rd team All-State by the Associated Press and 2nd team in the coaches poll.

Hop, Von and Dana, took one more step that indicated what they had in the back of their mind for these girls. They stayed in Bowling Green through Saturday night to watch the final game.

The pre-game show for the Sweet Sixteen championship is spectacular. The giant trophy and banner are brought out for display as the teams are introduced and the spotlight and fireworks add to the drama. The Lady Comets were both impressed and saddened. Tears filled the eyes of most of the girls as they knew they could have been out on that court going for the big prize. It was a dream that they resolved right then and there would become reality in March 2000. They wanted to be in the spotlight on Saturday ready to play for the big banner. Hop also had dreamed of such a night, longed to bring the title back to Olive Hill, and hoped his girls had gotten the message. Kandi recalls that there was no doubt the team understood that they should be there next year.

The closing Comet basketball banquet celebrated a fantastic year with a record of 29–4. Seniors Wendy Debord and Kerri Day were honored. Kandi Brown led the team in scoring with a 19 per-game average and shot over 45% from the three-point line, a new team record for a season. Kayla Jones averaged eight points and six rebounds; Meghan Hillman, eight points and seven rebounds; Cathy Day, nine points a game and Megen Gearhart, ten points per game. A solid, productive team, a total package, that would return all starters in the fall for a determined quest for "the banner."

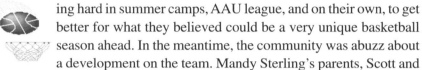 While the world was worrying over Y2K, the Lady Comets were working hard in summer camps, AAU league, and on their own, to get better for what they believed could be a very unique basketball season ahead. In the meantime, the community was abuzz about a development on the team. Mandy Sterling's parents, Scott and Paula, had come to Coach Brown and staff in the off-season to announce their intentions of moving to Olive Hill from Ashland and hoped Mandy would be welcomed on the Lady Comet team for her senior year. They rented a home that they discovered was right next door to Hop and Sharon. Kandi was called upon to take the lead in assimilating Mandy into the program. Mandy had also been at the closing night ceremonies at the State tournament the year before, and her dreams paralleled the Comets, to be a part of something special in 2000 and play in that final game. Kandi said it was great to have Mandy on board, because she "certainly dreaded playing against her."

Hop knew with the performance of last year's squad that the expectations for the team would be high for 1999–00, and now with the addition of Sterling, it appeared the Lady Comets could be virtually unstoppable, if the team chemistry was not upset by the coming of a former opponent. Some fans and parents expressed similar worries, but they proved unfounded, because Mandy was readily accepted. The Gearharts visited and told the Sterlings that Mandy would be totally welcomed as a Lady Comet. They realized it was simply going to make the team better.

Hop began to bring the dream of winning a state championship clearer into his mind, but never went public with his belief that this could be the team that would put Olive Hill on the map. The girls were undefeated, 27–0, in their summertime action. But he couldn't quash the thoughts of folks in the community, who felt confidently that this team would go all the way.

The problem in December, would be the starting lineup, since it had been set, worked well and all players were back from the previous year. It would be impossible to keep a scorer like Sterling from starting, so Hop solved the problem by announcing that Cathy Day and Kayla Jones would share the fifth spot, starting every other game. Hop would later say that the acceptance of those two girls of this new situation greatly contributed to the overall team spirit and eventually the championship season.

He had also made it clear that while Mandy had been averaging well over 20 points for Ashland as their main scorer, she probably wouldn't have that kind of opportunity on offense with this team. She understood and quickly learned the system and impressed everyone with her defense and passing. It worked out fabulously and Sterling told reporters and friends that she was very happy at West. Coach Brown said parents and fans seemed to adopt the former Kitten into the fold and most of the reason was that Mandy was "just a super kid as well as a good player," Mandy said that it was a great transition with no problems.

Hop told friends and reporters early in the season that this was the "most conditioned team" he had ever had, and they have "experience and a lot of leadership." He constantly emphasized the intelligence of the girls in the classroom and the fact that they were simply "great girls on and off the court."

It was a year of expectation among West Carter basketball faithful, and a job for Coach Brown to keep the team focused just on the next game, with everyone talking about a State championship. His philosophy had never been to look ahead but just to think of playing one good quarter at a time.

With Sterling and the continued improvement of Hillman, the Lady Comets seemed to have all the components for a championship, for sure. They had size and strength inside with Brown, Jones and Hillman. There were four players who could nail a 'three' anytime with Gearhart, Sterling, Brown, and Day. There was the coach on the floor in Gearhart, whom Hop once said, "knows as much about basketball as rabbits know about running." They had the ball handling and defense. Did they have the heart, and could they get through the season without injury? Those would be questions that flashed into the minds of fans, coaches and players.

The early polls were predictable, with West Carter rated at number one in the state. How could this be? A 16th Region team considered the best in the state in girls basketball? The 1987–88 team that had started it all in Olive Hill, could never even imagined a state championship, let alone foreseen a time where it was expected.

The pressure and hopes of the community did not faze the girls, as they knew they had the talent, but realized it also took a lot of luck and solid play to achieve that ultimate goal.

The West Carter Lady Comets of 1999–00 were the best girls basketball team the area fans had ever witnessed. No team in the region even came close to beating them. West boys coach, Grady Lowe, said "I've never seen any team compare to them."

The game with Russell on February 10th was hailed as a sign of a possible chink in the armor, as they were held to 56 points and only beat the Lady Devils by 18!

While Hop Brown has never had the reputation of "running up the score" on any opponent, he was faced with the task of making sure his starters received good playing time, while always being conscience of what was happening on the scoreboard. The starters generally played the first and third quarters with substitutes alternating in and out the other two quarters and many times playing most of the second half of games.

The scores were incredible—114 to 33 against Elliott Co. were the most points scored by a West Carter team. They scored over 90 points eight times during the season and averaged 74.5 points per game and held their opponents to 42.5, the best winning margin in the state statistics.

West breezed to another EKC championship in regular season and in the December conference tournament beat Bath Co., East Carter and Russell by an average of 47 points! The Lady Comets took the title game over the Lady Devils 91–37, as Kandi Brown scored her 2,000th career point with a 29–point performance.

People flocked to see them play, not because the outcome was in doubt, but just to watch a new level of girls basketball, a thing of beauty. Fans sat in awe of not only their fantastic shooting ability, but their teamwork, hustle and defense.

The girls went to the Lady of the South Invitational in Allen Co. for the first time. The opening game against the Cookeville, Tenn. team resulted in a 65–60 win. They defeated Warren East and Scottsville easily, before meeting Hart Co., ranked third in the state. Mandy Sterling and Kayla Jones had been sick during the tourney and several of the girls were at less than top-notch. Still they held a seven-point lead at halftime and appeared ready to take the tournament championship. But Hart Co. came on strong in the third quarter to deal the Lady Comets their first loss 52–46 and knocked the Lady Comets out of the top spot in the state-wide poll.

They returned home to sweep three opponents in the Ashland Invitational and win the championship over Betsy Layne 74–46. In the semifinals, the Lady Comets had beaten Montgomery Co. 72–54 and then in regular season would whip them again 72–44. They rolled over Ashland on January 10th at Blazer gym, 83–46 as Mandy Sterling blistered her former teammates with 28 points and eight treys, a new school single-game record.

Only East Carter seemed capable of coming within 20 points of the Lady Comets and they had lost by margins of 28, 26, and 22 in three season games, heading into the District Tournament.

West closed out regular season play with a 91–29 drubbing of Greenup Co. and then opened the post-season by taking Lewis Co. by a similar margin 91–28 in the opening District game at Lewis Co. Middle School gym.

The District title game saw the Kandi-Mandy show at its best with Brown scoring 22 and Sterling 26, to lead the Lady Comets to the District championship 74–55 over East Carter.

The first round of the Region found Mandy and the Lady Comets playing her old team, the Ashland Kittens. Sterling was held to two points, but her teammates more than took up the slack, this time, with a 64–36 victory. It was on to Morehead for the Region final four and a chance at the so-called "3–peat."

Russell came into the game with a good 19–12 record and two stars, Natalie Dial and Samantha Nester, hoping to slay the giant. It was no contest, though, with the Comets using a well-balanced attack to claim the victory, 66–41.

East Carter had advanced to the finals with easy victories over Rowan and Boyd to earn a chance to try to stop West Carter one more time . . . their fifth encounter of the season.

The 19–point winning margin over East in the District final had been the closest the Lady Raiders could come to a challenge of West, but there was still a glimmer of hope for the 21–11 team, some way, a miracle might happen.

The hopes of Hager Easterling's team were quickly dashed by the Lady Comet scoring machine with a 69–45 victory, led by Sterling's 22 points, and the 16th Region championship was going back to Olive Hill for the third straight year, the first time a team had ever accomplished the three-in-a-row. Five Comets made the All-Tournament team—Jones, Hillman, Sterling, Gearhart, and Kandi Brown who was named the Most Valuable Player for the third consecutive year, another region record.

It was simply an incredible record-setting season. They stood 34–1, and ranked second in the AP and Lexington newspaper polls, behind Hart Co. It was dream year, with great cooperation from community, parents and fans. Hop reflected later that most years, you always have some little team or parent problem creep up, but not that season. Everyone got along fabulously, as there was unity, a singular focus for all those involved—win the State championship. He also realized they had been "very lucky" without a major injury or illness issue during the season.

The team could do it all, with six players capable of scoring 20 points on any given night. It seemed the girls just took turns making the big plays in games. The freshman floor general, the slick Penny Gearhart who could drive to the bucket and set up the others or bury the three-pointer; Kandi Brown, the best all-around player the region had ever seen; There was Meghan Hillman, the leading rebounder and consummate post-player; Kayla Jones, the scrappy warrior on offense, defense and especially the boards; Add in Mandy Sterling, the long-ball specialist who could whip a beautiful pass with precision. Cathy Day was the stabilizing force on the team, great shooter and defender. It was a perfect blend of youth and age, exuberance and experience, and all orchestrated into a beautiful basketball symphony by Hop Brown, Von and Dana, backed up with a cheering bench led by senior Shanna Shelton.

The quest for a state title began on March 23rd with West having the best record of all the teams in the tourney. Marshall Co. and legendary coach, Howard Beth, had only one loss and was in the upper bracket with Lexington Catholic and Jackson Co. West would play Harrison Co. in the Thursday afternoon first round game. If they won, Hart Co. would be the likely opponent in the quarter-final for Friday.

The coaching staff, learning from past tournament late-nights and excited girls playing poorly, decided not to take the girls down to the tourney until Thursday and then head home to have them sleep in their own beds that night, if they won. They would return to Richmond on Friday afternoon and then plan to spend the night for the Saturday games.

Harrison Co. was 28–3 and was also a team that featured a coach's daughter. Senior Camyrn Whitaker played guard for her dad, Mac Whitaker, and was the spark plug for the Fillies. West had known for a week they would meet Harrison in the opener and Hop and staff had been adjusting their match-up zone defense to try to stop Whitaker's dribble penetration. He wanted the defense to "pinch" in and shut her off from the inside.

West went out and took care of business with a 68–52 victory, despite Whitaker's 26 points. Kandi Brown's 22 and Penny Gearhart's 20 led the attack and the Hart Co. game loomed for Friday night. Hart had not been that impressive in their first- round victory, but the girls knew it was the most important game of their life and there could be no letdown.

Hart Co. featured a Miss Basketball candidate in Leslie Logsdon and while the Lady Comets did not have a week to prepare for her as they had Harrison, they knew what to expect from the previous meeting where Hart had handed them their only loss in the Lady of the South Tournament. It was time to avenge the only blemish on their season and make it to the final four.

Coach Brown decided to start Kayla Jones, who was bigger and stronger, instead of the smaller Cathy Day, even though it was Cathy's turn in the rotation.

Both teams seemed to have early-minute jitters and the pace of the game was deliberate. The score was 10–7 in favor of Hart Co. after the first quarter and Hart had stretched the lead to 16–9 in the second quarter, before Brown hit a couple of big buckets. The Lady Raiders, of coach Tommy Adams, maintained a three-point bulge at halftime.

A rare three-pointer by Meghan Hillman put West ahead in the third quarter 24–23 and the crowd went wild when Hillman jumped high in the air after the shot dropped into the net. She said after the game, she thought maybe she shouldn't have shot it, but then when it swished, she couldn't contain her glee. A big shot behind the arc by Gearhart made the game 32 all at the start of the fourth quarter, after a nip-and-tuck third period, but seniors Brown and Sterling, both had four fouls on them.

Hop took the gamble though and started them both when the huddle broke for the fourth period, telling them not to foul. They didn't. Cathy Day's baseline shot with 1:23 left in the game was the twelfth and final lead change and the definite turning point, as West finished the scoring at the line with four in a row by Kandi Brown to seal the big victory 50–44. The shot by Day was one Comets fans remember well, and Day said people still remind her about it, years later. It did the trick in the big game.

Since West had overwhelmed most season opponents, some questioned whether they would have the composure to win the close ones or play from behind, not having any practice at being challenged in the final moments. They proved they could play to win, either way.

West shot 12–18 from the line but Hart Co. struggled at 10 of 23. Logsdon led the game scoring with 25 points, but Kandi Brown was 9 for 9 from the free throw line, finishing with 18 points and took her team to the Saturday morning final four at the grand Sweet 16. Kandi had acquired the nickname, "Money" and with her at the line, West fans knew it was like money in the bank.

Only two other 16th Region girls teams had been this far, Russell in 1976 and Rowan Co. in 1981. Now, the Lady Comets were set to play Louisville's DuPont Manual, Saturday morning for the right to advance to the title game. Manual had won the second game Friday night clobbering Muhlenburg North 62–39.

While Hop stayed around to watch that game, the girls went back to the motel. It was part of Dana Smith and Von Perry's strategy to keep the girls isolated from the hoopla of the tournament and fans and intent on the business at hand. Von said, "we really didn't want them to see the other teams and how athletic they were." They simply wanted the girls to concentrate on themselves and not on the talent of other teams.

The Louisville Manual-West game was set to tip-off at 11:30 AM, and the girls arrived just in time for their game, as Shelby County had surprised the favored Lexington Catholic in the first semi-final that morning.

Cathy Day scores as the Lady Comets avenge their only 2000 season loss, with semi-final win over Hart Co.
photo courtesy Mason Branham, Olive Hill Times.

Manual quickly opened up a seven-point lead on the Lady Comets, but a pair of "threes" by Brown closed the gap and enabled West to hold a four-point advantage at the quarter break. A couple of long bombs by Sterling in the final moments of the second quarter assured a five-point lead at intermission. But it was the guard play of Gearhart that was helping to set up the scorers. The little freshman quarterbacked the team to perfection with her driving lay-ups and pinpoint assists.

Manual came back to grab a one-point lead with 6:16 to go in the third quarter, when West accelerated on a 14–0 run to grab control of the game. They ended it up demonstrating their free-throw shooting prowess scoring the last ten points from the stripe to win, going away, 73–55. West wound up 16 of 18 from the charity line and placed four girls in double figures, led by Brown's 22 points with Sterling adding 19, Gearhart 16 and Hillman 11.

The Lady Comets were playing on Saturday night at the State and just one step away from their goal. While the team was joyful, they held their emotions and went quickly back to the motel to rest while Hop Brown addressed the radio audience. The Olive Hill folk, not already at the game, were heading for Richmond, and all across the 16th Region, fans waited eagerly for the tip-off that night.

In the scheme of their plans, the West staff had actually figured to be playing Lexington Catholic, if they made it to the finals. Catholic, the defending state champion, had handed West that discouraging two-point decision in the first round the year before and with the Hart Co. loss avenged, the Lady Comets would have a chance for some more payback. But Shelby Co. (27–5) had upset Catholic, 54–50.

Coach Hop Brown knew the Lady Rockets of Region 8 presented a special problem with 6'4 LeNita White anchoring their center position. In trying to describe the problem to the folks back home on the radio, Hop exclaimed that she was the biggest girl he'd ever seen. . . . "she's as big as. . . . as big as Chris Perry," referring to the Comets venerable public relations man who was standing nearby helping the WUGO radio crew. The folks listening in Olive Hill got a laugh and got the message. But Hop, Von and Dana, set down to draw up the plans.

They would bring Meghan Hillman, who was about three inches shorter than White, out on the floor to take her away from the basket. Then they would rely on Gearhart to push it up the floor and run the team quickly, wearing down the big gal and her teammates.

Dana Smith had begun a practice of composing poems before each tournament game to get the girls fired up and ready. The last line of her poem *Going for the Gold* that each girl found in her locker read:

> Long practice, summer camps, hard work, sweat and tears
> THIS is the moment we have been waiting for all year
> Together as a TEAM, we KNOW what we can do.
> There's a State Championship waiting for YOU!

A record crowd of over 6,500 people packed McBrayer Arena that night for the big game, including, many folks thought, almost all the population of Olive Hill and half of Grayson. Many estimated over 2,500 Carter Countians were there. Attendance records were set at three of the four West games. Never had a county basketball team been in this position, one game away from a State championship. A 16th Region girls team had not accomplished the feat in modern girls basketball, since revived in 1975.

The pre-game ceremonies that the girls had witnessed one year early was now theirs to behold as they were introduced in the spotlight. The banner

West fans are some of the most dedicated in the state and pack the stands at the Sweet Sixteen
photo courtesy Mason Branham, Olive Hill Times.

and trophy were displayed, the fireworks went off, and to the winner would belong the glory. When Hop Brown gazed at the banner being lifted back to the ceiling, he thought to himself, that the banner had to go back down I-64 to Carter Co. "I wanted that banner, so bad, " he remembered and when he started to do a little dance, the team loosened up from their nervousness, huddled up, and got ready to play.

West unveiled their strategy shortly after tip-off sending Hillman out behind the arc where she drilled a three and put the Lady Comets on the scoreboard. Hillman hit another long one, midway through the period to give West an 11–4 lead. West was on top 18–13 at the end of the first eight minutes of action, but Shelby Co stood strong and went on top, two minutes into the second period. West came back to hold a three-point halftime advantage. Shelby County never led in the second half, but the Lady Comets couldn't pull away either, as Kandi Brown had to sit down in the third quarter with four fouls.

Hop sent her back into the game with 5:19 remaining in the fourth period and West hanging on to a two-point lead, taking a chance, rolling the dice, but confident in her ability to "play smart" and not pick up that fifth foul. He said it was time to get "Money" back into circulation.

She quickly hit a jumper to extend the lead to four and the fans started to feel good. Shelby County did not score a point in the final three-and- half minutes of the ballgame and again, West iced the victory from the free-throw line.

It wasn't until, with :08 showing on the clock and Kandi Brown arching the final shot of her high school career into the net from the free-throw line, that the bench and the crowd knew for sure this was it—mission accomplished, dream fulfilled -STATE CHAMPIONS!

When the buzzer sounded it was 58–50 and the stands exploded with cheers. Brown finished with 19 points, and the sophomores, Hillman and Jones, had combined for 26 points and 20 rebounds and neutralized the inside game of Shelby Co. Although they had not shot as well as the other three games, West committed only six turnovers for the game. It was truly appropriate that when Kandi returned to the line-up in the final quarter, she hit a bucket, a three, and then wrapped up the game at the foul line. The one who had taught Dad so much about the importance of free-throw shooting, gave him the prize he had longed for, at the line.

The vision of Kandi Brown jumping into the arms of her dad was especially memorable as father and daughter celebrated together a dream come true, a once-in-a-lifetime moment. She was named the *Herald-Leader's* Tourney MVP and Megen Gearhart and Mandy Sterling also were selected All-Tournament team members. In addition, Kandi received the *Courier-Journal*'s Joe Billy Mansfield Award, that has been awarded since 1975 to the player who excels in basketball, academics, sportsmanship and citizenship. It was only the second time in history that the same player had won both awards. (*1992– Christina Jensen, Mercy)

All the Lady Comets donned their State Champion T-shirts and raised the trophy high, the trophy they had coveted from last year's ceremony and pledged to themselves to bring back home. Tears of joy and elation flowed freely that Saturday night in Richmond but the party would only be a taste of the accolades that would soon come to this special team.

Similar thoughts rolled through the minds of Hop Brown and Von Perry. Hop thought of all the years he had dreamed of playing in a boys state tournament, while a player in Olive Hill, and his life-long desire to see Olive Hill have a championship, and now he had been a part of winning it all, the Sweet 16! Von Perry remembered the early days of West girls basketball and all the devastating losses and her stated Senior ambition- "to someday coach a West girls team to a state championship." It was an emotional storybook climax to a record-breaking season.

The buzzer sounds and Meghan Hillman and Mandy Sterling start the State Champi-
onship celebration, Hillman and Sterling both move on to college ball. Hillman as
West's all-time leading rebounder.
photo courtesy Mason Branham, Olive Hill Times

Folks knew it was truly a special moment for Sharon Brown, to see Hop's dream come true with Kandi being such an integral part of it all. Kim Brown was on the floor to celebrate, while sister, Karla, yelled and shed tears, holding son Dalton, in the stands. Marla and Mira Gearhart, who had thought only of a goal of winning one game at the State, now joined to celebrate with the little sister that was always begging them to play ball with her. Kim Brown and Brenda English felt it was a team, "destined to win it all." Kim declared that the teams of her era never thought they could compete with the big teams in the state and now, here they were, "little West Carter of Olive Hill, State Champions."

Many other recollections of their old playing days flooded the former West players, men and women, as they joined the floor celebration. They shared in this unforgettable moment with family and faithful fans who had seen the girls program rise in popularity and proficiency over the previous decade from that first exciting trip to the State Tournament in 1988.

It was just "a magical carpet ride" said Hop Brown as he conducted an emotional post-game radio interview that paid tribute to the wonderful fans and to his old coach Jack Fultz, who had brought the boys team so close to this championship moment but never achieved it. He wanted to be sure the win was shared with all of Carter County and the region and not something to cause hard feelings or resentment. He was grateful that the girls play brought some respect to the 16th Region and eastern Kentucky.

He thanked the many Grayson fans who were supporting them and said, "We brought one home for the 16th Region, we're not the doormat anymore." "I am just so happy for these girls, they played so well all week and all year with so much heart. People don't realize how hard these girls worked all summer and all season long to accomplish this." And "these are intelligent young ladies, with basketball sense, as well. They play so unselfishly and that's what it takes to win, and every girl, right down the bench accepted their role so graciously, this was a total team effort, with no jealousies, no problems. These girls got along so well, it was an amazing group of young ladies."

In his usual light-hearted style, Hop noted to the media, "I heard Hollywood Henderson won the lottery last week with $58 million and I've got the same kind of feeling. But that money will be soon spent; I'll have these feelings forever." He admitted that as the final buzzer went off, he didn't know what to say, or what to do. The king of the one-liners was truly speechless.

Hop did tell Ashland reporter, Mark Maynard, he was a little disappointed that nobody asked him. . . . "What are you going to do now?" He was ready with an answer from the TV commercial for that . . . "I'm going to Disney World." And he really wouldn't have been kidding, this time, as he was helping escort the West Senior trip to Disney World in Orlando in a few days.

The girls were ecstatic as they came to the radio mike to express their pleasure of a moment they would cherish forever. Hugs, high fives, and hurrahs were the order of the night at McBrayer Arena. Hop noted, "No one can say we backed into this championship, as we beat four very good teams this week." It was a championship that might have been expected by many fans,but took big-time plays on the court, each day, to accomplish.

As for all her individual honors, Kandi said they were meaningless, compared to the feeling of winning as a team—a State Championship.

Principal Jim Webb of West Carter, and one of Hop's best friends, was especially proud and felt that the team would indeed go down as one of the best ever in Kentucky history. He also noted that the girls were simply great kids, deserving of this victory. "They are outstanding students with over half the team at 4.0 GPA and never missing school." He also marveled at the great fan support. "This team has brought the community together," Webb noted. Certainly the city of Olive Hill, racked by political controversy and lost jobs for many years, needed some good news and a rallying point. The West Carter Lady Comets provided a source of pride that brought the whole area a wonderful feeling.

Supt. of Carter Co. Schools, Larry Prichard, called it "one of the biggest thrills he has had" in watching the girls magnificent season. He lauded their hard work as they truly made Carter County schools proud.

The county, of course, had never had a State champion basketball team. The only similar elation had come in 1984 when the East Carter baseball team, under veteran coach, J.P.Kouns, had won a state title. Only the Ashland Tomcats boys team had ever brought home a basketball championship to the 16th Region, the last one in 1961.

The intense pride was evident on Sunday when the caravan rolled into Olive Hill escorting the school bus that brought home the new State Champs to Holbrook Complex - West Carter for a special gathering of family and admirers as over 1,500 fans packed the gym.

The huge "State Champions" banner had been put in place, as Baxter Stevens, Chris Perry, Jason Parsons, Jeremy Webb and Jeff Garvin had worked preparing the gym for a special "Welcome Home" rally.

Coach Hop Brown was happily startled at the turnout for the team, "I've been to two carnivals and a horse show in this town and haven't seen anything like this." It had truly welded the community together to embrace a great team and a marvelous achievement. The fact that the victory had become a bonding element for the town he loved, pleased Coach Brown as much as anything.

The coaches and players had an opportunity to express their appreciation to the fans, even as the crowd that gathered in the gym wanted to share the moment of victory with the girls. Cheers and applause rained down from the stands for the girls and their entourage. Hop has referred to it as certainly the most wonderful moment of his life and the community would have to agree. It was made especially meaningful as Hop's mother, Betty Brown, made her first trip to the high school gym to greet Hop, Kandi, and the team. She told them she was proud, but also cautioned Hop about whether he had really been working too much.

A state high school basketball championship is truly unique in Kentucky for you share it with no one else, no classifications by student population. All schools start with an equal opportunity in March and only one emerges as the best. West Carter was one of the smallest schools in the State Tournament, at less than 600 students, and had come away with the big prize.

The presentations and additional honors to the team in the post-season were numerous. City and County officials declared it "Lady Comet" week. The girls were guests of Governor Paul Patton, in Frankfort at the Capitol, and presented to the State legislature for special resolutions by

Senator Charlie Borders and Representative Robin Webb, who had played on the first East Carter girls teams in her high school days.

There was a special Lady Comet day at the mall in Ashland and congratulations poured in from everywhere. The state road-markers welcoming folks to Olive Hill, "Home of the State Champion-Lady Comets," went up quickly. Globe Hardwood Co. gave a new trophy case to make room for all the big hardware. Addington Bros. and Terry Stamper Landscaping combined to put a beautiful marker and garden in front of the gym.

The town of Olive Hill, population 2000, which heretofore had been known by markers as the home of country music singer-songwriter, Tom T. Hall, now had a sports distinction few small towns ever know. Mayor Jack Colley, called it "the best thing that has happened to our city. We are so proud of you, and this is something you'll remember for the rest of your life."

The coach's mailbox and scrapbook would overflow with cards from fellow coaches, fans, friends and just plain citizens who had been touched by the story of this first-ever girls champion for the far eastern part of the state. Everyone wanted a chance to congratulate and celebrate with the young ladies, who had brought the fans so much joy and excitement for the year. Boosters said it was no trouble raising thousands of dollars from county businesses to buy the girls rings and jackets, as everyone responded willingly.

Marvin Gearhart, who saw all three of his daughters play in the State tourney and now had his youngest win it, said, "it's been the most enjoyable week of my life." He reported the girls were confident and while the parents were all nervous, Megen kept telling him, "Dad, don't worry, it's gonna be alright."

One group of students who were especially happy were the primary class at Upper Tygart Elementary School, where teachers Connie Hillman and Leigh Williams had started a program with their students that incorporated Lady Comet basketball into their studies with visits from the girls as special pen pals and mentors, starting in November and continuing through the season.

Each Lady Comet had been paired by Hillman, Meghan Hillman's mom, with a group of students. The fifty kids corresponded during the year and kept track of the progress of the individual players and the team. Their lesson plans included reading newspaper articles about the team, calculating travel mileage and statistics to learn math, writing letters and tracing their travel on road maps. The Lady Comets even stepped in to the physical education classes to demonstrate their basketball skills. The second and third graders had a real inside view of this great championship season.

The girls learned the excitement and the pressure of having little kids look up to them as heroes and the time they took to help the youngsters also taught them many valuable lessons.

Indeed many adults saw and admired the qualities in the girls unselfish play and their determined work ethic. They wore the mantle of heroes and people of all ages could appreciate what they had accomplished.

The *Daily Independent* in a March 27th editorial praised the work of Hop Brown, " Coach Brown has created a powerhouse by building teams that are fundamentally strong and feature players who know their roles and perform them well." The editor also noted the improbability of such a title by the small school. "West Carter's title is a tribute to all small schools from Pikeville to Paducah. With approximately 575 students, West was one of the smallest schools in the tournament. By winning it all, they again helped silence those who say Kentucky high school basketball should divide its schools by enrollment."

West Carter finished with a 38–1 record, the most wins by a team in state history. They had avenged their only season loss with a Sweet Sixteen victory over Hart Co. and were the obvious number one team in the state and some say, maybe the best that had ever played in the State Tournament. They were listed as number 11 in the Midwest by Fox Sports and 49th in the nation.

The statistics bore out the superiority of the squad. Their scoring average of 74.5 was the best in the state. They shot 48% overall from the field and 70.3% from the free throw line and hit more three-pointers than any team in Kentucky, shooting 40% from behind the arc. Kandi Brown averaged 17 points and six rebounds a game. Sterling clicked at 14 per game, Gearhart 12.5 per game and set a Comet record for assists in the season. Meghan Hillman averaged 10 points and seven rebounds. The fifth spot also was in double figures with Jones and Day sharing time, Kayla averaged eight points and Cathy six per game. Balance and teamwork were certainly key words for this elite team.

Kandi Brown scored 681 points to set a season record and her career total stood at 2599, number one in Lady Comet history. She would also head the all-time list in total rebounds, deflections, as well as three-point and free-throw percentages. She was the Player of the Year in the EKC, and the Region. She was selected the *Daily Independent* newspaper's Player of the Year. Kandi was named first-team All-State and chosen as one of the top 25 girls ever to play in the State Tournament. She was *USA Today* All-American, honorable-mention. It seemed every possible award came her way, but one- "Miss Basketball in Kentucky." That honor went to Jenni Benningfield, of Louisville Assumption. Her team had been runner-up in 1999, but failed to make it to the Sweet Sixteen for 2000. Kandi, though, took the disappointment in stride, saying nothing could compare to having the team win the championship. She would rather have that experience anytime over individual awards.

Mandy Sterling had also surpassed the 2000 point mark during the season and was selected second team All-State in the coaches poll and Megen Gearhart, third team. Brown, Sterling, Gearhart, Jones and Hillman were All-EKC, first team. Those five, plus Cathy Day were selected as the *Daily Independent's* All-Area team, the only time six girls from one team had ever been chosen. Coach Hop Brown was the Conference, Region, Area and State Coach of the Year, and was selected the *Daily Independent's* Sportsmen of the Year in the inaugural season for the award.

Seniors Kandi and Mandy were chosen to play in the Ky-Ohio All-Star game and Kandi became the first Lady Comet ever to play in the Ky-Indiana All-Star series.

Principal Jim Webb, brings home the precious hardware to West Carter

photo courtesy Mason Branham, Olive Hill Times

For Hop Brown, his last daughter had wrapped up a stellar high school career, and together they had achieved their dream. A full basketball scholarship at Dad's alma mater, Morehead State University, was waiting for Kandi. He called himself, truly blessed and fortunate beyond his wildest dreams.

The 2000 season had an incredible impact on all those associated with the team, the school, and the community. It was truly a love affair of epic promotions—Hop Brown, Lady Comets, Girls Basketball, State Champions, that was the talk everywhere. An unforgettable year etched in memory of folks to savor forever.

Mark Maynard, sports editor of the *Independent* of Ashland, in his column called it a win of a lifetime.

He wrote:

> Years from now when some of these players from the 2000 West Carter girls State championship team are bouncing grandchildren instead of a basketball, the memories of these last three precious days will flood back.
>
> They will remember this week as the time of their lives, a time when playing basketball was the most important thing they ever did, a time when they achieved one of life's ultimate goals.
>
> They will tell that grandson about the Lady Comets miraculous 38–1 season, about the exasperating championship game win over Shelby County, about the fireworks before the introduction, about the celebration that turned a small town upside down.
>
> That grandson will nod his head as he sees the twinkle that remains in Grandma's eyes. She will remember it like it was yesterday. Great memories, golden memories, delicious memories. . . .
>
> He, too, will know how special this basketball team was to a school, a community and even to an entire part of northeastern Kentucky. He can hear that in his grandmother's voice, as it cracks with emotion, remembering how a group of teenagers—some barely old enough to drive, some still with a two-year wait before getting their license—came together in a crescendo of hoops and hurrahs.
>
> West Carter is special today and special tomorrow. They are legends in the making. The day of March 25, 2000 is now a day that will live in West Carter sports history forever because it's the day the girls state basketball championship came to Olive Hill, Ky.

He continued:

> The reason the Lady Comets were so successful and such a worthy State champion was their team play. Unselfishness was their trademark from November to March. They truly cared for each other and they put winning above individual achievement.
>
> Hop Brown's status as one of the coaching legends is now secure as well. He deserved this State championship, too. He embraced each victory at the State because he didn't know what tomorrow would hold.
>
> When Kandi Brown sank two free throws to make it 58–50 with 8.2 seconds remaining, her dad called time-out and gave her a bearhug of a lifetime. And the celebration had started. It hasn't ended yet and probably won't for decades to come. Way to Go West Carter . . . You're a great champion.

Olive Hill resident and poet laureate, Paul Salyers penned his thoughts-

> What is that great procession
> that's within our little town?
> It's the Champion Lady Comets
> and their leader, Captain Brown.

> They have just returned from Richmond
> where they won the tourney stakes,
> as they beat the four best teams there
> for each girl had what it takes.

> Megen Gearhart took the dribble,
> Mandy Sterling made the pass,
> Kandi Brown did everything
> and Meghan Hillman, owned the glass.

> Kayla Jones was Meghan's help-mate
> backed by ready Cathy Day,
> every player played her part well
> what is left for one to say?

> What about the tireless Captain?
> Everybody calls him "Hop"
> he is such an humble leader
> here is hoping it won't stop.

> This is his redeeming moment
> of the present and the past
> he'll remember it forever
> for great moments always last.

> As they ride off in the sunset
> this past picture comes to me,
> these girls in another battle
> and once more again I see;

> Meghan Hillman work the backboards
> and Kandi has another steal
> Mandy hits another quick trey,
> I can't believe all this is real!

> Megen Gearhart starts a fast break,
> Cathy hits a needed shot
> and hard-working Kayla Jones
> is forever on the spot.

Everybody loves these ladies
and in truth, I love them, too
not just because of this great feat
but for what they say and do.

So, enjoy your achievement
This is real, and not a dream
All those other teams were skim-milk;
The LADY COMETS were the cream!

                                    Paul Salyers, 3–15–00

There was even a song or two composed for the new queens of roundball. The chorus of one went like this:

A little bit of Kandi shoots the three
A little bit of Mandy at the top of the key
A little bit of Penny passes the rock
A little bit of Kayla on the block
A little bit of Meghan rebounds and scores
A little bit of Cathy dives on the floor
A little bit of Shanna plays the "D"
A little bit of Lady Comets makes you believe.

Everyone had their own special memory or memento of the Championship run. The State Tournament programs signed by the staff and girls were
cherished possessions. Naturally, everyone had to have a State Champion
shirt. The local paper, Olive Hill Times, sold a boatload of congratulatory ads
for special souvenir editions, with stories and pictures composed by Mason
Branham, who had followed the girls game since its early days with Coach
Brown. He put together a remarkable tabloid for the fans and dubbed it—
"West is Best." The Ashland and Lexington newspapers were gobbled up,
also, to preserve those precious headlines, columns and pictures.

Meanwhile Coach Brown pondered his future, in the late Spring.
Should he go out as a champion, and step aside to devote time to following Kandi's college career? Was it time to consider a move up in the
coaching ranks?

His close friends and assistants, Von Perry and Dana Smith, urged
him to stay. They would relieve him at practice when he wanted to watch
Kandi, and they pointed out the talent coming back. More trips to the State
seemed apparent. And in the back of his mind, Hop toyed with the vision
of another title in 2001. He announced he would return as Lady Comet
coach for his 23rd season.

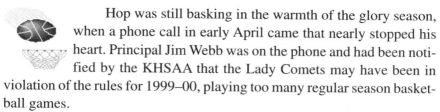 Hop was still basking in the warmth of the glory season, when a phone call in early April came that nearly stopped his heart. Principal Jim Webb was on the phone and had been notified by the KHSAA that the Lady Comets may have been in violation of the rules for 1999–00, playing too many regular season basketball games.

Julian Tackett, Assistant Commissioner, had advised Webb that they would have to make an inquiry after a member school had reported to the KHSAA officials that West appeared to have more games than allowed by statute. Webb said the school would launch an immediate investigation itself and file a report.

Hop and the staff had always been meticulous in counting games and abiding by the rules. How could this be? Past teams had even cancelled some late season games to avoid the overage. The problem for coaches comes with the interpretation of how participation in tournaments are handled. Since a team doesn't know how many games they will play in a single-elimination tourney, the KHSAA allows those tourney games to count only as one scheduled game, a double elimination tournament can count as only two games, regardless of how many are actually played. But a team is only allowed to count two tournaments a year in the shortened formulas. If another tournament is played, it must count all the games.

Jim Webb and Coach Brown took a long look again at the schedule and the rule (Bylaw 25) to determine if there had indeed been a violation. Hop had inquired about his three-tournament schedule during the season with the KHSAA and was told he was O.K. But apparently there was some miscommunication and some misinterpretation of the rules regarding counting tournament games, because upon further study, the West Carter staff concluded that indeed they had played 26 regular season games, two over the limit of Bylaw 25.

On April 13th, Jim Webb wrote the letter to the Kentucky High School Athletic Association making them officially aware the violation by West Carter of *Bylaw 25, section 7 (4) limitation of seasons.* Webb called it "an honest oversight on our part and occurred when counting tournament games and involved an incorrect interpretation of the rule." The staff had thought the Ashland Kitten Invitational Tournament which they played in January could count as one game under the rule, but in fact they would have been required to count all three games, when they won the tournament championship.

Jim Webb, in his letter, cited the schools past excellent record, apologized for the error and said they were ready to accept whatever penalty was imposed. He asked that, if possible, the matter be dealt with privately so as not to further embarrass the school.

A long, tense, wait now began, and while based on past experiences, it did not appear the KHSAA would take away the state title, that did not keep the West Carter staff from worrying and wondering.

Finally on July 17th, Jim Webb received the notification from the KHSAA that the violation had been confirmed and West had actually played in 30 regular season games, or 26 using the tournament format rule, two more than the maximum.

While the Bylaw states that schools that violate the provision are ineligible for tournament play, the Bylaw 24 states that there are no forfeits in state tournament play. Therefore since the violation was discovered after the tournament, those ineligibility provisions were not strictly applied.

However, several penalties were imposed. West Carter was fined $200 and was forced to return to the association the amount of mileage reimbursement given them for the 2000 State tournament, a total of $230. Any statistical records on aggregate wins by the team were vacated, meaning West Carter would no longer be officially 38–1 for the season and would not hold the all-time record for girls basketball. Individual records would not be affected, but all team statistical records would be officially expunged. The basketball program at West Carter was placed on probation for two years. That would not affect post-season play unless further violations occurred.

The maximum number of games for the upcoming 2000–01 season would be reduced to 20 with a limit of two tournaments played in any format.

The last sentence of the ruling was the one that brought the sigh of relief. It stated in regard to the State championship—"Since the violation was self-reported, and certainly does not appear to be a willful disregard for Association rules, removal or vacating of the championship is not applicable."

The official news release made the issue public around the state, on July 19th and while the sanctions appeared bearable to West Carter fans, the whole matter placed a small blemish on the season, and caused some bad publicity to the girls program that had been bursting with nothing but good feelings for years.

CHAPTER 6

THE AFTERGLOW

The start of the 2000–01 brought additional notoriety to the Lady Comets, as they were picked again to repeat as the Region champs and of course, as defending State champions, would have a big red target on their back all season. State-wide polls put them among the top five in Kentucky. Losing the two seniors, as the Kandi and Mandy show had moved on to the college ranks, meant the other four would have to elevate the level of play and that fifth starting spot needed to be filled. The pre-season cover of the *Daily Independent* featured Coach Brown and the four returning starters with the headline, "Four on the Floor." Megen Gearhart and Meghan Hillman were voted the top two players in the region by area coaches, and both were considered All-State candidates. Hop joked with the *Daily Independent* reporters that Hillman, developing into a strong low-post player, was receiving more mail than Dear Abby, with colleges expressing a high degree of interest. He also said he believed Gearhart, still just a sophomore, to be the best guard in the Commonwealth. As for the rest of the region and state gunning for the Lady Comets, he remarked, "that's the way we like it."

But his main emphasis to players and fans alike was that the Championship was special and great, but was history, and this was a total new season. He said, " I try to teach the team to live for today, not in the past."

Senior Cassondra Glover, seemed to get the early nod as the fifth starter, since she had really improved in AAU ball, where again the girls had put in a full summer. Coach Brown touted her as a strong rebounder. Sophomore Brooke Mullis was described by Hop as "the most athletic player" he had ever had. Freshman Stephanie Hall, was also in the running and displayed tremendous outside shooting ability.

Glover got the start as the season tipped-off against Fairview and West routed the Lady Eagles 89–27. The Lady Comets easily won their first five games including their eighth straight EKC Tournament championship, handling East Carter 73–51 in the title game. Glover stuggled with

The girls don their championship shirts to lead the home folks in the Celebration in Olive Hill. Most girls return to the State Tournament in '01 and '02 but fail to pick up a victory.

illness early in the season and was replaced in the starting lineup by Brooke Mullis. All five starters hit in double figures in the EKC championship against the Lady Raiders and West appeared to be on their way to another flawless season.

They went to Lexington's Bryan Station Classic for a rematch of the State championship with Shelby Co. and won again, 58–53, eerily similar to the 58–50 score at Richmond in March.

West came back home to take on Raceland, December 11th and while the Rams were easy prey 90–40, Brooke Mullis fell early in the game with a knee injury, that turned out to be a season-ending ACL tear and surgery awaited.

The Comets were invited to the Prime Time Classic at Lexington Catholic over Christmas. The tournament brought together 32 of the best girls teams in the state and West met Knott Co. Central in the opener and won 61–47 with Glover back in the starting lineup replacing Mullis. The Comets "big four" were playing well, with Day, Jones, Hillman and Gearhart each averaging in double figures and taking turns at being the leading scorer. West beat Clinton Co. the next night 85–84 and went on to the semi-finals where they disposed of Louisville Mercy 55–51, setting up a showdown with the host team, Lexington Catholic, two days before Christmas.

The game was not as close as the '99 State tourney contest as the Lady Comets could never get untracked and went to the free-throw line only four times on the night, while Catholic shot 16–21 from the charity stripe and won it- 52–39. That loss broke the Comets winning streak at 37 in a row, dating back to the Hart Co. loss in December of 1999, the third best in state history, behind Laurel Co. and Whitesburg.

West started off the new calendar year with a win at East Carter 59–47, but Hop and company could see the Lady Raiders were improving with the development of 8th grader, Kasi Mullins, already considered one of the best guards in the state at that age, and freshman center, Kim Stapleton, was also coming on strong. The two rivals met again on February 1st at West gym, and Mullins and Stapleton combined for 28 points as West won by only six, 51–45. By this time, Coach Brown had decided to go with Steph Hall at that fifth spot, the third player he had used in trying to find the right person to make his unit a solid five.

West suffered their second loss of the season, again at Lexington Catholic gym, when they were beaten 56–53 by Mt. Juliet, Tenneesee in the Kentucky Challenge games, but they closed out the season with four straight victories and again finished regular season play without a loss to a 16th Region opponent, entering post-season with a record of 20–2, well shy of previous year's wins because of the KHSAA sanctions that limited their games that season.

West drew Lewis Co. for the opener of the District and whipped the Lady Lions 74–36 with Glover, Hall and Jenise James sharing time in the fifth spot and combining for 14 points to go with double figures from the other four starters. The stage was set for another big East-West battle in the District finals at Grayson.

While West had won three times in the season, it was obvious they would have their hands full with the Lady Raiders, who were making strides each game and who had the look of determination when the ball was jumped up before an overflow crowd.

Many had come to watch the battle between the veteran state tournament player, Penny Gearhart, against the young talent of Kasi Mullins at guard. Then there was the match-up with West's other All-State candidate in Meghan Hillman at center, versus the young freshman, Kim Stapleton.

It turned out to be East Carter's night, as they jumped out to an 18–6 first quarter lead. And while in years' past they had folded in fear against the great tradition of the Comets, this time they displayed some real confidence and rolled to the upset victory, 57–52 with Mullins scoring 23 and Stapleton 16, both besting the West counterparts.

Truly a shocking night for West fans, to see the State champions lose to a region team for the first time since December of 1998 and the first loss to East Carter since that District championship game of 1997.

For Coach Hager Easterling and his young team, it was a real time for celebration, not just of a District championship but of beating the defending State champs and proving to themselves that they were capable of possibly winning their first-ever region crown.

Deborah Bondurant, a senior for East, said it was a "truly exciting moment, because our group had never beaten them."

The "fab four" of West—Day, Hillman, Jones and Gearhart were selected to the All-District team and while they had suffered a loss, the season would continue and they would go on to the Region as a runner-up, while the Carter Co. fans awaited another East-West battle in Morehead, when a state tournament trip would hang in the balance.

Coach Brown had privately thought that this team could repeat as State champion, even without Kandi and Mandy. He had four of the six starters back and saw some star potential in at least five other players on the roster, making it the deepest team he had ever had.

Losing Mullis for the season had been a sad blow, and now they had to approach the Region tournament with a blemish on their record and the knowledge that it wasn't going to be nearly as easy getting to the Sweet Sixteen this year as the last three years.

But Coach Brown was still confident, and shrugged off the loss, congratulating East for a great game, and basically pointing to the next week as the game that really mattered. He knew it is tough at the top and when you're number one, everyone is gunning for you.

West went on the road for game one of the Region to take on the Russell Lady Devils. Before the Russell game, Coach Smith was again ready with her poems to spur the girls on to bounce back-

Ready to Run

Load the bus, down the road, we are ready to arrive
The heart of the CHAMPION will come alive!
We may have stumbled but we did not fall
One game at a time, winner takes all!

> So hold your head high and remember to smile
> We will claim victory over Nester and Dial!
> The Devils will be the first victim of three
> Good defense, move your feet, nothing will be free.
> No guts, no glory, hard work, heart and soul
> As a team together, we only have one goal!
> This is the time we have waited for, to get it done
> Step up, Lady Comets, and get ready to make a run!

Russell stayed close for two quarters before the Comets pulled away and made that run for a 69–50 win to advance to the final four at the college floor in Morehead.

The Ashland Kittens had played West Carter pretty tough during the regular season, losing by three-point and ten-point margins. They posed a dangerous obstacle in the semi-finals for West in their quest for a fourth straight region title.

But the Kittens were never into their game that night, and West jumped on them early to post a 50–36 win in a game that did not, however, please Coach Brown in the least. Yes, they would be in the finals against East Carter, who had beaten Menifee Co. and Boyd Co. to advance to the championship, but the play on the floor against Ashland was not what the West coaching staff had wanted to see. For the first time since their incredible region run had begun in '98, they saw flashes of individual play and the wilting of what had seemed to be a cohesive team spirit. Were some girls suddenly going after individual glory instead of looking at the team goals? Was their dissension between the older and younger players?

Cathy Day was the senior starter, and while always a steady force, was not one to assert herself to direct the others. The two hot college prospects, Hillman and Gearhart, were considered the heart of the team's offense, but at times they seemed to ignore each other. There were rumblings in the city of bickering among parents and fans. Finger-pointing was replacing the great united spirit of the year before. What would happen now that they were to face their cross-county rivals with everything on the line?

There was a lecture after the Ashland game, with a challenge to remember that you don't win games unless you play as a team. And there was also the subtle reminder that three-straight years, West was the Region champion, and now State Champion. Did this talented team want to be known as the one that lost, the one that didn't allow the mighty Lady Comets to at least try to defend their State crown?

The girls pondered those points that night, and at a team meeting the next day, as they prepared to work out any problems, right the ship, and sail on to Bowling Green.

The big game with East marked the second straight year it had been an all Carter County final and the fans were primed for a wild one, between two of the state's top ten teams. When the smoke had cleared at Johnson Arena, West was still tops in the county and made it four regional titles in a row, with a 63–55 victory.

The Lady Comets came out with fire in their eyes and zoomed out to a 19–point early lead, and then withstood a furious second half comeback by the Lady Raiders to claim the big win. Kasi Mullins, almost single-handedly kept her team from falling flat, with a masterful 30–point performance. But West Carter's inside duo of Jones and Hillman was overpowering in scoring and rebounding, finishing with 25 points and 30 rebounds between them. Coach Brown praised, not only his team's great board work, but their determined defense against East, especially the gritty work of Jones and Day. That defense, combined with balanced scoring, led by Gearhart's 18 points sent the Lady Comets back to the State. Team members agreed that this one was especially sweet since it meant showing everyone they could bounce back from that District loss at East.

Kayla Jones told the radio audience, that the team had pulled together to show who was indeed the better team. Cathy Day, the lone senior starter, said the speech about not being remembered as the team that lost in the Region to East Carter certainly motivated them. Penny Gearhart was named the Tourney MVP, and Hillman, Jones and Day were also selected All-Region. Gearhart admitted East had applied some good pressure, but she and the girls certainly wanted to get back to the State as defending champs.

It was a big celebration again for West fans as they began to use the word "dynasty" freely referring to now, four region titles in a row and five out of the last six years. Truly it was a disappointing night for the Grayson faithful, who were dreaming of a first-ever trip to the Sweet Sixteen. On the post-game radio show, Coach Easterling expressed his dismay at the slow start, but credited his team with an intense comeback and he pointed out the Raiders outstanding record of 29–5, with four of the five losses coming to West.

Coach Brown when asked if it ever got old, winning every year, he replied, "Oh no, because each year is different and winning is something that never gets old with me. I just love it for these girls and the fans."

For West, it would now be a long eleven-day wait before tournament play opened. The KHSAA had signed an agreement to keep the girls state tournament in Bowling Green, and it would have to follow the boys tourney each year.

The Lady Comets had never won a game in Diddle Arena at Western Kentucky and now they faced the task of meeting Hart Co., in the opening round, the team they had beaten the previous year in Richmond in the quarter-finals. For sure, Hart Co. would be gunning for them. West took a 25–3 record into the tourney with Hart Co. at 24–9 even though the *Lexington Herald's Cantrall ratings* had Hart Co. at number two in the state behind Jackson Co. and West Carter at number nine.

The game tipped off on Wednesday night, March 21st and it was quickly apparent the Lady Comets had not brought their renowned shooting eyes. Part of the problem they faced was a Hart Co. defense that had Coach Tommy Adams put his taller girls out on the perimeter. Krystal Gardner was especially effective with five blocked shots and Laura Shelton kept Gearhart frustrated all night, as Penny suffered through a 5–22 shooting performance. The Comets hit a miserable 26% from the field. Neither could they display their state-leading free throw shooting ability as they got only seven chances at the line. They lost 51–39, a total almost 30 points below their season scoring average.

Coach Hop Brown, one of Kentucky's greatest girls coaches, took his team to five straight State tourneys and eight in all.
photo courtesy of Mason Branham, Olive Hill Times

Coach Brown, after the game, told the media that the defense definitely caused the Lady Comets problems and probably contributed to their poor shooting. Kayla Jones turned in a sharp performance with 12 points and 12 rebounds, but once again the Lady Comets couldn't get past that first game, and many felt, as they had in 1999, that a first round win would have meant a chance to play on Saturday night.

Hart Co. lost to Muhlenburg North in the quarter-finals and Lexington Catholic, defeated the favored Jackson Co. Lady Generals. Catholic went on to win the title, Saturday night, for the second time in three years, with a 36–34 victory over DuPont Manual.

Megen Gearhart was named AP 1st team All-State and Meghan Hillman made 2nd team All-State in the coaches poll. Gearhart also took the EKC Player of the Year honors. Cathy Day was selected by the Kentucky Association of Basketball Coaches poll as Senior Player of the Year for 16th Region. The Senior class of Nikki Burchett, Leah Frazier, Cathy Day, and Cassondra Glover had achieved an overall record of 119–18 and the first-ever class never to have lost a regional tournament. They were perfect in the EKC and, of course, were a part of the 2000 State Champs.

Gearhart led the team in scoring for the season, with a 17–point per game average and shot 87.1% from the charity stripe, the best in the state. Kayla Jones averaged 13, and again shot 60% from the field. Meghan Hillman tossed in 12 and Cathy Day, nine points per game. Steph Hall led the team in 3–point percentage with 43%, while Jones and Hillman both averaged nine rebounds per game.

The team's overall free-throw percentage of 77% was the best in Kentucky, again. Senior Cathy Day, closed out her career making the top five in West Carter history in three often-unheralded but important categories—steals, deflections and assists.

The staff reflected on the year of being known as the State Champion finishing 25–4, but failing to advance beyond the first round of the Sweet Sixteen. It was disappointing for sure, but certainly, the future was still bright. The team would have the bulk of the scoring back - Hillman and Jones for their final year, and Gearhart for her junior season. They just might have a decent shot at another banner in 2002.

 Carter County basketball fans were truly revved up for the 2001–02 season, and not for boys basketball, but for the girls. Both county teams were picked to be among the best in the state and were definitely the cream of the 16th Region crop. The two teams returned the bulk of their players for the new season and after meeting each other in the Region finals in the past two years, observers figured Carter to be the true hotbed of girls hoops, but who would prevail this year—East or West? Could this be the year East finally knocked West out of the top spot?

The Lady Raiders, however, had suffered a set-back in the Spring, when their senior starting guard, Lindsey Newland, was seriously injured in an Easter weekend auto accident. She made a slow but remarkable recovery to be able to at least come to the games near the end of the season, and with the help of teammates entered the action on her senior night to dribble out the clock to a standing ovation.

Coach Easterling lamented her loss with the comment that the team was minus a lot of toughness when Lindsey was lost for the season. On the positive side, her determined battle for life certainly emotionally charged the team and inspired many people all over the county.

Once again, it figured to be a real duel between Mullins of East and Gearhart of West; Stapleton vs. Hillman on the inside. Those four and Kayla Jones of West were considered the best players in the region. Then you add competition for strategy between Coach Brown and Coach Easterling, actually very good friends, and you had a recipe for another exciting year in Olive Hill and Grayson.

Coach Brown in pre-season radio shows, talked about his solid three returning and then Steph Hall, whom he said was sort of "thrown to the wolves" the previous year in replacing Brooke Mullis after her knee injury. Now Mullis was back and strong and Hall had the experience of a year of varsity and summer ball to round out a solid starting lineup for the Lady Comets. Hop felt he truly had three All-State players in Gearhart, Hillman and Jones. "Kayla doesn't get the publicity of the others, but she's got a tremendous nose for the basketball and is always around it," Hop said. "Gearhart just lives and breathes basketball and is the best in the state, and Hillman well, she will be difficult to stop in the post."

Hillman took pressure off the recruiting season by announcing she would sign with the University of Cincinnati to play college ball, the first Lady Comet to go to a major college outside the Ohio Valley Conference. Her mother, Connie Hillman, said the family visited and considered Evansville and Xavier, but liked the coaching staff at Cincy and the location. It would be a big challenge, but Meghan figured it best to go and try at a big school, than to never know if she could make it.

Hop knew his team, again, was at least top ten in the state and if there was improvement during the season, the Lady Comets could challenge the very best. He realized Lexington Catholic would be good again, but also pointed out that Muhlenburg North probably had the best talent of anyone. Little did he know his forecast would bode ill later for the Lady Comets when they would draw the North Stars in the first round of the State Tournament.

A big addition to the West schedule for 2001–02 was the All-A Classic for small schools in Kentucky. West Carter High School's student population qualified them as a Class A school now and they agreed to participate for the next two years in the 16th Region and State Tournament to crown a small-school champion in Kentucky.

The first tourney on the schedule, though, was the EKC and East and West were paired against each other in the opening round game at East Carter. West was 1–0 after burying Morgan Co. 79–28. East was 2–0 and felt ready to dethrone the perennial EKC champs.

The game was close all the way until the fourth quarter, when Gearhart scored ten of her game-high 20 points and gave West the victory 47–39. That virtually assured another EKC tournament trophy for West as they beat Morgan 87–35 in the quarterfinals, destroyed Raceland 92–29 in the semis and then defeated Russell in the championship, 64–52.

West followed their ninth straight EKC Tournament championship with a victory against Lexington Henry Clay and wins over Rowan and Boyd before they entered the Prime-Time Classic at Lexington Catholic in December.

The Lady Comets put together back-to-back victories over Campbellsville and Louisville Mercy. Gearhart had scored 31 points against Mercy and the whole team seemed to be hitting on all cylinders, as Coach Brown was bringing along 8th grader Brandi Rayburn to complement Jenise James as his super-subs.

Then, before the Lexington Christian game came word that Meghan Hillman's grandfather, John "Waxie" Hillman had passed away, failing to recover from heart surgery. Meghan's parents came to Lexington on that night of Dec. 22nd to deliver the news in person. It saddened the whole team, because he had been such a huge fan, never missing any games. Meghan says her grandfather, was always there after each game, win or lose to tell her she was the "best on the floor." Now the decision had to be made, would she stay or go home ? She knew "Waxie" would want her to play, so she suited up for the game that night against Lexington Christian.

She lasted two quarters, but broke down emotionally and did not play in the second half. West won the game for her, 51–38 and now faced host Lexington Catholic, the defending State champion, in the semi-finals. The team pondered the idea of forfeiting, but decided to stay and play. Hillman went home that night with her family, but returned the next day to join the team and take the court against the Lady Knights.

Catholic jumped out to an early lead and was on top by five at half-time. The Lady Comets made a determined comeback though and took a four-point edge into the final period and went on to win, 54–45, spoiling Christmas for the host team.

West now had to take on Covington Holmes, that night, for the over-all championship of the 36–team tournament. Holmes featured Erica Hall-man, who would become Miss Basketball for that year, and also a strong inside game. The two teams battled hard and close for three quarters, and were tied 34–all going into the fourth period, when suddenly the Lady Comets suffered an unusual late-game collapse. Ball-handling, defense, and shooting abandoned them completely as if they had run out of energy, in the face of an emotionally-sad week and their fifth game in four days. They lost 67–50, allowing an unbelievable 33 points by Holmes in the fourth quarter. It was an inexplicable finish to what had been a great tour-nament for the Lady Comets, but they went home to rest, take time to embrace the Hillman family, celebrate Christmas, and prepare for the East Carter game on January 3rd.

The game against the Lady Raiders at West Carter saw an unusually large crowd for a regular season girls game, with East sporting a 12–2 record and West 12–1. It was 14 all after the first eight minutes of action that night. But the second quarter was disastrous for East's hope, as they managed only eight points and West went on to win 61–41, despite a nice third quarter rally by the Lady Raiders. The Lady Comets showed balanced scoring and great teamwork that night, flashes of the kind of smoothness that can win state tournaments.

The first experience at the Touchstone Energy All-A Classic Region Tournament was an easy time for West, as everyone expected. They won their first ever 16th Region All-A championship handily with lop-sided vic-tories over Rose Hill, Raceland and Bath Co.

Before their trip to the All-A State at Richmond, West had to play East again in Grayson on January 26th. It turned into a real barn-burner, with West Carter's great free throw shooting preserving a close victory 65–60, as

Gearhart and Hall paced the scoring. But after the second quarter, the minds of many of the Lady Comets were distracted, as a few minutes into that period, Coach Brown suddenly turned to Von Perry and said he felt ill, like he was having a heart attack. She turned to Skip Christensen near the bench, and he left with Hop to the locker room. Hop confided in Skip, that the pain in his arm was intense, and that his head just had a rather blank feeling, unable to concentrate. Hop had never been sick in his life and never spent a day in the hospital, but he was quickly taken to Kings Daughters Medical Center in Ashland by ambulance, as a precaution, given the history of heart trouble among the men in the Brown family. Dr. Paul Lewis, his friend and family physician in Olive Hill, who was at the game, came to the locker room and immediately ask for an ambulance to transport the coach, even though by that time, Hop said he felt fine and was really completely normal after the brief episode.

Tests were conducted for a possible heart attack, but all proved negative and it was chalked up to possible stress. After a couple of days in the hospital bed, Hop declared himself fit and ready to go on to the All-A State tourney at Richmond with the team. While he seemed fine physically, Sharon, Von, Dana, and others close to him, recall him becoming rather forgetful. Sharon says, she remembers saying "I told you that" a lot during the late winter and early spring. He also seemed to have difficulty remembering names, but he just thought it was old age and long hours taking its toll.

When the Lady Comets came into McBrayer Arena on the campus of Eastern Kentucky University on Jan 30th, the coaching staff and players had that nice déjà vu attack with their first trip back to the floor where all the school's dreams had come true two years earlier. They had a sneaky feeling they could win a state championship of a different kind here and use it as a springboard for the bigger Sweet Sixteen.

The All-A Classic had been started in 1980 as a northern Kentucky area tournament for small schools. In 1990, the tournament expanded to a statewide championship with 16 boys regional winners, outlined along the same plan as the KHSAA tournament. A girls tournament was started in 1991 with a field of four sectional winners, and expanded to full 16 boys and girls teams in 1993. It remains a privately-funded and operated classic that includes academic and athletic competition each year for the smaller schools in Kentucky.

West was considered one of the three best teams there, with number one-rated Jackson Co. figuring to be a likely opponent if the Lady Comets made it to the Sunday afternoon final.

It turned out to be just that way, as West defeated Owen Co. in the opener 43–34 despite only seven points from Gearhart, their leading scorer. Jones and Hillman dominated down inside and it was on to the quarter-finals.

Gearhart came back strong to pace the attack with 22 points against Louisville's Holy Cross Academy and West led from opening tip to buzzer for a 49–45 win.

West and Newport Catholic brought identical 20–1 records into the semi-final game and Coach Brown and staff knew the Thoroughbreds of Region 9 were a tough test, as they had been runner-up to Jackson Co. in the tournament a year earlier.

The Lady Comets took the win 52–48, but it was a huge struggle and a great ballgame, The showdown with Jackson Co. at 1 pm on Sunday put the Lady Comets into another State championship game at Paul McBrayer Arena.

The Lady Generals featured 6'6 sophomore Sarah Elliott, and senior guard Leah Moore, to match up against the Comets' Hillman and Gearhart. Both teams came out flat with Jackson taking a 12–5 first quarter lead. West never got out of the doldrums, though, and the Lady Generals went on to an easy 64–41 win. The Comets rallied briefly late in the third quarter but couldn't sustain it. Hillman got only six shots on the night and failed to score a field goal. Jones was held to two field goals, while Gearhart finished with 18. Elliott and Moore led the Lady Generals with 29 points between them, to take their second consecutive All-A Championship.

It was a State runner-up trophy for the Lady Comets, but a miserable showing, shooting only 28% from the field in a key game and certainly not duplicating their performance on that floor in 2000. Second places are never highlighted with the Lady Comets and no sign of such an accomplishment hangs in the gym or office at West. Hillman and Gearhart brought home All-Tournament trophies from their first All-A experience.

West finished the regular season play with a record of 26–2 with only the two tournament losses. They had a close call with Ashland in February, winning 45–42, in a game that saw Hillman and Jones score only nine points between them. In that game, Penny Gearhart surpassed older sis, Marla's, record for career assists.

Then came the District Tournament draw and a fate the Carter Co. fans dreaded actually happened. East drew West for the opening round of the post-season. Despite being the two best teams around the region, one of them would not be at the tournament in Morehead this year.

Repeated attempts over the years to seed district draws based on season records had been rejected by Lewis Co. and Elliott Co. representatives and the pairings are left to luck, rendering the regular season records virtually meaningless.

West Carter hosted the 62nd District opener to a packed house for the East-West girls elimination game. It had been a year since East had pulled off that big district win and hoped for a repeat surprise. The game had all the trappings of a regional championship, and even though both coaches wanted to quash such talk, fans knew the winner here would in all likelihood be headed to the State Tournament.

The two teams battled even through the first eight minutes with the Lady Comets going down low to Mullis and Hillman. By halftime, West had taken a 29–25 lead and in the end, the long hours of free-throw shooting paid off again, as the Lady Comets hit every one of their charity tosses in the fourth quarter, when the Lady Raiders, trailing by eight and nine points struggled to rally. For the game, West was 15–18 from the foul line, while East had only three attempts, hitting two. Mullins and Stapleton scored 23 and 18 respectively for the Raiders, but West had four players in double figures, led by Gearhart's 22 and claimed a 61–53 victory.

It was a huge game for the West Carter program, but they still had to win the District and then take care of business at the 16th Region Tournament.

The District championship game went easily to West, 73–47 over Lewis Co. with Meghan Hillman pouring in 27 points. All five Comet starters were named to the All-Tournament team, and the Lady Comets were on a roll, poised for an incredible fifth straight region championship. After the season, Lewis coach, Kevin Lewis, announced he would step down following what was his seventh season.

Lewis Co. had never won a District title, but had been runner-up, 13 times. Elliott Co. girls had never won a tournament game at the District.

West hosted Raceland for the opening round of the 16th Region Tournament and handled the Lady Rams, 86–35.

At Johnson Arena in Morehead, West faced Ashland in the semifinals, but this time there was no let-down similar to the regular season squeaker. West ripped the nets and throttled the Kittens offense, taking a 62–40 victory, using balanced scoring led by Kayla Jones's 15 points.

Boyd Co. looked to derail the Sweet Sixteen-bound Lady Comets in the final, but again the girls turned in a gritty performance, and raced to a 63–48 victory. Gearhart had 26 points that night, joining the 2,000 point club in her junior season. West hit 24 of 31 free throws mostly in the fourth quarter, as Boyd Co, playing from behind all night, desperately tried to catch up in what became a very physical game. The state's best foul shooters proved again that you win games by canning those free throws.

The Lady Lions of Coach Pete Fraley, rallied to within six points at the end of the third quarter 39–33, but West's ball-control offense forced the Lions to foul down the stretch. Meghan Hillman had a big double-double night.

Hop Brown had brought the old lucky "fish tie" out of the closet for the game, but in the end, he credited the great shooting and poise with the incredible fifth consecutive regional title for his girls. The Lady Comets would take a ten-game winning streak to the State Tournament at Bowling Green. This year, the girls knew there were probably several teams at the Sweet Sixteen who were better, but they just wanted to get down there, fight hard and see what happened.

Megen Gearhart was again the Regional Tourney MVP, with Jones and Hillman also selected All-Tournament.

The 2002 Girls Sweet 16 opened March 20th at Diddle Arena, with West Carter drawing the very team Coach Brown had said in the pre-season might be the best in the state, Muhlenberg North.

It was the only team West had ever defeated in a state tournament, aside from their 2000 Championship run. But that victory had been in '98 and in Richmond. The Lady Comets were determined to break the Diddle Arena jinx against the North Stars.

West actually had the third best mark among the sixteen entries. Teams like Sacred Heart and Jackson Co. were ranked ahead of the Lady Comets, and the Muhlenberg game, with their record of 25–6 as champions of the 3rd region, was considered a toss-up. A victory in the first round would pit them against the winner of the weaker 15th and 14th region teams, and a possible chance to advance to Saturday's final four. Everyone felt sure they would be staying a few days.

When the game tipped off, it looked like the ghosts of Diddle had vanished and West jumped out to a 16–4 lead at the end of the first period. But, once again, the normally good-shooting Lady Comets lost their touch in a big game as they faced a torrid North Star defense, and scored only 13 points in the next two quarters to trail by one, 30–29 going into the fourth period. Gearhart failed to score a field goal in the second half, and while the Lady Comets had gone down low to Hillman to start off the game, she netted no points, in the paint, after the first quarter. But her three-pointer with 4:22 remaining in the game put the Comets in front by four. Muhlenberg got two free throws and a field goal to tie it up 36 all, with still three and a half minutes in the game. The two teams struggled in the final moments to score.

The Lady Comets, who had only five turnovers through three quarters, committed five mistakes in the fourth quarter as they repeatedly threw the ball away and with it opportunities to pull out the victory. They did not score a basket in the final four minutes and had only one Gearhart free-throw in the book that pulled them to within one at the 1:23 mark. The Lady Comets were forced to keep fouling the Stars until they reached their first bonus shot at :31 on the clock. They missed it, but West turned the ball over again. Another missed free throw by Muhlenberg gave them a final crack at a basket, with just eleven seconds left, but the Lady Comets couldn't get a shot off. Muhlenberg had opened the door for West, but that night, the girls simply couldn't walk through it for the win.

For the second year in a row at the State tournament, the offense turned sour in the face of a strong defensive effort of the opponent, and the Lady Comets walked off sadly again, this time saddled with a 38–37 loss to the North Stars. West finished shooting just 29% from the field and only 3–19 from long-range. Only Hillman was in double figures with 12 points, while Gearhart was held to a season-low of five points.

After the game, Hop had few explanations for the collapse other than to commend Muhlenberg for their defense and scratch his head about another cold shooting night at Diddle Arena. West was forced to lick their wounds after the first round for the second consecutive year against an opponent they felt they should have beaten, with a point total far below their season average. Fans could only shudder in disbelief at another terrible first-round showing. It seemed as if they had been destined to play well at the "Big Show" only one year, 2000. Sacred Heart of Louisville captured the State title that Saturday night.

The team took the long trek from Bowling Green back to Olive Hill after their disappointing performance and logged in for the season with an excellent record of 31–3. It was the third 30–win season in West history and the tenth consecutive season of 20 or more wins for Coach Brown's teams.

For Meghan Hillman and Kayla Jones, the game was a tough way to end a career, but who could deny the accomplishments of the Senior class that included Chelsa "Moe" Hamilton and Robin Butler. They had a 90%

victory percentage in five seasons, and a State Championship ring. They were the first team to win a Sweet Sixteen game in their 8th grade year and the only team to win it all. These seniors never tasted defeat in a regional tournament, carrying home five big trophies.

Hillman finished the season averaging 11 points and eight rebounds a game, while Jones, averaged ten points and seven rebounds. Hillman with 1,722 points and Jones with 1,527 put them in the top ten of all-time career Comet scorers. Jones shot 89% from the free-throw line for the year, including 30 in a row, right behind Gearhart's 90% which was tops in the state. The team's overall free-throw percentage of 81% was best in the state and set an all-time record, besting their own record of 76% the previous year.

Meghan Hillman and Kayla Jones finished one and two in rebounds in West Carter history, owning the backboards during their careers.

Post-season honors again were numerous, as Gearhart, Hillman, Jones and Mullis were named All-EKC. Penny Gearhart was named EKC Player of the Year, with Brooke Mullis, selected as Defensive Player of the Year.

Gearhart was selected AP 1st Team All-State. The coaches poll All-State team listed Gearhart, first team, Hillman, second-team and Jones, honorable mention. Gearhart and Hillman were selected to play in the Ky-Ohio All-Star series and Hillman was selected as the KABC 16th Region Player of the Year, with Hop again as Coach of the Year. Hillman received recognition as a *McDonalds* All-American.

Coach Hop Brown also was inducted into the Kentucky Association of Basketball Coaches *Court of Honor* and a brick with his name engraved now graces the KHSAA headquarters courtyard in Lexington.

The Daily Independent newspaper chose Hillman and Gearhart as Area Co-Players of the Year, in what seemed a fitting climax to a year of relying on the "two megans."

Megen Gearhart would be back for her sixth and final season as a Lady Comet, along with starters, Stephanie Hall and Brooke Mullis. As they did after the 2000 season, the team would have to find a way to cope with the loss of two all-time greats, this time, in Hillman and Jones. Hillman would pursue a college career at the University of Cincinnati. Jones would go down in Lady Comet history as one of those players who truly gave it all, every night.

It would be hard to replace the inside blue-collar type work of those two young ladies. But as it would turn out, however, the team and the school were going to be dealing with something far more serious than that.

CHAPTER 7

THE FAREWELL

Hop Brown received a prestigious honor after the 2001–02 season as he was asked to coach the Kentucky All-Star team in their annual series with Indiana. He agreed with the stipulation that he could name Von Perry as his assistant. The Lions Club officials agreed to his request and in mid-April the two began preparations to hold try-outs in Georgetown. It was a fulfillment of a dream for Hop to be able to direct the Kentucky girls in the two games against the Hoosier state.

In the middle of the night, a couple of days before they were to leave, Sharon heard a thud in the bathroom and rushed to see what had happened. She couldn't get the door open, as Hop had fallen against it. She continued to bang the door gently against him, until he finally came to and she was able to enter and see blood on Hop's face from a cut. He had apparently struck the sink as he passed out. Her attempts to get him to go to the hospital right then were unsuccessful. She now suspected there indeed was a health issue beyond stress, and Hop himself felt he must have heart problems to deal with, similar to what had plagued other men in his family. Sharon called Dr. Lewis, who immediately ordered a series of tests for the following week, after Hop insisted they go on to the tryouts, although he admitted to Von that he felt rather strange, and asked her to drive them to Georgetown.

His problem of remembering names seemed to worsen after the bathroom episode and when he returned to Olive Hill he went for an appointment the next week. On April 22nd Hop went with Sharon to Kings Daughters Medical Center in Ashland.

The first of the tests was a CAT scan, and about thirty minutes after Hop had been taken back into the room, the word came for Sharon to join them for consultation. The doctors had found a mass in his brain, and immediate surgery was needed. It was scheduled for the next day. Family, friends, and fans were notified and prayers began all over the county for the coach. Dr. Jeriel Boyer would remove the tumor and determine its exact nature.

The surgery was performed and while the lemon-sized tumor was taken out, the worse possible scenario emerged. The doctors determined it to be cancer- glioblastoma multiform—stage 4, the worst kind. It was attacking Hop's brain and it now was apparent that the cancer, not the heart or stress, had been the source of his recent problems.

The prognosis given to Hop was very grim. The cancer was a fast-growing type and the tumor would come back, it was just a question of when. Only ten percent of patients with this type of brain cancer lived beyond one year, the family was told. The sad news quickly spread through the shocked community. Their beloved coach was suffering from a terminal illness. The family remained optimistic, though, as the tumor had been removed and radiation treatment was started in early May with thoughts that if anyone could beat the odds, it could be Hop.

The community didn't want to believe the news and sports and school officials all over the state offered support. Supt. of Schools, Larry Prichard, recalls that it was the "hardest time of my life to find out the grim news" but knew there would be plenty of family, community and state support, and Hop's attitude would help pull him through.

Hundreds of cards, letters and phone calls came pouring in to the coach after his surgery. He pulled through the initial operation well, and was his usual laughing, joking self the next day as he greeted family, friends and players. However, an allergic reaction to one medicine caused a period of disorientation and depression and several very difficult days.

Hop recalls being asked by the doctor what day it was and he replied, "Tuesday," since he knew he had surgery and figured it was that day. It was actually Saturday and the days in between were just a "blur" in his mind. He remembered nothing of the various episodes of unusual behavior, nor anything he had said during the week.

He was released from the hospital, April 27th to return home to Olive Hill and a flurry of gifts, visits and well-wishes from coaches, teams, family, hundreds of fans and friends and just in time to celebrate his son, Kyle's eighth birthday, the next day.

Hop's thoughts were about getting better, continuing to coach, and most of all asking the good Lord for more time to spend with Kyle. He was pretty sick for about a month and suffered from frustrating bouts of mental confusion and the inability to remember names. This was especially exasperating for Hop who knew and loved so many people and now simply was unable to recall their names.

In May, he began a series of chemotherapy and radiation, that Hop was determined would not make him sick. While he avoided the nausea often associated with those treatments, he found it brought on periods of weakness. He wanted desperately though to defy the odds, and told the doctors, he would prove them wrong, he would live more than a year.

He admitted that fear had a grip on him and he didn't want to leave the house or let Sharon out of his sight. It would be weeks before he agreed to go anywhere. He missed working outside in the summer, as he always kept his grass, his neighbors and his Mom's yards in shape. It was a real victory when he was able to do some yard work and go next door to visit Tex, and down to hang out at his friend, "Pud" Fishers, car lot.

He was determined to still play some role in the All-Star games even though he realized he was not fully capable at the time. He accepted the idea that Lexington Catholic coach and friend, Greg Todd, would practice the team and take them to the series with Von remaining as assistant. Hop would come only for the day of the games, June 15th and 22nd. The plan worked to everyone's satisfaction and the Kentucky All-Stars won the game in Owensboro, but lost on the road the next week in Indianapolis.

Hop was able to assist on the bench and his decisions and instructions in the final minutes of the game helped the All-Stars pull out a dramatic last second, 79–77 victory over Indiana, after trailing by 17 points. The girls had dedicated the game to Coach Brown. They truly seemed inspired by his presence. Tara Boothe, the team's center from Highlands High, who led the way with 25 points, said, "we wanted to win it for Coach." The team shot only 50% from the free-throw line, truly uncharacteristic for any Hop Brown team, though.

Greg Todd stated after the series that Hop had a tremendous influence on winning the first game and nearly pulling off the upset in the second game. Todd told the *Lexington Herald-Leader,* that "he just willed us to victory." Kentucky was the underdog and had lost 15 out of the previous 18 All-Star contests.

Hop admits the same strategies, though didn't work as well in the second game, as the Hoosiers took the victory in their home territory.

Hop was feeling well enough by the July 4th weekend to participate with his girls in the annual Olive Hill Homecoming parade. Former players crowded on to the float for the trek down Tom T. Hall Blvd on a hot summer day. Hop also did a radio interview and a TV interview while accepting the WSAZ-TV 3 Huntington, "Hometown Hero" award from Tony Cavalier, the popular weatherman.

Hop and staff began their normal preparation routine for the upcoming season, with Von and Dana taking the girls to summer camps and competition. Hop had decided that he would make this, the 25th season, his last year of coaching, if indeed it might be the last year of his life. He had actually planned to go two or three more years until eligible for teacher retirement, but now opted to buy out those remaining years, all the while hoping to get completely well.

His friend, Jim Webb, had planned to retire as principal at West Carter, but with Hop approaching his final year, the coach asked him to stay on and Webb consented. Jim knew Hop needed only a few wins to reach the 500 milestone and he was hoping and praying he would feel good enough to take the team to that mark.

In late June, Sharon had heard through a cousin about a doctor at Duke University in North Carolina who specialized in brain cancer and had experimented with various approaches for treating glioblastoma. After several attempts, she finally was able to arrange an appointment with Dr. Henry Friedman. Dr. Friedman was an avid womens basketball fan and when he heard about Hop's condition and that he was a famous Kentucky girls coach, he was especially excited to help and the two developed a good rapport. Friedman also contacted Duke coach, Mike Krzyzewski, who worked with the V Foundation, named for the late great coach, Jim Valvano, in helping and encouraging cancer patients. Valvano, who coached North Carolina State to a national championship, lost his year-long battle to cancer in April of 1993.

Coach K made a phone call to Hop. Hop recalled answering and hearing the coach tell him that he wanted to talk with him and for Hop not to say anything for the next fifteen minutes, just to listen. It was a combination of lecture-sermon-medical consultation and Hop called it, "very special." Coach K even tried to convince him he would be a Duke fan, when he came down there and met the staff. Those words were of course, quickly rebuffed by Hop, the lifelong Big Blue Kentucky fan, but was still "truly touched" by the call and concern. "I told him, I had been a UK fan for 42 years."

That phone call was followed by others from Coach Rick Pitino, Kyle Macy, and Tubby Smith, all urging their fellow coach to hang tough, fight hard, and be assured that many, many folks were standing beside him. Macy, coaching at nearby Morehead State, expressed his admiration for the accomplishments of Hop's teams as well as his work for the sport itself.

Hop said it was exciting to hear from those people he had long admired and was moved by their talks. He was appreciative of all the many well-wishers who stayed in contact with him.

Another call was especially surprising for Hop, when the phone rang one day, and sportscaster Dick Vitale was on the other end. Vitale had heard about his situation from Coach K, and wanted to express his thoughts of encouragement and offer to meet with him. Hop said it was great speaking with him and afterward said he appeared to be very genuine. He promised to send Hop some tapes, books, and autographed posters and indeed they soon arrived. He proudly displayed those in his office as he began to develop a nice friendship and great respect for Vitale.

Hop made the first of what would be several trips to Duke University Hospital and was very impressed with the people and the facility. One of the medical assistants, as it turned out, was playing ball with Mandy Sterling at Barry University in Florida. The planned personal meeting with Coach K, had to be cancelled, though, when Krzyzewski was called to be at the White House to meet with the president that day. Dr. Friedman prescribed a series of pills, experimental chemotherapy, to slow the growth of the cancer. The doctor had successfully prolonged the lives of other patients, by as much as three to five years. Hop returned to Olive Hill with some renewed hope and a host of new friends.

By the end of the summer, Hop was feeling much better, eating well, and feeling confident about being able to fight through the illness and its aftereffects. While he was grateful for all the prayers and support, he wanted to deflect all the attention away from his physical condition and just get back into the gym.

Other than his new shorter hairstyle, because of the surgery and chemotherapy, Hop gave the appearance of business as usual for the upcoming season as school began in August. The summer had obviously been emotionally draining, but he was determined to continue teaching and coaching every day. He had only missed two days of work at the school in his life, a day each, to attend the funerals of two of his older brothers, Glen Arnold in 1981 and George Russell in 1992.

 The first of December brought a nice promotional piece and picture on the front cover of the *Daily Independent* girls basketball tabloid, of Megen Gearhart and her quest for the Miss Basketball honor in her senior year.

In addition, Gearhart had taken care of all recruiting speculation before the season started by announcing she would stay close to home. The 5'6 senior point guard would attend Morehead State University on scholarship and join Kandi Brown as a Lady Eagle and they would share one year on the team together in 2003–04.

Later on, in January, Gearhart was named the *Tony Curnutte Memorial Sportsman of the Year* by the *Daily Independent*. The award, given annually by the newspaper, was named after the late popular sportswriter for the Ashland paper. The editors noted not only her on-court accomplishments but also her 4.0 grade point average, church and community involvement.

She was lauded as a mentor and role-model for the students and her work to raise money for the Marvin Hicks Scholarship Fund, named for the East Carter janitor, killed by a student in 1992.

Gearhart responded graciously, pointing out that she had been blessed with a great team and thanking her family for steering her life in the right direction and for the relationship God had in her life. Her coach, Hop Brown, had received the *Sportsman* award two years earlier after leading the team to the State championship.

Ashland football star, Arliss Beach, who signed with Kentucky, was recipient of the award in 2002.

The team knew this basketball season would be different and determined to help their coach battle his illness even as they went to war on the court. Each player had a personal slogan for Hop painted on their basketball shoes. Their collective arms were around him, even as they had felt his support for so many years. They all admit it was difficult but because Coach Brown remained upbeat, they tried to keep their spirits up, as well.

Coach Perry commented, "Every girl was a little scared, because he is just like a father to them." As for her part, it was also very hard, because, "he is like a brother to me, and has taught me so much."

The season began with a staff addition, as Tex Andy English, a student at Morehead, became the third assistant on the bench, in a move designed to groom him for the years ahead, to assist after Hop's departure. He had grown up next to the Brown family and Lady Comet basketball was in his blood.

West Carter, despite the loss of Hillman and Jones, was picked again to win the Region, in the coaches poll. That pick would likely have gone to East Carter, with their starters expected back from the previous years great team, but circumstances had dramatically changed when All-State candidate, Kasi Mullins' father, Rory Galloway, had advised Coach Easterling he was going to move to Jackson County, and Kasi wound up playing summer ball with the Lady Generals, essentially making them a state champion contender, for sure, since they had already been picked in the top two or three.

However, that didn't last, as before the basketball season actually tipped off, Kasi moved back to Boyd Co. and sought to enroll there and play for the Lady Lions. Her eligibility was now in doubt, being in three schools in the span of less than six months.

She was not allowed to suit up for Boyd Co. pending eligibility decisions by the KHSAA, so coaches were unsure whether Boyd should be considered the number one contender for the region title. It now appeared, if Kasi played, Boyd and not East Carter would be the biggest challenge to West during the season. In an ironic twist, the guard who had been the best scorer in East Carter history would now become a major stumbling block in the Lady Raiders hope of a Sweet Sixteen trip.

Coach Brown knew his Lady Comets would probably be a quicker team but also felt the region itself would be very competitive with four of five teams capable of winning it all.

The season opened for the Lady Comets with the EKC Tournament and easy wins over Russell and Rowan Co. Penny Gearhart began her senior season and certainly was impressive with 34 points against Rowan Co. The tournament title game was set and would feature East vs. West at Rowan Co. gym.

The Lady Raiders lost the game, but only by five points, 68–63 seemingly sending a message that they were still a very competitive team even without Mullins. Freshman Ashley Baldwin had been inserted into the backcourt lineup and Coach Easterling felt the team chemistry was right and the talent present for a good season.

For Hop Brown, it was his team's tenth consecutive EKC title and it got his "farewell season" off to a good start. He felt his illness had not affected his coaching ability, other than the problem with names. For some reason, the part of his brain that gave him immediate name recognition just was not the same. He resolved the problem by trying to keep a card with the girls names and numbers on it in front of him in practice and a scorebook handy when going on the post-game radio show or newspaper interviews. Sometimes, though, he just had to resort to calling numbers. In addition, he was cautious in conversation because the word he wanted was just not there on his tongue or the wrong word would come out.

The staff had replaced Hillman and Jones in the lineup with the previous years' faithful subs, senior Jenise James and freshman Brandi Rayburn. The team would rely heavily on the scoring ability of Gearhart, Hall and Mullis and hope James and Rayburn could provide some rebounding strength and develop additional offensive punch as the season progressed.

The Lady Comets lost to Bryan Station in mid-December, and got ready for the Prime Time Classic at Lexington Catholic, the week before Christmas with an overall record of 5–1. West beat Covington Holmes and

Rockcastle Co. before meeting Lexington Catholic in the semi-finals. The host team was determined to gain some revenge from the loss West had handed them in their own tournament the year before, and whipped the Lady Comets 69–43. Catholic had been rated number two in the state behind Louisville Sacred Heart.

West closed out the tournament beating Mercer Co. to finish 3–1 in the event, as Gearhart scored a personal high of 35 points. The team came back home and proceeded to overwhelm Morgan Co. 93–28 with five players in double figures, to tune up for the January 6th EKC game with East Carter.

West had not lost an EKC game in ten years and had an incredible 76–game conference winning streak coming into the game in Grayson. It was a determined East Carter squad, that took the court that night and quickly built a big 17– point first half lead before West fought back hard in the second half only to lose the game 56–55. The big win by East ended the regular season conference dynasty of the Lady Comets and virtually assured that the Lady Raiders would be the EKC champions for the season, a title they had not won since 1978. Coach Brown commended the Lady Raiders after the game, saying he couldn't see any other team in the conference beating them.

The Lady Raiders, who many thought would struggle during the season, now had a 14–3 record, and a top-ten rating in the AP state basketball poll, and went to first place in the regional poll, ahead of West, the first time that had happened since the poll's inception by the Ashland paper.

Hop's last visit to the rival gym was marked by special ceremonies, as Coach Easterling presented him with a beautiful hand-stitched Lady Comet afgan for his retirement and the county crowd, East and West, embraced the coach with loud applause. He quipped that it was about time the people in Grayson gave him something. In a more serious note he acknowledged the friendships from both Grayson and Olive Hill he had cherished through the years and how nice the folks in Carter County had been to him, through the past quarter-century of basketball.

Four days after the East game, West Carter suffered a home loss to Ashland Blazer 54–52, two straight defeats to region opponents for a team that had dominated the region in regular season play for eight seasons. West again started slow and dug a hole falling 18 points behind then put on a furious second-half comeback, only to suffer the loss. Fans were beginning to scratch their head at what could be wrong. Penny Gearhart was not shooting well, and had been going regularly for treatment for a sore back, but Hop and the coaching staff remained confident the team would recover their strong form and Gearhart discounted the fact that any physical problems really contributed to her shooting woes. In reality, though, she was experiencing pain, and it seemed only her sheer desire to keep playing for Coach Brown kept her on the move.

Part of the team's problem was the obvious emotional struggle all the girls were going through in watching the illness of their coach progress. Many times they would get down in the game, muster the strength for a comeback, but sometimes falling short. Coach Perry later called it a "tremendously difficult time." She herself felt the intense stress of what was happening to Hop but resolved to bear up for the sake of the team. It was just not the same happy-go-lucky atmosphere of past years.

Hop was still struggling with names and would suffer some spells of disorientation but Von and Dana were always there to assist. He also had uncharacteristic bursts of anger and would realize that he was not in total control and it embarrassed and frightened him. The fans and players realized the change was not the 'real Coach Brown.'

He remained his old friendly self, his knowledge of the game still sharp, but was often apprehensive in talking with reporters for fear he would say something wrong when he had one of his memory lapses. He continued to do his radio shows, though, but would often ask afterward, if he had said anything out of line. The brain disease was definitely impacting his quality of life and coaching style. He simply had to slow down his conversations with people, keep them short and punctuated most of them with "Coach Brown luvs ya." or "good to see ya, brother."

West headed for the All-A Region in late January for the second year in a row as the heavy favorite. They captured the title easily with wins over Rose Hill, Elliott Co. and Bath Co. by an average margin of over 40 points. The All-A championship was their second in two appearances and once again they would be going back to Richmond and the Touchstone Energy All-A Classic.

The win over Elliott Co. at Menifee Co. gym in Frenchburg marked Coach Brown's 500th career victory. Hop spoke after the game to the crowd, saying, "I'm really not responsible for those 500 wins, if I was, I'd have to be responsible for those 199 losses and I don't like that idea. I've always had good coaches, parents, good kids and a great community, but really the next game is what is important to us, to get 501 wins."

He was given a plaque by Principal Jim Webb and plans were in the works for a more formal presentation during the special night, set for February 1st in Olive Hill.

On that night, by a vote of the Carter Co. Board of Education, the basketball court at West Carter gym would be officially named—-*John "Hop" Brown Court.* Principal Jim Webb explained that it was just the right thing to do, and not just because of the illness, but because no one had impacted girls basketball and West Carter sports more than Hop through 25 years of coaching and bringing the town a state championship.

The last week of the month, West faced off against Boyd Co. in a rematch of the previous year's regional final. Before the game, Coach Pete Fraley and staff presented Hop with a rocking chair for his retirement, noting his great contributions to the game, and their long friendship.

The Lady Comets lost the game 65–60, despite a 32–point performance by Penny Gearhart. At that time, Boyd Co. was still not able to suit up Kasi Mullins. The KHSAA had ruled her ineligible to play citing the transfer rule. Many observers seemed to think that she would not be playing against either East or West that year and believed the ineligible ruling fair. But the family had hired a lawyer and a court injunction forced a decision by a judge who, after testimony, declared Kasi eligible to join the team in February.

In a strange turnabout, West played Boyd again, Feb 21st at West with Mullins playing, and once again Gearhart had 32 points. This time, though, the Lady Comets won it easily, 65–51.

In Hop's final visit to district foe, Lewis Co., the school presented him with a special set of "King of the Court" bears for his office and Gary Kidwell, lauded Brown's great career in presenting a beautiful Kentucky plaque. Kidwell was a long-time Lewis Co. boys coach, athletic director, and was serving as commissioner of the Eastern Kentucky Conference, as well as broadcasting games on the Vanceburg radio station.

The special night for Hop Brown was set aside as the home game with East Carter. Some wondered why an easier opponent was not chosen. Hop, however, didn't want it any other way. The great rivalry over the years and the fact that East was now one of the best teams in the state made it appropriate that the Lady Raiders should be the foe on Hop Brown night.

The game, itself, actually was anti-climatic to the pre-game ceremonies and West was determined to give their coach a win on "his night." They did it with relative ease 55–43, as it seemed it was destined that Hop's team should have a good win on this special occasion.

The ceremonies were carried live on WUGO radio and Lady Comet public address announcer, Doug Calhoun, served as the master of ceremonies. The presentations and testimonials were numerous. Former superintendent, Harold Holbrook, talked of first hiring the coach, even when he didn't want to be involved in girls basketball. Former principal George Steele, spoke of his friendship and how Hop cared deeply for each girl that played for him and taught them great lessons beyond basketball.

Local legislators, Senator Charlie Borders, Representatives Robin Webb and Rocky Adkins, County-Judge Executive Charles Wallace, and Mayor Danny Sparks all made declarations of their support and lauded the great efforts of Hop's 25 years of coaching.

Adkins, a former Elliott Co. basketball great, who played at Morehead State, recalled doing his student teaching in 1983 under Coach Brown. He reported Hop must have had a great deal of confidence in him, as he handed him a piece of chalk, a book, showed him the blackboard and left the room with the admonition to jump in and teach.

Local businessman, William Waddell, staunch supporter of the program, handed Hop a $500 check, a dollar for each win, and Jim Webb presented a beautiful plaque honoring the special night and his 500 wins. Webb told the crowd that Hop Brown had literally help change girls basketball in the county, region and indeed in the state.

Paul Lewis represented the area basketball officials in chiming in with their respect and admiration for Hop's great career and his cooperation with the referees.

One of the highlights of the evening were video messages shown in the gym, from Coach Kyle Macy of Morehead State, and Hop's favorite player at U.K., University of Kentucky coach Tubby Smith, Louisville coach, Rick Pitino, and an enthusiastic speech from sportscaster Dick Vitale, who of course, declared Hop Brown to be "awesome, baby!"

Von Perry spoke of her many years of association with Hop and family and what his mentoring had meant to her, to the Lady Comets, and girls basketball in general.

Hop, Sharon, and the family- Kim, Karla, Kandi and Kyle, observed and listened, seated at center court, as they heard the words—"Coach Brown, for all you have done for our community and our school, for the State Championship, and the quick-witted comments to the press. For the screaming in anger and the hugs you give generously. For your inspiration, your success, your dedication, your humility, for you.. from this day forward the court at

West Carter High School shall be recognized as John "Hop" Brown Court." The Brown kids participated, as they pulled off the sheets from the official wall signage on each end of the floor declaring it - *John "Hop" Brown Court.*

The outbursts of applause and standing ovations were plentiful all evening. At the conclusion, Hop, obviously moved, took the mike to express, not only his thanks, but his love for every person there.

Many folks worked hard to make the ceremonies a success, and it had gone off well. Chris Perry, who had helped initiate the idea said he was pleased with all the assistance that went into making it a special night. Hop later expressed that it was such a nice thing to do and very unexpected, but "he was kind of embarrassed" by it all and joked that he hoped it wouldn't put lot of pressure on his son, Kyle, to play ball on a court named after his dad.

Local sportswriter, Mark Maynard, said in his column that the ceremony was "classy, timely, and emotional." He wrote, "Brown, one of the most popular and beloved girls coaches in state history, deserved a night all his own."

Hop put his thoughts in a letter published in the local paper:

> Dear Friends,
> The year so far has been a whirlwind for all of us. So many of you have approached us with kind words and best wishes or sent cards, letters, gifts and encouraging notes that have meant so much to us.
> Having the basketball court at West Carter High School bear my name is an honor that is overwhelming and immensely appreciated.
> Reception from area schools and their expressions of thoughtfulness, prayers, and love regarding my impending retirement are tremendous as I think of all the people who have crossed my path. It is really quite humbling when my family and I consider how many people we have had the chance to befriend over the years. I just hope that the impact of my family and I have had has been one that is positive and beneficial to you.
> Please know that as the year is coming to an end, Kyle, Kandi, Karla, Kim, Sharon and I are forever grateful to each and every one of you and we ask for your continued support and prayers in the coming years. I've said it countless times to many of you and I mean it more today than ever, I love you all!!
> *Coach John "Hop" Brown and family*

West was to open play in the All-A State, Feb 5th against Whitesburg, a team they had not seen since the mid-90s. The night before that game in Richmond, though, Hop and Sharon had been invited to Rupp Arena for the Wildcats game with Florida. They were guests of Coach Tubby Smith and before the game, Hop had the opportunity to finally meet Dick Vitale who was working the nationally-televised game that night.

During the game on ESPN, Vitale mentioned Coach Hop Brown of Olive Hill was at the game, and spoke of his State championship, his battle with cancer, and also related to the audience how Kandi Brown, at Morehead State, was leading the nation in free-throw shooting.

The next day, Hop headed on to McBrayer Arena to join the team. The opener with Whitesburg was a close one with the Lady Comets pulling it out in the fourth quarter 55–51 to advance.

They now would face Newport Central Catholic in the quarterfinals, two days later. They fell to them in a close battle, 52–51 and were heading home without any trophy this year, after being state runner-up, a year earlier.

The Lady Comets returned to the county and finished the year with six straight wins, including avenging their loss to Ashland, beating the Kittens at Blazer 48–43. They seemed to be shooting better, playing well, and perhaps peaking at the right time for their post-season dreams of another state tournament appearance. They returned to a top ten spot in the *Lexington-Herald* girls rankings.

The final home game of this season would now be a special one, the last time Hop Brown would coach on what was now "Hop's" court and the final game for Penny Gearhart and the two other seniors, Jenise James and Brooke Mullis.

It was scheduled for Thursday night, Feb. 27th, but a threatened snow storm forced Bath Co. to call and say they wouldn't make the trip. The game was rescheduled for Saturday afternoon, the final day possible and everyone prayed for good weather.

The senior ceremonies began at 3 pm. The day was made especially exciting as Gearhart needed just 17 points to break the all-time scoring record at West Carter surpassing Kandi Brown. Everyone knew it would be his last game to coach at his beloved school, but the spotlight was on the seniors and not Hop that night. The three seniors were honored along with exchange student, Janine Solik, who had logged some playing time with the JV team.

Gearhart made quick work of the quest for the record, scoring 17 points in the first quarter and play was stopped to present the ball. . . . 2601 points! She finished her senior night with 23 and the Lady Comets breezed to victory over Bath 61–35.

Penny said, after the game, that it felt good to get it all out of the way early, and her teammates were very supportive. Coach Brown said it was difficult to think about it being his final game in the gym but the team had other goals and he would challenge them to take the school back to the Sweet Sixteen, another time.

West began their hoped-for journey to Bowling Green with the District action at the Elliott Co. gym and easily disposed of Lewis Co.,71–45 with Brandi Rayburn scorching the nets that night with 22 points. The stage was now set for another East-West duel in the championship.

The West-East battle was a nip-and-tuck affair providing some real excitement for a standing-room-only crowd at Sandy Hook, with the Lady Raiders in control down the stretch, looking like they had the victory clinched, when Gearhart took over. Her two free throws in the final seconds gave West the win 48–47, and another District title. Both teams advanced to Morehead for the Region and a forecast by many that they would meet again for the fifth time of the season, with the state tourney trip on the line. All five West starters made the All-Tournament team.

Coach Brown admitted that East Carter had played well enough to win that night and his team struggled, before snatching the victory from the jaws of defeat in the final moments. The Lady Comets got the breaks on a night, that it seemed fate would not allow anything but a championship in Hop's final District tilt.

The Region pairings ended up matching West vs. Morgan Co. and East drew Boyd Co. for a first round game. For the first time, school officials had decided to hold all games at Johnson Arena at the university instead of allowing the District winner to host a game. The gender-equity issue had been brought up, so the format of the girls and boys would be identical.

A couple of days before the regional opener, Hop became ill with a sore throat, dehydration and general fatigue. He had been taking more experimental drugs and with his immune system weakened, his energy was gone, his blood count fell and antibiotics were also reacting on him, creating blisters throughout his throat and mouth. He was miserable, could barely talk and unable to eat. Eating had become a tricky situation anyway, as he had developed sugar problems and the levels became difficult to regulate.

He sent his team off to Morehead with Von as coach and the charge to win the tournament, and he would join them when he felt better.

Dana began working on those famous poems . . .

Magic Carpet Ride
The magic has started but we don't need a magician
Our reputation goes hand in hand with our tradition
Lewis was first and it was an easy test drive

East brought it all and sometimes you survive.
Morgan is our foe, roll out the welcome mat
We know there are many ways to skin a cat.
One game each night, three to a crown
It's time once again to lay some smack down.
Focus on our goals because they will come true
Tough times don't last, but tough people do.
Jump in the wagon and don't forget to feed the mule
It's on to Morehead, we don't even need to car pool.

The girls and coaches were having fun with the "mule train" theme after some rowdy city fans at Ashland, earlier in the year, had made fun of their rural roots by throwing out some insults and proclaiming they must have "ridden in on mules."

It would be the first tournament game Hop had ever missed and only the second game he had set out in his career. He had missed the Raceland game in December after a round of chemotherapy.

He listened to the game on the radio as George Bellamy, coach of Morgan Co, who had announced his retirement, sent his girls out to try for the upset, by holding the ball in a stall tactic. The score was tied 8–8 at the end of the first quarter and the Lady Cougars actually had a three-point lead in the second period. Von was starting to get worried that her first coaching job in a regional tournament would be a disaster.

West took a halftime lead of four points into the locker room, and came out in the third quarter to watch Morgan go to the stall game again for three minutes. But Steph Hall broke it open, nailing three treys in the period to open up a 20–point lead by the end of the quarter and West went safely into the semi-finals with a tally of 58–29. Hop had kept in touch with Von, Dana, and the girls, from his house via cell phone during the evening.

Before the game, the Morgan Co. girls had presented Sharon Brown with a plaque for Hop designating him as the "Coaching Legend" of the 16th Region. Coach George Bellamy agreed, telling the GO radio audience, that his friendship with Hop was a cherished relationship. "he has done more for the level of girls play in this region than anyone could imagine. His influence is statewide and we wish him the best."

The anticipated match-up with East in the championship game did not happen, though, as the Lady Raiders lost to Boyd Co. in the first round, 54–44, with their old teammate, Kasi Mullins, leading the scoring for Boyd.

The semi-finals would not be played until the following Monday, March 17th, giving Hop, five days to regain some strength, while the boys teams completed their tournament at Johnson Arena.

When Monday night rolled around the Lady Comets had a date with Ashland in the semi-final, a familiar scene, for sure, as the two teams had been semi-final opponents, three of the previous five years, and met in the first round and finals the other two years. The last victory by the Kittens over West in a tourney was in 1997, the only year West had not won the championship in the previous seven years.

Ashland's lineup had been weakened, though, when their center, Ashley Renfroe, injured her knee in the District and would not play at all. Coach Brown again was too sick to make the trip and hoped by staying at home one more night, he might be able to join the team on Tuesday, if they made the finals. He talked to the team from his phone at home before they left the locker room at West and Von reported to the media at Morehead that the girls were fired up and ready. They came out on the floor, though, with a bad case of jitters and struggled through the first half, being beaten badly on the boards and on the floor by a hustling Ashland team. West trailed at the half by a count of 28–26. The second half, though, belonged to Penny Gearhart when she seemed to take the team on her back and say, "we're going to the finals, follow me." She finished with a career high 37 points, including 6 of 10 from the three-point range, and 11 of 11 free throws.

The play of all the Lady Comets became more intense than the tentative efforts of the first half, and they claimed the win 67–57. The performance of Gearhart was eerily reminiscent of older sister, Marla's, identical 37–point night against Ashland in 1996 to carry that team to the Region championship. Now Penny had brought them to their sixth consecutive championship game and only Boyd Co. stood in the way to make it a perfect run for her and give Coach Brown what he wanted, one more state tourney trip.

The senior girls of Jenise, Brooke and Penny had devised a cheer with which the team broke huddle each time with the cry "Coach Brown." Dana Smith had developed the theme for the girls. . . . *H O P—He's Our Power . . .* and the phrase was emblazoned on t-shirts and banners. The team had embraced the idea that they were going to help Hop fight his battle for life and likewise they would give their all for him on the court.

The Boyd Co. game presented special problems as the Lady Lions were a very physical team, pretty deep on the bench, and for the previous three weeks had Kasi Mullins at point guard, who was slowly rounding back into form after being idled by the ineligible ruling for most of the season. West, however, had beaten them by 14 points, just three weeks earlier.

Coach Pete Fraley had now brought his girls team to the final four every year for his seven years of coaching and yet had never won it. Boyd had won championships three times, the last one being in 1993. Oddly enough, either West Carter or East Carter had stopped him each time in the previous six years. Boyd had lost to West in the 2002 championship and were the victim of West Carter's big win in 1998 to start their string of five consecutive titles. There was plenty of incentive in the Boyd camp to end the West Carter reign and take home the trophy. Fraley told the media before the game, that it was time for a different team to win it.

Everyone knew what would motivate the Lady Comets that night . . . they had to win it for Coach! Then there was the drama of "Kasi vs. Megen" one more time. The two guards had battled hard for three years, while Kasi was at East Carter, and now they meet again in the finals, with Mullins wearing a red jersey.

It would have been hard to find too many Carter Countians rooting for Mullins that night given her unceremonious exit from East, reportedly over her father's disagreements with Coach Easterling, and now her return to menace the Lady Comets after getting the legal ruling to be obtain eligibility, just a few weeks earlier.

You didn't have to remind people of her talent, especially Hop Brown. She had kept in touch with him all summer, during his illness, but truly he had expected to see her in a Jackson Co. uniform, not back in the 16th Region again. He had an enormous respect for her skills.

Von Perry would be called upon to lead the team, again. Hop was still weak, but hoped to at least make the game to sit on the bench and offer encouragement. He knew the team would be in good hands. Von had been with him for 21 seasons, and had helped build the West offenses and defenses through the years. The coaching philosophy and style were nearly identical and with Dana and Tex by her side, they would not miss a beat.

Hop walked slowly onto the floor to a cheering crowd and the girls broke huddle ready to give him a victory. But something happened, as it seemed their sentiment and enthusiasm didn't translate into smooth play. Again they seemed nervous without the usual confident aura of a Lady Comet team.

The first quarter was sloppy, the team disoriented, and shots would not fall as the Comets dug a hole for themselves against some very tough Boyd defensive tactics. Hop, protesting a referee's call, jumped to his feet in the first quarter, and then crumbled on the floor. Play was halted for a moment, as family members and trainer, Lisa Hatton, rushed to his side and helped him back to his seat. They remained near him for the rest of the game. The West girls seemed frightened to see their beloved coach in such a condition. They went to the locker room trailing, 23–19.

As she had the night before, sheer determination emanated from Penny Gearhart in the second half, and when her shot fell at 1:25 remaining in the third quarter, the score was tied. The Lady Comets were back in the game and trying to get the momentum to swing their way. There was "fight" back in those eyes and they would not quit.

But Boyd Co.'s Jennifer Swann buried a corner "three" at the end of the quarter to put the Lions back up by six and that spelled doom for the Lady Comets. Swann had some key defensive plays and was later named the tourney's Best Defensive player. Boyd's tactic of double-teaming Gearhart was something she had become used to seeing during the year, but it was proving effective.

West shot poorly all night and managed to hit only 2–15 shots in the critical fourth quarter as they desperately tried to pull out the victory forcing up any kind of shot. Boyd sought to control the tempo and the Lady Comets were forced to foul as they watched the clock tick away on the game, their season, their dream. Kasi Mullins repeatedly went to the foul line and helped seal the win. She finished with a team high of 18 points and Boyd took the title, 65–53.

Brandi Rayburn and Penny Gearhart combined for 46 of the 53 points as the other three starters were able to manage only seven points between them.

As the seniors left the game, Coach Brown was there to meet them, hug them, and reassure them through their tears. For the first time since 1998, there was a new

A tearful end to an Era, Hop and Megen's final game

16th Region girls champion and the Lady Comets would not be making plans for the state tourney trip.

It was a total emotional letdown for the Comet faithful. They had sadly witnessed an end of an era. The last game of Coach Hop Brown, the end of the incredible region championship streak, and the final game for the Gearhart family in a Comet uniform.

For twelve straight years, a daughter of Marvin and Judy Gearhart had helped lead the Lady Comets onto the court. Marla, Mira, Megen posed for a final photo at the end of the game after Megen had been named the tournament Most Valuable Player, by a unanimous vote, her third consecutive trophy. Brooke Mullis, Brandi Rayburn and Steph Hall also were named to the All-Tournament team. Later in a move indicative of her loving character, Gearhart awarded her All-Tourney trophy to her friend, Ashley Renfroe, of Ashland, who had been unable to play because of the knee injury. Megen stated that Ashley surely would have been on the team had she been in the games. The two girls had played AAU ball together and known each other since the sixth grade.

West was accepting the Runner-up trophy for only the second time in history, in a year when the Championship one would have meant so much. Gearhart told the radio audience after the game, that it was sad, it hurt, and she just had to be ready to accept whatever God's will would be. She would close the book on her fabulous high school career and now play on that same court in the fall as a Lady Eagle.

A tired, and obviously weak, Coach Brown, was helped from the floor after the post-game ceremonies and Coach Von Perry reported he was feeling very ill. She commented that the team just seemed so tight with their shooting, but lauded Boyd Co. for strong defense and effort. "Give them credit, they came ready to play." Perry said. "This hurts really bad, these girls are devastated. It couldn't go on forever, though, but life will go on." Her post-game radio show was an emotional one as she recounted the accomplishments of her friend and mentor, Coach Brown. "He taught more than basketball, he taught all his players about life and about living good moral lives. He loved and cared for each one of them. His retirement leaves mighty big shoes to fill," she noted.

The whole town of Olive Hill seemed lost without a trip to the State tournament. Later, feeling better, Hop expressed the sentiment that maybe he should not have gone that night to the championship game. "It was the final game, and I wanted to be there, but I felt so bad, and maybe my presence upset the girls. They just didn't play well."

West had lost only one other time in a regional title game, but Hop said this particular one really hurt and he couldn't forget it. It kept him up all night. Losses tended to do that to Hop through the years, but in the past few months, he had been sleeping well after every game because of his illness and medication. That night, however, he couldn't get out of his mind how he wished he could have been well enough to have helped more, but he knew his mind and body just hadn't cooperated.

He had truly longed to get back to the Sweet Sixteen one more time. "I really wanted to play Clinton Co. in that first round at the State." Hop said. "I think we could have beat them." The Diddle Arena jinx would remain, perhaps to be broken, another day, another year.

The Boyd Co. girls lost to Clinton in the first round of the State, 74–54. Sacred Heart edged Lexington Catholic in the final to take back-to-back State championships.

Hop felt that if he could just get well, he would like to come back and coach more, but for now he had to concentrate on his health and family and especially being with Kyle. At the end of many seasons, he would often relate that he was ready for practice to start again, the next day. "I'm gonna miss it, that's for sure . . . I just love this old Roundball." It seemed he could never get enough basketball.

Hop received many gracious tributes in the hours and days after the final game. He was once again voted EKC Coach of the Year, Daily Independent Area Coach of the Year, and *Lexington Herald-Leader* State Coach of the Year. WUGO honored him with a *Silver Mike* award, noting his 25 years of not only being the longest-standing and most successful girls coach in region history but for 25 years of *Coaches Corner* programs on the radio. His long-time friend, East Carter boys coach, Charles Baker, was likewise honored, as Baker had retired the previous fall after 26 years as head coach with the Raiders.

A special section of the local newspaper, *Grayson Journal and Olive Hill Times* featured his career's accomplishments and a pictorial tribute by sports editor, Denver Brown, to the final game- A Wondrous Legacy.

The honors poured in for Senior Megen "Penny" Gearhart as she was selected EKC Player of the Year and 16th Region Player of the Year by the Coaches Association, *Daily Independent* Area Player of the Year and first-team All-State in the Associated Press and Coaches poll receiving the most first-place votes.

The ultimate moment came, though, when in Lexington on April 18th, Coach Brown was able to present her with the famous #1 jersey to wear in the Ky- Indiana All-Star series as *Miss Basketball of Kentucky,* the only 16th Region player (boy or girl) ever to receive the highest sports honor in the state. The award had been given since 1956 with the boys and since 1976 with the girls.

Twice before, West stars, Kandi Brown and Meghan Hillman, had fallen short in the voting by coaches for the Lions Club All-Star honor, but this year they announced it was the closest vote ever, but Megen had won, edging Lexington Catholic's Chelsea Chowning.

It was a proud moment for Marvin and Judy Gearhart and sisters Marla and Mira, who certainly had helped little sister develop her skills with the backyard games and hours in the gym. Megen credited the great support of her family and a lot of hard work with achieving the coveted Miss Basketball title. Dad said he felt she certainly deserved it and he would have been disappointed had the vote gone any other way. He was proud for the person she is, not just for what she had done. "Megen is a better person than she is a ballplayer. No matter what, you don't say anything bad about anyone. She is such a loving and caring person."

She had helped the team to five consecutive Regional titles and the State Championship. She broke school records in career points at 2,711, in assists at 850 and steals with 481. She also set the school record for season free-throw percentage 90.1% in the 2001–02 season, the best in the state. She had been All-District, All-EKC and All-Region, five times, and 16th Region tourney MVP, three times. Her off-the-floor accomplishments were many as well, including maintaining a 4.0 GPA in school.

Coach Brown called Penny a "prime-time player, a truly incredible person on and off the court." He expressed his pride in her "not just because of her basketball, but because of what a special, sweet, loving person she is." Rival coaches were very supportive of the award knowing Gearhart's great gift for the game of basketball. All of Olive Hill and Carter County joined in the chorus of congratulations for "Penny." Fans were overwhelmed and somewhat surprised that a 16th Region gal could actually win the honor in a state-wide poll.

Even Megen told the media that maybe now people would realize that with hard work, someone from a small town could win. The notoriety of her five straight state tourney appearances with the Lady Comets and the popularity of Hop Brown and the program had made the Gearhart name and her basketball savvy known throughout the state.

Megen also noted that it had been her dream to bring Coach Brown, one more regional title in his final season. The team had failed that, but maybe this honor, "would make him feel a little better."

Hop looked forward to being able to watch her play some more with his daughter, Kandi at Morehead State. "She will just get stronger and better, and I know they will love her at MSU. She is such a talented and versatile young lady."

Supt. of Schools, Larry Prichard, noted that his career in the county started about the same time as Megen's basketball career and he wished he could have accomplished as many goals as she had. "She is the ultimate graduate," he said, " a great person, good student and outstanding athlete." Prichard said he felt that with the close votes in previous years for Brown and Hillman and now Megen winning the Miss Basketball award, it should open up doors for other girls in the eastern part of the state.

Hop Brown's last girls basketball banquet was held on May 4th at Carter Caves. The senior class of Gearhart, James and Mullis had achieved a final record of 120–16 for their four-year careers. Gearhart led the team in scoring for the year with an average of 21.4 points per game and 4.3 assists per game. Her 33 free throws in a row during the season broke the old record of 30 set by Kayla Jones the year before. Mullis averaged 12 points per game and paced the team in rebounds at eight per game. James averaged five points and five rebounds per game and had the best free-throw percentage at 88%.

Steph Hall, who led the team in three-point shooting, including seven in one game, Brandi Rayburn, and Leigh Audra Perry, would form the nucleus for the first team of a new era in the fall.

The Lady Comets finished 26–7 on the year, and averaged over 65.8 points per game, the third best in history. The free-throw shooting continued to set state records, being the best for the year at 77.5%. In addition to Gearhart, Hall and Mullis received All-EKC honors.

Hop's final senior class presented him with a plague that read:

Dr. Suess had a Hop on Pop	*Jenise, Brooke, & Penny*
We had a Pop named Hop	have been quite a crop
Who took us to the top	but like all good things, it comes to a stop

Coach John Hop Brown formally tendered his resignation to Principal Jim Webb and the school council, on May 5th, 2003, almost 25 years to the day after he had accepted the appointment from Supt. Harold Holbrook.

Coach Brown said it had been a wonderful 25 years with so many special moments and he wished he could go on. He lauded the wonderful support of the parents, players, his family, his assistant coaches and so many fans and friends. He knew he was leaving the strong program he had built in good hands.

A public reception for Megen and Coach Brown was held on May 22nd at West Carter cafeteria, where a large crowd turned out to offer their congratulations and farewell to two basketball icons of the town, who had brought fame and pleasure to the community. The town now made room for another basketball welcome road sign- "Olive Hill- the *Home of Ky. Miss Basketball, 2003, Megen Gearhart,"* which was unveiled that night by State Representatives Robin Webb and Rocky Adkins and Mayor Danny Sparks.

Sparks noted how all the girls and Coach Brown had brought such positive publicity for the city of Olive Hill. Coverage of the coach and the West girls team had been extensive from area media, including Lexington, Ky. and Huntington, W.Va. television stations.

Rocky Adkins talked of his many memories watching Hop play and doing his student teaching with him. He commented that Coach Brown's gym was really a classroom about life, where he taught the girls great lessons. He applauded Gearhart's great work at point guard, a position he played in high school and at Morehead, where she was going to attend.

Robin Webb noted her early playing days in the infancy of girls basketball at East Carter with no budgets and how Hop had been a leader in Title IX enforcement for equality for girls. She presented him with some Cleveland Brown mementos obtained from famous Brown quarterback, Tim Couch. She also presented Gearhart with a Legislative declaration in honor of her accomplishments and said "My own daughters could have no better hero than you, Megen." County Judge-Executive Charles Wallace spoke about the great pride the whole county has had in the Lady Comets through the years.

Principal Jim Webb and Olive Hill Chamber of Commerce president, Don Lykins, presided during the evening. Webb said the #35 jersey would hang in the school in honor of Miss Basketball, and presented a framed uniform also to Penny, to a standing ovation.

In her response she read a statement about her final year as a Lady Comet. Her remarks were not about herself or her award but her great love for Coach Brown.

> There are many lessons to learn in life, and basketball has taught me many. Several people have influenced the lessons I have learned and one of the greatest teachers was my coach, Coach Brown. I always knew there was more to life than basketball, but the complete understanding

of that did not sink in fully until I heard Coach Brown had cancer. I learned to focus on the more important things in life. The most important thing going into this season was to make it the best I possibly could, so Coach Brown would be happy and proud with the team he was graduating with.

I have also learned there are bigger battles than the ones that appear on the hardwood. I have seen this man battle every day of the season. Many would have just given up and quit, but as he preached and established in me that quitting is not the answer, he has practiced this in his everyday life. Witnessing this every day helped me perform to my utmost abilities to please this man. In many games this year, we were faced with the opportunity to lay down and quit, but we decided to push forward, as we have seen Coach Brown do many times. Although we did not win all of those games, we did not quit and I believe Coach Brown can be proud of that.

I have never been so heartbroken for this man than after the regional final game, this year. You could see the determination in his eyes the whole year of wanting to make it to the State Tournament, one last time. I just wanted to give him that chance. In the last moments of Coach Brown being my coach on the floor, I felt so helpless and overcome by anger, because I realized I did not accomplish the most important thing I had focused on all year and all I could do was let the tears flow.

It took me many weeks after that game for me to realize the meaning of Coach Brown's favorite quote- "Winning isn't everything, but wanting to is." I know Coach Brown knows how bad I wanted to win for him and that is how I know now that Coach Brown isn't ashamed of his last season here at West Carter. I love this man with all my heart and would do anything for him, but when I fall short, the empty spot in his heart can be filled with the knowledge of me wanting to do it for him.

As you can see, you can learn many lessons in life. I am very thankful and fortunate that I had not only a good coach and friend, but also an excellent teacher in the game of life.

There were few dry eyes in the house that evening. Coach Brown spoke briefly about the wonderful support from the community and the great girls he had over the years. "The reason that I never had any trouble with them was not me, but you parents. I loved them all and they were confused enough to love me!"

He talked about the championship team, but also about the fact that he felt confident in his heart that the Lady Comets were the best team in the state in 1999 and 2001, also.. "I never told that to the girls or the public. I didn't want to get fired, if you guys knew that, you would have said, Hey Hop should have won this thing for three years and he only did it once, how did he keep his job?!"

He closed with- "I appreciate and love each and every one of you . . . we're goin' come back next year and have a good team, I'm quite sure."

Just as they had been so supportive through the years, Olive Hill area businesses joined together to sponsor the event. It seemed somewhat appropriate that the beloved coach and the great star said farewell to Lady Comet fans together, even as the adoring community expressed their heart-felt "thanks for the memories."

The reception came just after the entire Brown family, eleven in all, had enjoyed a week's vacation on the island of Caye Chapel, just off the coast of Central America. It was provided by the Addington family companies who operate the resort. Larry Addington and family, originally of Sandy Hook, had been huge benefactors of civic, school, and sports programs throughout Northeastern Kentucky.

John Smith, son-in-law of Larry Addington, was the son of J.C. Smith, a former Olive Hill Comet basketball star, who had died of cancer. John and Hop were friends and the Addington group had been very supportive of basketball in Olive Hill and Carter County.

On May 28th, the West Carter High School site-based Council announced that Von Perry had been hired to the position of head girls basketball coach, after serving for 21 years as assistant coach to John Hop Brown. The move was expected by the sports community and Jim Webb was quick to point out that Von had certainly "paid her dues" and he was confident the great tradition of West Carter basketball would continue under her leadership. Perry was excited about continuing the work of Lady Comet roundball and said few things would change, as she had learned from the 'master' and expected to keep his philosophies in place. The players knew their styles were so similar that the transition would be pretty seamless. Dana Smith and Tex English were hired to assist Perry.

Then on the eve of the Kentucky-Indiana All-Star series, a quite ironic and disappointing twist to the season came, as Penny Gearhart announced she had been told by her doctor not to play the June games, because of her lower back problems.

She had often discounted the problem through her senior year, and played through the pain, not wanting to focus attention on her physical ailments. Her treatments by a chiropractor had continued during the season. In all her career, through six seasons as a varsity regular, she had missed only two games. The grueling year-round schedule of games since her elementary years seemed to have been exacting a toll on her back.

Now the situation grew worse and in early June, running became difficult. Doctors advised her to forego the games, and focus on getting better for the beginning of her college career. An extremely disappointed Gearhart said, "It's every player's dream to be in this game, it's such a big deal, and not playing is really killing me." She felt, however, that some rest to ensure a good start of her college career was the priority now.

Her beloved coach had one year earlier heard the bad medical news and cancer surgery prevented him from participating fully in those same All-Star games that he had dreamed of coaching after being awarded the honor. Now one year later, Miss Basketball would not be able to help her state play in the big rival game and would be relegated to the end of the bench to cheer the team on. The All-Star team, with Gearhart watching, beat Indiana in the first game, but were whipped soundly a week later in Indianapolis.

Despite our best efforts and fertile dreams, life events are not always what we had hoped for or anticipated. Coach Brown had tried to teach his girls to deal with wins and losses in a gallant way, resolving to win with dignity and accepting defeat graciously.

Now both coach and star player had to deal with circumstances that were not a part of their winning plan. Coach Hop Brown didn't envision his 25th season being his last. He loved roundball so much, and the bond he had built with his staff, players, media, fans, officials, and friends was simply so strong, he didn't want to let go.

The 2003 season became the "farewell" to the man who graced the sidelines for the West Carter Lady Comets for a quarter of a century and left an enduring legacy.

A fitting tribute to the coach, the man, the legend—was written by Go radio's Tim Carper.

HOP

The sidelines will seem so empty
Without you dancing around,
For 25 years we've always seen
The man known as Coach Hop Brown

We've shared in joys and sorrows,
More wins than there were defeats,
But you never took the credit,
It was your team who accomplished those feats

In humility you led your girls,
Teaching basketball, but also life,
Making sure that they could handle
Winning, losing, adversity and strife.

Your accomplishments are too many to mention
This page won't hold them all
Husband, father, mentor, friend
And a legend in basketball.

You've given so much to so many
You've always gone the extra mile
But the most important gift you leave
Are memories that bring back smiles.

What a magical carpet ride you led
2000 State Champs you were
and who can forget Li'l Penny
Your underwear was older than her.

Quotes were always your specialty
How we loved to hear you say this,
"Winning isn't everything, but
wanting to is."

The fish tie, the match-up zone
"Shoot the 3" you yelled
Coaching your daughters was a thrill
With pride your chest was swelled.

An now the era has come to an end
Your whistle hangs silent on the hook
The clipboard gathers dust on the desk
Along with a towel and old scorebook.

But that which continues is more important
Than trophies, championships and wins
Life lessons, relationships, memories
Family, humor and friends.

Hop was feeling pretty well and with Sharon and Kyle attended the annual Olive Hill Comet reunion in June at Carter Caves State Park. The opening part of the program was a time to roast and toast the coach. The event is attended each year by former players, cheerleaders and all those associated with the Olive Hill basketball program through the years and presided over by Coach Fultz.

In the early morning of June 23rd, three months after closing out his final season, Hop Brown was taken by ambulance to Kings Daughters Medical Center in Ashland, after a seizure left his body weak and his mind jumbled. He was unable to walk and doctors told him he would likely never see home again, instead recommending he go to their life care facility. The cancer seemed to be sapping life from him and it was difficult for family and friends to see the once vibrant coach in that condition.

But after three weeks of rehabilitation, he again proved the prognosis wrong and returned home, fighting back with the same veracity that characterized his career.

Part of the many former players who gathered to pay honor to Coach Hop Brown at a special reception.

THE ALBUM

The 2000 Banner belongs to West Carter gym, and the Lady Comets, one of the greatest teams to play in the Sweet Sixteen.

photo courtesy Bluegrass Imaging

Tim Harris created a special keepsake print highlighting the State Championship scenes

1988-First Regional Championship and trip to the State Tournament
Front- V. Perry, T. McGlone, K. McDowell, K. Brown, B. English, M. Greenhill,
A. Mays, Coach Brown.
T. Zornes, G. Taylor, M. Tackett, S. Rayburn, S. Layne, C. Barker, S. Porter, C. Lowe,
L. Clay
photo Don Hall Photograhy

The Lady Comets return to the State Tournament with the 1996 squad
Front- Coach Brown, K. Brown, J. Faulkner, A. Branham, W. Dean, Mi. Gearhart,
B. Collingsworth, V. Perry
B. Barker, S. Maggard, C. Jones, J. Jones, G. Brown, J. Justice, Ma.Gearhart, K. Ray-
burn, C. Damron, W. Whisman.
photo courtesy Visual Sports Network

Posing at the start of the historic season— Coach Brown and daughter, Kandi, who would become State Tourney MVP and Dad, the Coach of the Year.
photo courtesy Bluegrass Imaging

Unveiling the Hop Brown Court at West Carter

Ky. Miss Basketball, Megen Gearhart, through the years of winning. Five trips to the State Tournament and All-Time Comet scorer

State Representative, Robin Webb, presents the team to Governor Patton at the Capitol to receive the special road signs as State Champions.

Von Perry, Hop Brown, Dana Smith, The winning staff

The Brown Family portrait—Karla, Dalton, Sharon, Kyle, Kandi, Hop, Gerad, Kim, J.T., Kelsey, Tim
photo courtesy Deer Creek Photography

Go radio's KJ interviews Coach after 500th victory and plaque presentation, with the senior girls

Coach Hop Brown's first team 1978-1979
L. Kiser, L. Messer, N. Rayburn, K. Kitchen, J. Sparks, E. Dahlenberg, Ann. Messer, Ang. Messer, L. James, K. Stafford, C. Bauers. (Brenda Reynolds- not pictured.)

The "Diaper Dandies," youngest team to win a game at Sweet Sixteen, 1998
Front- L. Perry, V. Perry, C. Hamilton, L. Pendlum, K. Day, S. Shelton, Me. Gearhart,
C. Day, Coach Brown
D. Smith, K. Jones, B. Baker, M. Hillman, K. Brown, Mi. Gearhart, W. Dean, S. Alcorn
B. Raybourn, J. James, Cc. Damron, H. Maggard, W. Whisman.
photo courtesy Visual Sports Network

Hop Browns Last Team-2003
Front—K.Brown, C. Burchett, S. Hall, B. Mullis, M. Gearhart, J. James, S. Cox, A.
Shelton, K. Perry
C. Hargett, J. Roe, Coach Brown, V. Perry, D. Smith, T. English, L. Webb, K. Waddell
K. Shelton, K. Barker, B. Rayburn, L. Perry, K. Burchett
photo courtesy Bluegrass Imaging

Chapter 8

The Players

Hop Brown has reflected on the many young ladies who have passed through the West Carter basketball program over 25 years and stated, "I never had trouble with any of the girls, they were simply good kids, obviously with good parents." An amazing evaluation and tribute from the coach, as he fondly remembered the young ladies who have worn the Lady Comet maroon and white. Such a statement is also a testimony to the discipline and pride he had helped build into the program. In addition, the girls were stars in the classroom as well as the gym floor. It's evidence that seems to reinforce research about the positive influence of athletics on the life of high school girls.

It's easy to characterize the West Carter girls basketball program as a family affair. Not only was there a family atmosphere created among staff and players, but the story of the team can be told by relating involvement of various families and their contribution of daughters to the program. West basketball became a true "sister act." The various eras of the team's history might be traced in a small way by talking of the Messer, Brown, and Gearhart sisters.

When basketball started at West Carter in the early-70s, few girls had ever held a ball, let alone played in a full-scale game. It was going to be a massive training job to bring a true program to the school.

Fortunately, there were some girls who had mixed it up on the court with the boys. The daughters of Tobe and Hazel Messer of Carter City, had grown up shooting hoops at the goal on the barn at their grandparents house. They learned to play softball, basketball and all sports. They loved to hunt and fish like the guys. Some would have referred to them as "tomboys" in those days.

With the help of the oldest daughter, Garnet Yvonne "Von" Perry, the first varsity team at West Carter took the court. Her fiery personality and red hair earned her the nickname, "Torch." That competitive spirit would play well with Hop Brown when he took her as his first assistant in the coaching ranks. She was the only one of the four sisters not to actually play for Coach Brown, but of course, would become the great co-pilot in his spectacular journey.

Angie, Annette and Lisa would all experience Hop's coaching touch in his early days and recall the big contrast when he took the reins. They all agreed that practices changed drastically, with running sprints, running the steps, conditioning and "lots and lots of hard work." Many of the early prospects who weren't serious about playing dropped out, of course. There was no need for the coach to make "a cut." The emphasis was also on learning fundamentals of how to dribble, shoot, pass and also about playing defense. In reality, the Messers concurred, "we just wanted to survive practice."

The four sisters played on the same team, one year before Coach Brown took over. Angie would get to play only one year for Hop, but the experience was a good one and she said, "we really enjoyed winning." She later came back to help mold the elementary feeder program by directing the first Olive Hill Elementary girls team, using many of the same drills she had learned in high school. She also coached at Grahn, Lawton and Clark Hill.

Annette played for three more years and became Coach Brown's first 1,000 point scorer. He called her his first "pure athlete, who had a lot of good basketball skills." Lisa Messer played four years under Hop and went on to coach for a couple of years at Upper Tygart, both the girls and boys teams. Mom and Dad Messer were faithful supporters and never missed a game.

The Messers helped to get the Hop Brown era off to a good start, then it would be two other trio of sisters, the Browns (Kim, Karla and Kandi) and the Gearharts (Marla, Mira, and Megen) who would elevate the program to its greatest heights, starting in 1986 when Kim Brown suited up for varsity. For the remainder of his coaching career until 2003, with the exception of the 1989–90 season, when Karla didn't play varsity as a freshman, Hop would have a Brown or a Gearhart in his lineup.

While his own daughters' careers didn't overlap, Mira Gearhart would have the opportunity to play a year with both her older and younger sisters. All the Brown sisters wore their dad's old Comet uniform number—41.

The Messer sisters agree that Coach Brown's strength was in his ability to handle individual people and motivate the team. "He totally changed girls basketball," they asserted. "He would let you know what he wanted, but he was really a softie, and worried about everybody. He would work you to death, but also be your biggest supporter." Annette remembered, "Boy, was he really big on conditioning."

None of the Messer girls played with the small ball, and Hop's hands weren't that big either and he empathized with them even as he tried to teach them the fundamentals. "He was serious about basketball and was such a motivator," they remember, "but also fun to be around, too." They recalled the day Hop decided to cut his mustache and took quite a ribbing about his "crooked nose," broken from so many basketball wars. With the upper lip adornment, few people took notice of the nose. So he quickly grew back the characteristic mustache.

Angie Messer Johnson took her passion for the game on to her elementary coaching and coached Hop's daughter Kim, at Olive Hill Elementary and was a big influence on her and Brenda English.

She says she also received some help from another Olive Hill basketball great, Gayle Rose, who starred for the University of Kentucky in the 1950s. Rose's daughter, Stacei, was also on the elementary team, when Rose taught them some full-court press principles and they began to torment other teams with it.

The Messer girls said they had to learn Hop's work ethic and also his "little sayings." He would come up with some things that maybe some of the girls didn't quite catch. Lisa remembers one time he told them to beware of their opponent because, "they ain't no can of corn, you know."

There was little money for the extras in those days and the girls remember getting one pair of socks and one pair of shoes for season play. "We painted the star maroon on those good ole canvas shoes."

The situation for the players gradually improved through the years as more money and more enforcement of Title IX equality provisions took hold. Title IX, a federal law, required non-discrimination in boys and girls athletic programs.

The Brown sisters agree that playing for their dad was fun and really quite a different experience for each of them. Kim took the brunt of dad's coaching wrath and was often chastised hard for poor play. Hop admits to being embarrassed when he sees some of the old tapes and how hard he was on Kim. "I just wanted to make her a better player," Hop remembered, "but I know it was rough on her. I was pretty awful, I've apologized and I think she has forgiven me."

He told her she had to work harder on her shooting, and in the summer before her junior year, she practiced every night 'til dark on their court at the house. The hard work paid off with not only more playing time, but she also developed into one of the best three-point shooters in the state.

Karla's early interest was in cheerleading but came out for basketball and developed into a very strong shooter for the team. She would be the only one of the Brown and Gearhart girls who didn't experience a state tournament as a player.

Kandi Brown literally grew up with her dad's coaching job and was the consummate "gym rat" shooting hoops from the time she was four years old and following Dad around, while he swept the floor and completed all his daily tasks. She was at every practice and went through the drills with the big girls, dribbling and running, and was manager of the team all through her childhood years.

She had enjoyed watching Kim and Karla hit the long bombs, and developed her own

Kentucky's all time leading free throw shooter, Kandi Brown, prepares to fire

Photo courtesy Mason Branham, Olive Hill Times

three-point shooting style. When Karla played elementary ball at Clark Hill, where former Lady Comet mentor, Mike Barker, had returned to coaching, Kandi got into a game as a kindergartner and hit the first shot she ever took, a 15–footer. She had been going to all the games to watch Karla, and Barker had dressed her that night against Grahn. She went on to play her elementary years at Olive Hill.

Kandi began dressing for the Comets junior varsity in the sixth grade. When she witnessed Dad yelling at Kim and Karla, it upset her, she admitted. When Kandi played varsity, Hop definitely had changed and admitted he had learned not to be too harsh with his daughter. he said, "I learned to relax a little and really enjoy Kandi, although I did get after her, a few times."

The Brown girls feel that there was definitely no favoritism while playing for Dad, and that often he seemed to bend over backwards to avoid any appearance of it. Basketball talk at home was never an issue. It was mostly kept in the gym, where he was Coach Brown, not Dad.

Kandi's outstanding career often led her to hear the opposing crowds taunts of "Daddy's girl" but she tried to ignore it and prove with her play what she was all about. Hop called her, "a totally unselfish player." "She didn't care about points, she was like me in that she just wanted to win."

Many nights, Kandi would settle for helping the team win with her deflections, ball handling and assists. She knew the girls looked to her as a leader and she wanted to build a team spirit and not look for stardom.

Kim had the opportunity to play college ball at Morehead State after graduating in 1989, but turned down basketball, saying she was simply "tired of ball." She looked back later and knows it broke her dad's heart and regrets the decision she made then. She has been able to live some of the college ball thrills though, through Kandi's outstanding career at Morehead with the Lady Eagles. Kandi, at 5'10, with all the skills and a keen knowledge of the game, was the perfect college prospect and set school marks for three-point shooting, joined the 1,000 point club there and was the nation's leading free-throw shooter, in helping the Lady Eagles to accomplish winning seasons. Kandi said it took a little adjusting to college ball, as it consumed so much of your time, and the game was more fast-paced.

The Gearhart sisters developed their skills under their father also, Marvin Gearhart, who played for Jack Fultz and loved the game immensely. He built his own full-size court at the house, which friends dubbed, "Marvin's Gardens" where the girls grew up shooting and learning key skills from their dad.

Marla started with basketball at Olive Hill Elementary, and was thrust into the point guard spot at West while only an 8th grader. She says her skills were in ball handling, speed and steals. She really had to work on her outside shot to develop more scoring punch. As her career developed, more responsibility was placed on her shoulders as point guard. The coaching staff, aware of her basketball knowledge, gave her freedom to call plays and she became the Comets first true—"coach on the floor"—type player.

Hop and Sharon say farewell to first daughter, Kim, at senior night

Marla says she loved being able to play with Mira those three years, because "we understood each other and it was a lot of fun playing together. "Mira was really a good player and could have played in college if she had wanted."

Marla did go on to college and enjoyed an outstanding career at Eastern Kentucky University, where despite missing her junior year to injury, scored over 1,000 points, and in her senior season, was second in the OVC in scoring and top 20 in the nation with an average of over 20 points per game. She was selected first team All-Conference for the Lady Colonels.

The Brown and Gearhart girls enjoyed a good relationship. Karla Brown played with Marla, and Kandi saw action with Marla in the 1996 season, and then teamed up with Mira for two more years. Megen joined them in 1998 when Mira was a senior and then played with Kandi for three years.

Mira calls herself "the lucky sister" because she got to play with both her older and younger sister and went to the State tournament with both of them. Her tendency was to help Marla and then be more protective of little sister, Megen.

Likewise, Megen points to being able to play with big sis, as an amazing part of her career, because she never thought she would get the opportunity. She also loved being able to play with Kandi and then move on to join her at Morehead. She said it is difficult to point out one memorable award, but would have to say that the Miss Basketball honor was "such a great accomplishment for me."

Megen believed playing basketball gave her true lessons for life, with having such great teachers at Coaches Brown, Perry and Smith for so many years.

While the Gearhart sisters learned a lot of fundamentals playing at home, they developed their team play under Coach Brown, whom they said was more than a coach, "he was your friend."

He didn't want any arguing on the team and Mira said they held a few team meetings during her years without the coach, to iron out some matters.

They all agreed that Comet players knew Coach Brown cared about them as he was always concerned about people getting enough sleep, getting good grades and not getting sick.

They knew the success of the Lady Comet program, though, was more than Hop Brown, it was also the long hours that Coach Perry and Coach Smith put in during winter and summer to prepare everyone and everything for the season.

To the Gearhart girls, Hop Brown was "always there for you, and faithful to the West Carter program for all those years." Hop called it a "true privilege" to know and coach the three sisters who had meant so much to the school. They were all "outstanding players and outstanding young ladies."

The assistant coaches describe the three as quite different- Marla was the jokester, didn't much like to practice but very competitive. She hated to lose. Mira was very accommodating and basketball wasn't the total focus of her life. Megen was quieter and a very loving person, but totally dedicated to the game, to extra work and to winning. Hop said that you simply couldn't keep Megen out of the gym. She came early and stayed late, and practiced every day, and between church services on Sunday.

Megen achieved more, but as Von Perry put it, "she also had the advantage learning from the older sisters and a more year-round program."

The Gearhart family shares in Megen's Kentucky Miss Basketball moment—Mira,
Marvin, Megen, Judy, Marla

The Gearhart girls are the only sibling ball players in the Region ever
to record over 1,000 points each in their career, with Marla and Megen
exceeding 2,000 and all three were named Most Valuable Players in the
16th Region tournament during their careers.

Marvin started working with Marla when she was just a toddler tossing the "nerf ball into nets" all over the house. He remembers even taking
her to games he was refereeing, while still in diapers. "She would sit still
through the games watching, but I think she listened to the crowd a lot,
because afterward she would say, - you stunk, daddy!"

Marvin worked the girls on his home court in the summer and in the gym
in the winter. He did a lot of welding work for the school system and when
there were snow days, his pay was getting into the gym to play basketball.

He says the girls argued a lot when he got on them, but he wanted to
get rid of their bad habits. They'd watch game films and critique everything. Gearhart said, "Marla was the natural boss. Mira was more 'laid
back' and Megen was able to take it all to a higher level."

Coach Brown credited Gearhart with helping both the boys and girls
basketball program at West. "He would do whatever you asked and got the

boys and girls playing against each other over at his place and developed a lot of good players."

The Brown and Gearhart sisters all shared great basketball ability, but were different in their various gifts and personalities.

There were many other "sister acts" that contributed much to West girls basketball. Janet Sparks played only the first half-season in the experimental year, but sister Julia was a senior on Coach Brown's first team.

Falissa and Janena Greenhill played together in 1983–84 but then gave up basketball the next year. Suzi and Samantha Layne were sisters who played together for two years. Amy Mays, whose career was shortened by knee troubles, did play briefly with little sister, Lori, who spent four years in a Comet uniform.

There were twin sisters, Stacy and Tracy Piper, who played together in 1992 , but Stacy was unable to play the following year due to injury and helped manage the team. The Day sisters, Kerri and Cathy, were together two years, then Cathy, the youngest, went on to star for the State Championship team and little sis, Julia, dressed JV for the 2002–03 team.

Shanna Shelton, a senior for the State Champion team, watched sisters Kelly and Ashley log minutes for the 2003 varsity squad and dressing for the end of the 2003 season were the Burchett twins, Kristin and Charla.

Two Jones girls made their mark on West basketball, as Carrie played three years of varsity including the '96 Region champion team. Younger sister, Kayla, was one of the "diaper dandies" with five varsity seasons and region championships every year of her career. She was a player Coach Brown called, "a real fighter and unsung hero on those great teams." Both Carrie and Kayla were among the best all-time free throw shooters.

The two younger Messer sisters, Annette and Lisa, helped lead the early Hop Brown teams.

Ginger Brown played four varsity years, including an outstanding season with the '96 Region champs. Older sister, Charity played two years varsity, 1989–91.

Other families contributed more than one offspring to the program through the years playing either varsity, junior-varsity, or serving as managers. Jessi Jones played on the '96 Region champs and was second-leading scorer on the '97 squad. Her sister, Jake, played JV ball. Becky Collingsworth was on the '95 and '96 teams, and older sis, Amanda, played JV ball and served as manager. Shannon Minor and sister Malissa each played two years for Coach Brown.

However all the girls who played at West relate that the bloodline or family name didn't really matter because they were all like sisters anyway, when it came to the team.

Besides Marla Gearhart and Kandi Brown, other former Lady Comets have made big impacts on college ball.

Brenda English played four years as a Lady Eagle at Morehead State. She said the transition to college ball was sometimes a "struggle" and there were coaching changes and losing seasons while she was there. She enjoyed it, though, and by her senior year was starting and averaged nine points a game.

Brenda had been almost like Hop's fourth daughter, and her father, Tex, said he and Hop sort of passed on their desire to win to their daughters. Tex and Hop were big buddies so he felt he could ask questions and offer his opinion on basketball matters and often did. Mom, Sarah Lou, did the video work for the team for many years.

In her four years at Rio Grande College, Michelle Tabor tied the school mark for most games played, set the three-point record with eight in a game, scored over 1500 points and had 500 rebounds. She was one of the best all-time free throw and three-point shooters. Her head coach, David Smalley, said Michelle came from a great family, a great program with Hop Brown, and had both the academic excellence and work ethic to make the big-time impact. Her team earned one trip to their national tournament, where they lost in the first round.

Michelle learned a lot about basketball from her dad, David Tabor, and her parents followed her faithfully through her high school and college years. She called Hop Brown "a truly great coach who cared about his players. He was always right there for me during my knee surgery and in rehab. He would come to the house and call and check on you."

Michelle had the opportunity in college to play against another former Comet, Stacey Carter, who stayed in Carter County to star for the Kentucky Christian College Lady Knights, where she won three National Christian College Tournament championship rings. She holds the school records for season free-throw percentage at 85.7% and for three-point percentage, also. She scored 1265 career points in four seasons.

Coach Brown and her college coach, Ron Arnett, both agree Stacey was one of the quickest defensive players they'd ever seen, and she loved to play defense as well as being a great shooter. While she was so active on the court, by contrast, Hop remembered her as one of the quietest and most reserved players he'd ever coached.

Meghan Hillman, with her good size and inside play, received the most attractive offer when the University of Cincinnati program gave her a scholarship. She attended only one year, logging playing time in thirteen games as a freshman, but transferred in the summer of 2003 to Georgetown and accepted a scholarship to play for them, believing she would be happier with their program and contribute right away.

Mandy Sterling of the State champion team, only played one year at West Carter, and wrote her name in the Lady Comet record book with her shooting and scoring. She said her transfer from Ashland was well worth it, and playing for Hop Brown, was "such a great experience, he's so wonderful to work for and easy to get along with. . . . the greatest coach I know."

Mandy accepted an offer to play at Barry University in Miami and averaged nine points per game her freshman season. Wanting to come back home, though, she transferred to Northern Kentucky University, but surgery on her leg ended her basketball career, after limited action there, and she became a student assistant.

Several Lady Comets participated in other sports and excelled at track and softball. Becky Collingsworth won three State track titles in Class AA, in the 100–meter hurdles in 1995 and in the long-jump in both 1994 and '95. Her sister, Amanda, won the 300–meter hurdle State championship in 1994. Brooke Mullis won a State track championship, when she took the 100–meter hurdles title in Class AA at the meet in May of 2003. That accomplishment coming after her knee surgery, two years earlier.

In the 1980s, Dana Smith, went to Cumberland College with the intent to play, but decided against it and came back to attend Morehead. Several colleges made overtures to Pam Biggs, but seemed to back away because of her lack of size. She decided to enroll at Alice Lloyd, but didn't stay.

Several other girls like Sheila Porter, Gina Taylor and Kayla Jones, all who played on state tournament teams and were members of the 1,000–point club, seemed to have college potential, but decided against basketball after high school. In many cases, where some girls might have played at small schools out-of-state, most just didn't want to venture that far from home.

While many good players didn't advance on scholarships, most Lady Comets had good academic credentials and a majority attended college and have settled down in society as wives and mothers with careers in the medical profession, social work, and many have become teachers. One took up high school coaching, as Lenore Sparks directed the Franklin Co. girls team in Frankfort from 2001–2003.

Two former players are memorialized with the annual Charla Bauers Leadership Award and the Cheri Nolan Duvall Determination Award. Bauers played for Coach Brown's first two teams, and Nolan played from 1980–83. Both were starters and loved by their teammates. They both passed away in 1994, Charla in an auto accident and Cheri from complications related to diabetes.

Stephanie Kiser, who played one year in 1991, was killed in an auto accident in 1996 and was said to have been one player who always seemed to be able to trade barbs with Coach Brown.

Certainly much was expected of every girl who became a West Carter Lady Comet, from obeying the rules and being a role model to others, to working hard in practice and dedicating themselves to winning.

But much was received in return as well. Each girl was cared for and respected by Hop and the staff. He was always open in expressing his love for each girl and his interest in their well-being was genuine. The "honey" with which he might have addressed the players, was heart-felt and they knew it.

The senior ceremonies and post-season banquets were always well orchestrated and were very memorable events for the players, support people, managers, and their families. The girls accomplishments and statistics were documented each year, excellent records kept, and each person recognized and honored with various awards.

 The State Championship in 2000 and then the final year for Coach Brown, following the discovery of the cancer became sort of "touchstone" events that brought all Lady Comet players together.

Every player that could get there followed the team to Richmond in 2000 for the title game and those unable to be there in person, were glued to the radio. When the final buzzer sounded and West Carter was the State Champ, it was a time of celebration for all former players. There were those who had been a part of the struggling years who never thought they could beat the big teams to win a Region championship. Then there were the Region champion team members, who thought that just going to the State was the ultimate dream. And at that one great moment, they all became believers and realized that all the hard work was worth it to build the program.

Many of the players who were at the game and joined in the wild celebration all said that it was unbelievable, that West Carter could do it. It was wonderful night for the older Lady Comets. Brenda Reynolds, who played on the very first Hop Brown team, was at the game and was so excited for her alma mater and for her former coach, as she thought, "he really deserves this."

Michelle Tabor, listened from her home in Russell, and was ecstatic with the accomplishment. Sheila Porter said there were hardly words to describe the feeling that we finally did it and the teams that went to the state in the late-1980s felt a part of it. Indeed, after the championship year, the first teams to advance to the state were brought back for a special night, to be honored as the ones "that started it all."

In a sense, every player shared a piece of the great banner and burst with pride to have been a Lady Comet. Many former players have always been among the Comets biggest fans and those who stayed close to Olive Hill could be seen at many games.

Then when news came that their beloved coach had a terminal illness, another emotional bond was formed, as former players sent get-well wishes and their prayers, visits, calls and cards meant so much to Coach Brown. Many just couldn't believe it was happening to the man who had been their second father.

Hop loved to have his players talk with him and desired to know as much as he could about them. He wanted to see their grade cards, know about what they were eating, and any problems they were having. "They were all such wonderful girls, and so smart, just outstanding students. If there was any one of them in any trouble, I don't remember it or they sure had me fooled."

Principal Jim Webb concurred with Hop's admiration of the girls, as he doesn't recall any academic or disciplinary problem with any of the Lady Comets in all those years.

Hop Brown wanted his girls to leave the program with more than trophies and basketball letters, but also with some lessons and memories they could carry with them.

Sheila Kay Porter remembered that his constantly pounding the idea of "team" into their heads truly helped them develop a sense of cooperation in life. "I learned to be tough under pressure and never give up and always give your best, no matter what."

Stefanie Rose, who was one of the Lady Comets best inside shooters, fondly remembers the great friendships with all the girls on the team. "Coach Brown knew the game of basketball, so I learned a lot, but I also learned about people being there for each other."

Pam Biggs declared that the hard work taught you a lot of lessons but Coach gave you confidence to take you through and "that stays with you after basketball."

That confidence built among players as the winning seasons mounted and the championships continued. Winning breeds winning and more confidence. It also creates a pride and tradition that everyone wants to continue. These were the kinds of thoughts that often carried the Lady Comets through tough games. Their experience and that Comet tradition, doubtless helped carry the team to victory on many a night, and made it difficult for opponents to break them down.

The pride in the program filtered down to the young kids who aspired to be Lady Comets and spread out into the community where people who never thought they'd care about girls basketball, followed the team, attended games, cheered the victories, mourned the losses, and admired those young ladies who proudly wore the Lady Comet jersey. Young girls came to idolize the stars of the Maroon and White.

Nancy Birchfield, stated it succinctly, "Being a Lady Comet meant much more than just wearing a uniform. There were things that were expected of you. They never had to tell you what all of them were, you just simply knew." Without a doubt, Coach required good grades, good conduct and a role model for your classmates. You were to be better than average."

Perhaps Megen Gearhart said it best:

> As I put on my West Carter Lady Comet uniform, I don't step into just any basketball uniform. I step into high expectations and have made the choice to carry on the tradition West Carter has made for them. As the tradition grows stronger, the expectations grow higher and the other teams' determination to beat West grows deeper.

Every team wants to beat West Carter. Every time I put on that West Carter uniform, I know there is a bull's-eye on my back and I better be prepared for war.

I take pride in having West Carter written across my jersey top. I take pride in the name West Carter has made for them: in the 5 consecutive Regional Tournament Championships, the numerous District Championships and the 2000 State Championship.

Why is it that every team wants to beat West, plays harder against West and gives it their all each and every time they are on the floor with West? It is because of the name West Carter has made, the higher level they have established for girls basketball, and the "never say die" attitude they carry with them.

When I take my uniform off for the last time, I leave it for someone else to wear. I hope they have the desire, determination, and dedication to carry on this tradition.

For any future Lady Comet . . . please take pride in the name written across your jersey top! If you put on a West Carter girls uniform, *it's not just another game.*

CHAPTER 9

THE STAFF

The success of the Lady Comet basketball program lies not only in the charisma, talent and hard work of Coach Hop Brown, but the care and compassion for the game and the team from assistants Von Perry and Dana Smith. Coach Brown has admitted, "we were successful because of them, they deserve a lot of credit."

Hop noted that their hard work and dedication year around was a major factor in building a winning program. "They are simply workaholics," Hop has stated.

For their part, Von and Dana, see it as a true labor of love—love for the game, the girls, and for their head coach, with whom they developed such a strong rapport, that they both were considered members of the Brown family. It was a united front and the players knew that the brain trust of the team was always of the same mind and purpose.

Besides the responsibilities of assisting Coach Brown with the varsity team, Von Perry was the mentor for the junior varsity program, which she started in 1983–84 season. The team was 5–5 that first year, but 6–4 the next year, the first of an incredible string of 19 consecutive winning seasons, for an overall record through Perry's career of 233–80, a 75% winning percentage.

The JV or B-team was a phenomenal 59–1 during the years 1993–96. The team practices with the varsity and learns the same plays, drills and procedures. Hop has noted that certainly having an assistant in charge of a JV program was the start of the turnaround in girls basketball at West Carter.

The feeder system for the high school team includes the girls program at West Middle School, headed up by assistant coach, Dana Smith. The girls who train under Coach Smith learn the fundamentals and the offenses and defenses they will need to know at the high school. Smith's duties also include coaching the freshman team which plays a separate schedule from the JV and varsity during the season.

Without question, this close coordination of the teams of Coach Smith to Coach Perry to Coach Brown, from middle school through high school, is a significant factor in the success of Lady Comet basketball. The longevity of that staff and the respect each had for the others was the major reason West Carter girls basketball could build a dynasty.

The West Middle School program under Dana Smith has enjoyed great success. From the beginning, she wanted to make it a carbon copy of the high school in practice, policy, and philosophy. The girls go through pretty much the same routines as the varsity.

Faithful assistant and new Head Coach, Von Perry

The school actually began as a junior high in 1989–90 bringing the 7th and 8th grade students from the elementary schools and the 9th grade students from the high school. The name Lady Warriors was adopted for the new school's team. The school calendar has their season going from August through the second week of November, prior to the start of high school games.

The first year, only a basic freshman girls schedule was played and the team went 4–0 behind Michelle Tabor. The next year's team in 1991 saw nine 7th graders come out for the team. Four of those would later become the 1996 high school Region champions—Marla Gearhart, Ginger Brown, Jennifer Justice and Kimber Rayburn.

The following year, a class made up of Carrie Jones, Jessi Jones, Summer Whitton, Amy Branham and Becky Collingsworth began a string of 34 straight victories going undefeated in their junior high careers. Then in 1993 and '94, the 7th and 8th grade teams had winning records behind best friends, Mira Gearhart and Wanda Dean. Kandi Brown began playing on the junior high teams as a 6th grader in 1994.

The school changed to West Middle School in 1994, when the freshman were sent back to the high school and 6th 7th and 8th graders were enrolled. The elementary team competition programs were eliminated when the transition to the middle school concept was complete. The last elementary team schedules and tourneys ended in the Spring of 1994. Many of the elementary schools were now gone with consolidation, as the Grahn, Clark Hill, and Lawton schools were all combined into Olive Hill Elementary that same year, Fall of 1994.

Instead of the individual elementary basketball teams for the 1st through 5th grades, a junior pro program was established with Saturday sessions teaching the youngsters fundamentals and playing games with teams using a lot of volunteers and a coordinator hired by the school system. Diane Greene, wife of former coach Bert Greene, took the job for the first couple of years, then Kenny Fankell became coordinator. He organized the elementary boys and girls into teams in November with the volunteers at each of the three schools and plays through January. They practice at their respective gyms a couple of times through the week and then gather on Saturday to play games at the West Middle School. In 2003, a county elementary tournament was reinstated competing with the schools on the east end of the county- Prichard, Star and Heritage.

Coach Smith says the loss of the elementary schedule meant that more basic skills had to be taught to the new girls coming in at the middle school level. Since the change, she has taken extra time three days a week to invite girls in grades 2 through 5 to come to the gym for workouts, after her regular practices. These girls then play some mini-games at the halftime of the middle school home games. All the extra work, Smith says, "helps keep those young girls who might be looking at soccer or volleyball, interested in being a Lady Comet." She brings the middle school girls into the gym in late July to begin practice for their season.

Part of the success of the program rests in the idea of building future stars for the Lady Comet program and that basketball is taken seriously by Coach Smith. Each girl signs a rules sheet along with their parents. Three unexcused absences from practice and a player is dismissed, but Smith reports no problems, when the girls know she means business. She has largely directed the program on her own since being hired, although Coach Brown and Coach Perry help out on occasion, attend games and offer advice. Occasionally, parents have given a hand, and since 1998, Kim Brown Johnson has helped by coaching the 6th grade squad.

No player is cut from the team, most leave on their own accord, because of the strenuous practice regimen. Smith says, "We spend a lot of hours in the gym, more than most middle school programs, and we get our kids involved in summer camps."

In 1995, future Miss Basketball, Megen Gearhart began playing as a 5th grader. The following year, Meghan Hillman and Kayla Jones joined the team. Jones was very skilled for her age, Smith reports, and rough from playing with the boys at Lawton. Hillman was 5'6 at the time and growing, but didn't know alot about basketball. That team, including Robin Butler and Chelsea Hamilton, went 43–0 during their middle school careers.

In 1998 West Middle joined the Ohio Valley Conference for league play among middle schools in the area. The Hillman-Jones group won the league championship and tournament. That same year, Megen Gearhart made the high school varsity as a 7th grader.

Every year, that West Middle has been in the OVC, they have been in the championship game in both the 7th and 8th grade divisions and won the 8th grade in 2000, and the 7th grade title in 2002. Smith's career record with the Lady Warriors has been a 78% winning mark at 392–112.

While the relationship between the three coaches has been amazingly close through the years and their work was like a three-legged stool holding up the area's premier girls program, the stool wobbled a little after the 1999 season, however, when it almost lost one of the legs. Von Perry abruptly handed in her letter of resignation to Principal Jim Webb, after the State Tournament loss.

Webb said he was totally shocked, but Perry indicated she was tired, somewhat frustrated and just did not feel like continuing. Webb held the resignation letter on his desk, called Hop and determined he wasn't going to accept the resignation. He figured surely the matter would work itself out.

Hop was extremely disappointed after the Lexington Catholic loss at the Sweet Sixteen and didn't want to talk much about it. It was as if he went into isolation and this was part of the frustration on Von's part.

When he learned of the letter, Hop immediately called Von for a long talk to try to clear the air of any difficulties. Meanwhile, Jim Webb had torn up the letter.

For her part, Perry says it was just a "difficult time" and she was tired more than anything else, as the job was very demanding on family time and she and Dana had so many responsibilities in caring for the program, from fund-raising to summer camps. She told Hop that she was just not happy.

"I wasn't enjoying basketball at the time," Perry remembers, "In fact, everything about it was getting on my nerves, and I didn't feel particularly appreciated." Hop told her pretty straightforward- "Von, if you leave, it will be a mistake." Webb and Coach Brown had the habit of calling her "Vonnie Mae" when they really wanted to make a point and she remembers both of them invoking the nickname in plainly telling her they wouldn't accept her resignation.

She decided to postpone any announcement until after the girls basketball banquet. By that time, she had indeed changed her mind and was certainly glad she did.

Perry's family life was totally absorbed with the basketball program. Husband Dan has been driving the team bus on all trips since 1987. In addition he worked full-time at a plant in Morehead, served as an elder for the Christian Church, and ran the clock for the home games. According to staff and players, it was Dan that kept them "pepped up" with his positive enthusiasm.

Daughters Leigh Audra and Kristin Danielle have grown up in the gym and loved to play ball. Leigh Audra became the first sub on the 2002–03 team in her freshman year and the first "second generation" Lady Comet in uniform.

Von and Dana's duties went beyond basketball, though. Von coached the girls track squad for the first four years of her high school teaching career from 1984–87, and then took over the softball program in 1988. It was slo-pitch at the time and the girls enjoyed some success and won the Regional slo-pitch title in 1996, the last year before schools were required to change to fast-pitch. She resigned as coach after the '97 season. Dana was assistant coach for seven years and head coach for three years before giving up those softball duties after the 2001 season.

Both ladies worked together in establishing another program that has become quite an asset to Lady Comet basketball- *The John "Hop" Brown Roundball Camp.*

The one-week summer basketball camp started in 1986, after some heavy persuading by Coach Perry and Sharon Brown for Hop to start his own camp. Perry remembers that he was very reluctant as they had talked about it for two or three years. She promised to do a lot of the work, since

Hop had a part-time summer job with Northeast Development that consumed much of his time.

The first year of the camp, 12 kids showed up, then 22 the next year,
and Hop thought about just dropping it. But after the Regional championship in 1988, over 80 girls enrolled. As the success of the team grew, so
did the popularity of the camp and the desire on the part of girls to get
involved in learning basketball. They have had as many as 150 campers
plus staff on hand during the week.

Hop did some personal instruction, opened the camp with a talk, presented the prizes and served as janitor, with the major part of running the
camp falling on Von, Dana, Sharon and the high school players themselves.

The program was offered to girls Kindergarten through 9th grade,
with the younger girls coming in the morning and the older ones in the
afternoon each day during the week. The camp was usually held the first
full week after school dismissed for the summer.

The program was "unique" according to Jim Kretzer, a Grayson parent, who brought his two daughters each year. "The players were very
involved and acted like they cared. It was as well run camp as you could
find," Kretzer remembers. His girls later played for East Carter and he
helped coach the East Middle school girls.

Most of the high school stars of the later years got their first indoc-
trination into basketball, Lady Comet style, at the Roundball Camp.

The camp continues every summer, and draws youngsters both boys
and girls now, from all over the area. Lady Comet players serve as instruc-
tors and counselors in what is the first week of a busy summer for them.
While they enjoy helping, it's pretty hectic and Coach Perry says, after five
days, it has left a lot of young girls determined never to have kids of their
own! Von says the players worked really hard at teaching the fundamentals
and then there would be scrimmage games, and always lots of prizes. Positive reinforcement was a part of the plan, rewarding the girls for hard work
and creating in them a desire to improve.

Von and Dana have big responsibilities with the varsity program as
well, especially in running the conditioning sessions and practice. They
also participate in mapping strategy, coming up with plays and, of course,
serving as mothers and counselors for the girls. That part of the job was
both stressful and fulfilling.

Von Perry says, "dealing with girls as basketball players can be com-
plicated, and we had to keep Hop advised about that. These girls go through

a lot of mood swings based on boyfriends, home life, their monthly periods, and it really affects how they play on any given night." She believes that accounts for such erratic scores in season competition sometimes, when you could beat a team nicely one night, and lose to them by 30 points, two weeks later with the same players.

Von and Dana tried to keep things calm and help Hop make adjustments as needed. They tried to tell him everything and deal with any problems quickly.

Dana took on the job of cutting newspaper clippings and keeping a basic scouting book on other teams through maintaining files on each team for the staff to use and also compiling the statistics for the Lady Comets. Coach Brown, called her, "a very intelligent person." Fans sometimes saw Von as the more vocal of the two but the girls indicate that Dana can get after them pretty good as well.

Both assistant coaches admit that through the years, their input into the coaching decisions have gradually increased as Hop became more confident in their opinions. His first years were marked simply implementing his own schemes, and he didn't ask for much advice, but in later years he developed more of a willingness to listen to ideas and incorporate them into the team. Von says, "with Coach Brown, it has never been an attitude of my way or no way. He listens to us and does it when he thinks it is beneficial."

Dana is single and has been merged into the Brown family, serving as friend and care-taker, early on with Kandi and then with Kyle. Sharon Brown says that she is "just like a member of our family." While Hop and Von motivate with their voice, Dana often does so on paper, with her unique poems she constructs and gives to players to challenge and spur them on.

At the start of the 2002–03 season, a third assistant coach was added to the staff for the first time. Coach Brown, realized that under the Title IX equality and based on the numbers in his program, he could have another coach. He called on the son of his good friend, Tex English, and asked Tex Andy English to come on board part-time while completing his studies at Morehead State University. He was familiar with everything about the program, having grown up with Lady Comet basketball and played a few years on the boys squad. Coach Perry said, Texy was a good player, but had health problems that kept him from reaching his full potential, but was very knowledgeable of the game.

The rest of the coaching staff welcomed Tex and complimented his efforts, "the girls love him and he sees the floor well and makes a lot of good suggestions and he is big help in practice." Tex Andy called his experience, "great learning from a good crew" and hoped to make a contribution for years to come.

Another familiar figure on the West Carter bench, since 1991, has been Skip Christensen. While born and raised in Nebraska, Skip came to live in Olive Hill from Florida, to take care of his mother, after the death of his stepdad. He had a family connection to Hop Brown, with Skip's stepdad, Ray Flannery's sister, married to Hop's brother, Glen Arnold. Skip had obtained employment at a warehouse but later worked on motorcycles for a company in Morehead and loved it, since he is a cycle enthusiast. Skip had no basketball experience but liked sports and played some semi-pro ice hockey.

Hop actually first met Skip, when he asked someone at the American Legion post, where they both hung out, who had painted a new sign there. He then asked Skip to make him some signs for West Carter basketball and he has been a friend and part of the West volunteer staff ever since.

Skip had attended art school and enjoyed doing decals, and signs. Skip says, "I do whatever needs to be done behind the scenes." He's the one who hangs all the plaques in the coach's office and sometimes fixes what needs to be fixed. Parents have offered to pay him, but he simply enjoys doing the work.

Skip attends all games home and away, rooms with Hop on the trips, and even comes to practice. The fans have called him, "Hop's bodyguard." Skip tells the girls, his job is "styling and profiling," as with his brush he paints their lockers, their shoes, designs logos, t-shirts, and puts the Lady Comet stamp on every piece of equipment. He constructs and illustrates the monthly calendar each girl's family has for the season, and does a lot of public relations and leg work for the team.

Coach Perry has said that he is one of the "most talented and intelligent people she has met . . . he does so many things for us."

Some fans have joked that, all the Lady Comets need is another manager named, "Jump" and we'll have it all in -Hop, Skip, and Jump!

The Lady Comets have had a good contingent of managers to assist the team through the years. These students do everything from carry water to keeping shot charts and shooting video. Carrie Hargett, managed the team for four years that included the State championship and the final year for Coach Brown. She says the championship team was a lot of fun and she was so glad for the team and coach, but the year of Hop's illness was pretty rough. "It was difficult for the girls as things were just not routine that year."

Hop with Skip Christensen, his right hand man.

The managers receive the same trophies, rings, jackets and are treated just like players when it comes to team events and the players are very respectful and appreciative of their work, according to Hargett and Wendy Whisman, a five-year veteran manager who worked through the entire Kandi Brown era. She was Kandi's best friend and loved the job. She was a cheerleader for Kandi's team in elementary school and then became manager at the middle and high school.

The job is not difficult, but is often time-consuming. The players wash and care for their own uniforms at home, but the managers do all the towels. There are generally four mangers each year to handle the chores and they take turns coming to practice but everyone shows up for the games.

Wendy was particularly close to the team, and to the Browns, spending a lot of time with the family. She says she still gets chills thinking about the State championship run. "It was so great, because it was always one of Kandi's dreams, but we never expected it to really happen." Wendy says. She went on to room with Kandi in college and became a manager for two years with the Morehead State team.

Hop has been like a father to her and the illness impacted her hard, but she and Kandi tried to keep the talk positive. Wendy said, "Coach always had something funny to make you laugh, and I felt loved and cared for just like his daughters."

The boys and girls teams have, through the years, shared a common West Carter Basketball Boosters club. Parents and friends join to raise money that is split evenly between the two teams. The staff works with the boosters in helping them to select and buy items needed such as shoes, bags, and sometimes uniforms. The Boosters fund the annual banquets and buy the jackets and trophies. They help with road trip expenses for both teams.

The money comes from a lot of hard work conducting fund-raising events, auctions, and chili suppers. The Boosters work the concession stands at games to reap profits and put together the game programs for the season, selling advertising to raise money. They also help put on two events in the pre-season that have become traditions.

The annual Maroon and White game is a pre-season scrimmage where the boys and girls teams take the floor for the first basketball event of the year. Also the annual Jack Fultz Classic is held in late November with boys and girls pan-o-rama preview games with area teams participating. They have also, in the past, sponsored Comet reunion games and even an East-West alumni game that drew good crowds.

Girls and boys squads maintain separate AAU accounts to raise money to send players to the summer camp programs. For the Lady Comets, this means a lot of hard work, as it can take as much as $10,000 to see that every girl gets to all the camps each summer. Fund-raisers, in which the staff and their families were very active along with parents and players, netted a lot of the money. The players could be seen in their spare time, stringing and weaving bracelets that were a big seller through the years at special events. It all brings to light a fact of sports—that good basketball programs require a lot of money, and for school teams that means a lot of extra-curricular work to obtain those funds.

The West Carter boys, through the years, have had several student managers and support staff who have stayed on long after graduation and helped with a lot of aspects of the program and the gym. Jim Webb says, "We have really been fortunate to have people who cared enough to volunteer their time for sports, for many, many years."

Jeff Roe has kept score for the boys since the early 1970s, and Baxter Stevens, Jason Parsons, Jeff Garvin, Chris Perry and Danny Stamper have been active in working with the athletic program, and helping at girls games as well when needed. Stevens' work was honored when local sports enthusiasts, Brad Baker, built a popular web site and chat room calling it Baxterpreps.com.

Sharon Brown has been the Lady Comet scorekeeper since 1991, taking over after different students held the position through the early years. It wasn't that the students weren't doing a good job, but Hop, as coach and husband, along with principal George Steele, felt it best to put Sharon at the scorer's table, to keep her from causing the referees so much grief during the games.

Sharon says, "the officials always wanted to know where I was sitting before the game, but after I became the scorekeeper they knew where I was, and they knew I had to keep quiet." She also kept the team statistics updated and available for Hop.

Sharon then had a triple role to play through the years . . . as coach's wife, scorekeeper, and also a parent. Other Lady Comet parents comment that Sharon was always good to do her part as parent, in the various jobs, projects and fund-raisers, even though she had the other duties. Connie Hillman, another parent, says that it was really tricky for Sharon to do it all, but she did.

Sharon, Von and Dana have a friendship that one has to describe as incredibly strong, and the three not only shared the common desire to keep the team on the right track but to help out Hop in any way possible. Their heart for service might simply be seen in the fact that all three are special-education teachers in the Carter Co. school system at West Middle and West High. It would seem their ability to work with youth and advise Hop is a key factor in the success of West Carter girls basketball. Observers seemed to agree that they were truly special women in the life of Coach Brown.

The staff has included a team trainer since 1996 when Sean Alcorn became the school's first one, through an experimental part-time intern program with Marshall University. The idea met with such success that the school system created a full-time position of athletic trainer for each high school, East and West. The trainer would serve all sports teams, through the school year, for boys and girls.

Lisa Hatton has been the West trainer since February 2000 when she and the coaching staff says it is one of the best things to happen for the program. Von Perry, noted, "it took a load off me, in trying to tape ankles and take care of injuries. Lisa really knows her stuff and she has been great for the girls. She can diagnose and act quickly and that has been a great advantage in the physical health of our teams."

Lisa came on board just in time for the State championship and she said, "That was a wonderful year, but every year has been great at West."

She drives 64 miles every day to the school from Hurricane, W. Va. where she lives, because she says, "I love my job."

For Lisa, its been amazing traveling around the state to trainer clinics and classes and when folks find out she is from West Carter, they immediately ask about Hop Brown. Lisa said, "He's a great coach, very competitive, and also always an advocate for sports medicine, because he takes to heart what you tell him and wants the best for the girls health."

Cheerleaders, of course, played an integral role in keeping up fan interest in the Lady Comets. It was certainly a difficult job in the early years, with few fans in the stands to respond, but became a coveted job when the team started winning the Region each year.

Martha Maggard, Barbara Tackett, Kaye Parker and Mitzi Tabor helped the cheerleaders in the early 1970s. Diane Tabor directed the squads for four years, then Diane Greene took the job in 1980 and coached both cheer squads for 14 years, while also handling her teaching duties. The job was a voluntary staff position for many years until small salaries were added for the cheer coaches in the mid-1980s.

Jeff Huffman, counselor at the high school, became cheer sponsor and coach, starting in 1994. Several have helped out with the dual squads during his tenure, including Rhonda McClurg, Teena Brown-Liles, Stella Patton, and Monica Zornes-Gee.

The West Carter cheerleaders whoop it up at the State Tournament.
photo courtesy Mason Branham, Olive Hill Times

Coach Brown has worked for several principals at West Carter, starting with Bill Calhoun, then George Steele, Madeline Sparks and Jim Webb. He had been under several school superintendents beginning with Harold Holbrook. Then came Dwayne Cross, Ross Julson, Cita Dyer and Larry Prichard.

When you say "Coach Brown" around West Carter High School, though, you have to be specific, because there are actually three others, oddly enough. But while they were all friends, they are not related at all to Hop, so he hasn't wielded influence to get relatives in place. Kevin Brown is schools' popular head football coach. Brian Brown, Kevin's brother, is assistant football and track coach, and Mickey Brown has also coached track.

Everyone agrees Coach Hop Brown was the general that led the Lady Comet troops but there were many first officers and a lot of buck privates who helped assure the victories and Hop was the first to acknowledge and thank those who helped in so many areas of service.

CHAPTER 10

THE COACH

The evolution of girls basketball in the 16th Region into a popular and well-played sport can be traced, in part, to the work of Hop Brown with the Lady Comet program for 25 years.

Without a doubt, the game changed dramatically from the mid-70s to the new millenium, and opposing coaches give a lot of the credit for improvement to the standards set by Coach Hop Brown for his team.

From the period of the late 1980s to 2003, it was clear that West Carter girls basketball had a dominant influence on the level of play and the popularity of the game in the region.

The Kentucky High School Athletic Association officials all agree that Coach Brown's influence was enormous, including the Commissioner Louis Stout and Assistant Commissioner Julian Tackett, during Brown's career. They have said, "Hop Brown is not only a legend in his part of the state, but a true pioneer in the sport. While he was famous for his clever wit and never-ending display of humor, his tactical knowledge and success in his tenure have clearly raised the bar for all girls basketball coaches in our state."

Girls basketball, as a sport, has always struggled to win the heart of players, fans and school officials in Kentucky, in what is the hotbed of the boys game.

The federal law known as Title IX was first approved in the Nixon administration and went into effect July 1, 1972. While developing the regulations, the Department of Health, Education and Welfare received thousands of comments before publishing the final document in July of 1974. President Ford signed the final draft of rules on May 27, 1975.

Title IX prohibits institutions that receive federal funding from practicing gender discrimination in educational programs or activities. The full implications and then implementation of the rules would be years in the making and of course, is still on-going.

Schools with small budgets simply tried to offer girls some sports activities as best they could, but without equal funding. Since girls basketball in the early years generated little revenue, the coaches had to find economical ways to conduct the program. To many school officials, it was often just a bother, with no real support.

Hop Brown was always at the forefront in seeking equality for his team, staying abreast of what other schools were doing and going to bat to get what he felt his girls deserved. He was not timid about talking with principals, school officials and legislators about the needs. Eventually, as his team found success and more public acceptance of the sport, West Carter girls were able to obtain solid backing from the business community of Olive Hill and Carter County.

Hop's home-town roots and personality enabled him to get sponsors that were willing to help out, and the Olive Hill merchants and fans became more generous as the team started winning and bringing home trophies.

He always expressed amazement at the amount of money the small-town merchants, friends and boosters were able to raise, when needed, to make sure the girls had what they needed for tournaments, trips, and

camps. As the team got better, the post-season State tournament trips each year became an expensive proposition, but people were always there to gladly meet the Lady Comets' needs.

As he saw need for adjustments in the sport itself, he became an advocate with those in power at the KHSAA. He was solidly behind those changes that sped up the game with the alternating-possession rule. He lobbied hard for making the smaller ball for girls mandatory, and of course, loved the three-point rule.

Hop even felt that a nine-foot goal would be right for girls play and advocated that change, that was never adopted, mainly because of the cost involved in

Cutting nets became a habit for Coach Brown and the Lady Comets...son Kyle hoping to learn the routine.

Photo courtesy Mason Branham, Olive Hill Times

having adjustable goals throughout all the gyms. His logic was that girls had smaller hands therefore a basketball, easier to handle, was needed, and they were certainly not as tall as boys on the average, so why not the shorter goal.

The first years of girls basketball in Kentucky attracted mostly women to head coaching positions. In the 16th Region, it was nine years before a team headed by a male coach won the championship. Russell, under Liz Trabandt, won the first two regional titles, Linda Meyers of Ashland the next two, Pam Traylor brought Boyd Co, back-to-back wins, after that, Claudia Hicks from Rowan Co. won two in a row.

Frank Sloan, of Ashland, broke the trend with a win in 1983 in the tournament at the new West Carter gym. Oddly enough, it would be at West Carter, five years later, that the next regional championship came to a male coach, when West took the championship. In the interim, Claudia Hicks had won back-to-back again, then Connie Greene took Ashland back to the title twice. When Hop and West won, they kept the tradition of two in-a-row going, winning the titles in 1988 and '89.

Into the fraternity of mostly women coaches, entered Hop Brown, from West, with the desire to build a strong program for his school. He was accepted and got along well with everyone, even though at the time, he considered himself pretty strong-willed when it came to his coaching tactics. He took some pretty hard losses against the ladies but said he liked all the coaches and never went into any game with a grudge or revenge on his mind. Hop recalled, "there never really was a team that I didn't like and I respected all the coaches . . . they were all good people."

Early teams were capable of winning big if they had just one good dominant athlete. In those years, players like Regina Carroll of Russell, Paula Hatten and Melanie May at Boyd Co., Karla May at Rowan Co.and Barb Harkins at Ashland, could lead their teams to a championship almost single-handedly racking up big numbers.

The city schools had a head start on the other teams, as many of those girls had been exposed to some girls basketball and developing practice schedules and feeder programs went smoother in those schools, than the start-ups in the rural and larger county systems, many of whom had trouble finding anyone wanting to play or coach.

Then as the other programs in the region progressed, it became evident that a team couldn't win with just one or two good players, and a concept of more team strategy, set plays, and a necessity of developing other athletes and role players emerged.

Jim Webb, boys coach and later principal at West, says he had doubts that girls basketball would ever be an entertaining game, but gives credit to Coach Brown for an attitude of refusing to tolerate mediocrity and losing. "Hop had confidence and he eventually was able to pass that on to the girls." That confidence and poise on the floor helped immeasurably as the girls began to take pride in who they were and face up to strong opponents.

While he has received many honors for his victories with the Lady Comets, Hop always deflected much of the praise, by saying he had not really won any games, and any coach really has to have talent out there on the floor. He acknowledged that he, of course, coached just as hard during the seasons with few wins as the seasons they posted better records.

Getting young girls involved in basketball, Hop realized, would be extremely important, and when the elementary schools in the county started their programs in 1980, it was a big boost to recruiting girls for the high school, who now had a little experience. Later the development of the basketball camps for girls, summer AAU teams, and the Jr. High and Middle School schedules all better prepared the girls to succeed in the sport.

Hop Brown brought ideas and practices to the girls that he had known as a player and were identical to boys teams. He placed heavy emphasis on conditioning, learning plays, and threw man-to-man defense into the mix, eventually shunning the traditional 2–3 zone that most girls teams employed. But first and foremost, his rallying cry was that team play wins games. Every player began to realize with Hop, it was all about "team."

He wanted to make the sport of girls basketball every bit as exciting as watching the boys in action and he worked hard at it, in those early years. The improvement in the quality of play was obvious in the Lady Comet statistics. While early teams were lucky to shoot 30% from the field, the 2000 team hit 40% from out behind the three-point line. The free-throw percentages and long range shooting of the Lady Comets in the later years, topped most all boys teams. Their average point-totals per game steadily increased while turnovers decreased and their play was as smooth and methodic as any boys game.

The coaching techniques he employed to build a winning tradition certainly changed over the years, Coach Brown recounted that "I was pretty much a slave driver, but I know I have mellowed and matured, through the years." That is not to say that his desire for excellence changed, he just realized some methods were better for girls.

Hop attributed some of his early mistakes to "youthful exuberance, I guess" and realized that a coach grows and adapts with age and experience.

He has definitely calmed down, where he used to be prone to tossing clipboards and kicking balls.

But, foremost, with Hop Brown, coaching was about winning, and losing hurt him deeply. He mourned every loss, often staying up all night until the morning paper arrived. He felt almost every game he lost, he should have won. He admitted also that "when I got beat, I didn't want to talk much, I was mad."

The staff doesn't really cut any players from the team, but some have been encouraged to take jobs as managers or helpers, when it was apparent they wouldn't get much playing time. No one has ever been 'kicked off' a team, although in Hop's early years he had told some to go home and think over their ambitions as a player, then went to them and encouraged them to come back.

Hop believed his ability to think and react during the game improved over the years. Von Perry, said, "He could have some pretty good animated speeches behind that locker room door." One of the changes in his final years in the huddle, was the job Von had of getting his chair out onto the floor and have the girls face him and surround him while he talked during the long time-outs. This took the girls eyes off the fans behind the bench and put them solely on Hop and also helped his "aching knees."

Hop wanted each girl to play with her head as well as her body, and one of his key reminders was "be smart." And he had the good fortune of having intelligent girls who could understand that and take what they had learned onto the court.

The practice sessions remained intense, but the hours of running long distances and running up steps and jumping over objects were replaced by more methodic conditioning and weight-lifting. The lifting program began in the mid-1990s and continues into the off-season as well. Each practice lasts about two hours and follows the same programmed pattern.

About thirty minutes of shooting practice opens up each session with a detailed regimen of quick shooting, one-on-one, and at least ten to fifteen minutes of three-point shooting. The practices are not radically different from other teams with the exception of the emphasis on outside shooting and the free throws. Coach Brown loved to have the girls shoot and watch the ball go through the hoop. His favorite word in practice was "boom" as another girl knocked down a great shot. In games, when he thought the three-pointer was going in, it was a foot stomp and the big "boom!"

The opening shooting period is followed by fundamental drills about pivoting, driving, lay-ups, ball handling, passing, and defense. There are six goals in the gym and they used them all.

In the middle of practice comes the free throws. Every player shoots until they hit five in-a-row. After they hit the five, they continue until they miss. When a player hits five-in-a-row they call out the accomplishment. Free-throw practice is not done, until the team reaches the stated goal of these "five-in-a rows." Most days it was 30 of them, but sometimes more, or maybe less if practice was running long. Coach Brown liked for the girls to shoot a hundred free throws in a day. Many of the girls can almost go on forever and both Penny Gearhart and Steph Hall have hit over 150 consecutive shots.

In the early years, the Lady Comets shot free throws at the end of practice, like many other teams. Hop Brown said he realized how important they are when he thought about the fact that a majority of your games are won or lost by six or seven points. The practice and emphasis on foul shots in the young kids has made West one of the most accurate free-throw shooting teams in state girls basketball history and a source of pride and hard work on the part of every Lady Comet.

Pam Biggs, twenty years after being a Lady Comet, said she can still hit those free throws she is so conditioned to them.

When Kandi Brown was in her elementary years, she entered the local Elks Club Hoop Shoot competition for free-throw shooting. She won the state championship and other girls have followed, with state honors— Stephanie Hall, Jenise James, and Brandi Rayburn. Leigh Audra Perry and Ashley Shelton have also competed, and Coach Perry's youngest daughter, Kristin, has won her state age group. Hop Brown's son, Kyle, also competed and won in his age category.

After free-throw shooting, it's strategy and scrimmage time during practice, some sprint running and skull sessions with Hop talking. The team generally runs through various plays they want to use in the game situations ahead.

Practice is serious business with the Lady Comets, and talking and joking is prohibited, a surprising reversal from the Coach's "out-of-sweats" personality. The last shot taken in the final play, must always be made, before the staff closes out the session with final words. In the early years, the girls were required to be quiet even on the bus rides to games, to ponder the action ahead and keep in tune with winning the game. Later on, they were allowed to listen to music.

Dana Smith says "we all have our particular duties in practice and games, and after so many years together, we know each other well and work as one. We all work to keep the girls focused in practice." Von Perry notes, "Hop enjoys teaching and showing the girls, but he always does it to instill confidence by being positive with them, not prohibiting them from doing something, but trying to tell them what they do well and show them how to do it even better." A girl was never told not to take a long shot, for instance, but was told what her best range was and then given her duties to help the team.

Perry has been given more and more duties over the years and allowed to make decisions, as Hop prepared her to someday take a head coaching job.

The Lady Comet offense might be described as varied, with plays designed to run against various types of defenses. There are about 40 offensive sets in the playbook, over 20 out-of-bounds plays, and about ten special plays. There are set plays for presses and, of course, various press defenses to learn.

The main defense is the man-to-man, but the girls also work on zones and especially Hop's own brand of match-up zone, that has been employed effectively over the last six or seven years of his reign.

These plays have names or numbers that may seem rather strange. . . . like Boyd, Owen, Duke, Kentucky, Vandy, Travis, Jordan—named after the individual or the team that may have inspired the play. Hop Brown admitted that many of the ideas are simply copied from other teams he has seen in action or played. "I don't claim to have a lot of original material," he said. "We pick it up wherever we can, and if we use it, we name it from its origin. For instance, one of our best out-of-bounds plays, we swiped from Owen Co. so we call

Hop, at final reception, with two of his favorite people—Warren Cooper, Jack Fultz

it Owen." He picked up things from the NBA and college, including going all the way back to Adolph Rupp and Joe B. Hall.

He was certainly one willing to learn from others whom he thought had good ideas. Hop and the staff had a real thirst for knowledge and attended every clinic they could and watched lots and lots of games on television and in person.

Some plays are named by what they resemble, like the 'banana' 'the horse and plow' 'twirlbaseline.' Von Perry recalled that in the past years, they could just yell out the play name and the girls could hear, but that was when you had few fans in the stands. When the noise level increased, they tried holding up big flash cards, organized on a metal ring to show the point guard what the bench wanted. That became too hectic and time consuming, so each play now has its own hand motion or number that is used to communicate to the team.

As the girls became more knowledgeable about the game and team philosophy, the captains and point-guards took a lot of responsibility of changing plays and making quick on-the-court decisions.

For the most part, it was not the practice to specifically prepare for a particular team in the regular season, but to simply prepare themselves to be at their best. The coaches did keep a good notebook about all opponents. Dana Smith would collect rosters, newspaper clippings, and keep this folder updated so that they would know the other teams and their players.

Hop, himself, subscribed to area and Kentucky newspapers and read those sports sections the first thing every morning and in the evening. He says that both Von and Dana had the knack for being able to watch other teams and remember key points. The opponent folders were often reviewed, and because of the extensive summer schedule, the girls and the coaching staff was pretty familiar with other teams by the time the season rolled around.

Other coaches soon learned that while Hop may not show you anything special in the regular season, you'd had better be on guard, come tournament time. That emphasis on tournament games was sort of the unspoken doctrine in the Comet camp, but it later included conference games, as well.

It was unlikely that Hop Brown would show everything in the regular season game, that basically has no meaning in Kentucky, unless it meant the conference title. It was not that he deliberately would lose any contest, but you did not throw the playbook at any team until crunch time in March.

Girls basketball, through the years, has morphed into a year-round job rather than just a winter sport. Success at any school depended on the willingness of coaches and players to devote full-time to building a winning tradition. The Lady Comets stay busy, as conditioning, weight-lifting, and shooting practice is a 12–month commitment and after the season is over, summers are taken up with camps and AAU team play. Hop felt you had to out-work your opponents in the summertime.

He worked hard and he expected the girls to do the same, and they were more than willing when they began to reap the benefits of that work through improved play and victories.

A typical schedule takes a Lady Comet to the Hop Brown camp right after school to work, then to the AAU tournaments, camps at Morehead, Eastern, Lexington Catholic, Georgetown and the West Carter girls Shoot-Out held in July. The mandatory dead period from late-June to July 9 gives the girls some time off. The age-based AAU tourneys that they participated in depended on the ages of the girls that particular year.

Hop Brown learned the importance of dealing with parents in the sport of girls basketball. His ability in that area has to be one of the key reasons for his success and longevity. Many a coach has thrown in the towel, in the face of all the jealousy and squabbling that, unfortunately, doting parents can cause over their offspring.

Parents can be pretty bold, many times, in their assertions of the need for more playing time for their child. Playing time was the most often-heard complaint, according to the coaching staff. "It wasn't very bad at all the first ten years, when we weren't very good, but as the team got better, the parents took more interest in seeing their player be more active," Hop reported.

One of the difficult jobs of coaching is getting parents to understand that the team concept produces victories. Unfortunately for many parents, winning as a team is not their top priority, but rather the performance of their daughter. Friends say Hop was really bothered by the issue of upset parents for awhile, but realized he just had to concentrate on the girls and do the best by each of them.

He believed that probably every parent has been mad at him at some time or another. Many of the parents deny that assessment, but admit they didn't always agree with all the decisions. Sharon Brown knows of times she wanted to defend Hop and would get upset when she heard things, but Hop would never let her say anything.

He learned to establish some ground rules in dealing with parent questions and concerns and resolve them as quickly as possible, the best he could. No parent is to talk with him about a player issue directly after any game. His office is open on Tuesday afternoons and on Saturdays specifically for parent conferences at which time, any issue can be discussed. He always has as least one assistant with him when talking to any parent.

A parent meeting is held at the beginning of each school year, where the calendar, program and expectations are outlined and questions solicited. Practice sessions are usually closed only at tournament time.

Marvin Gearhart, whose three daughters played for Hop, says that everybody questions some things every now and then. Connie Hillman agreed that people hold a lot of opinions but the girls never got involved or argued over strategy. Any problems anybody had were usually short-lived.

As the team continued to win the pressure mounted and that, many parents agreed, contributed to high expectations and some degree of stress. Everyone felt though, that there was nothing but respect for Coach Brown and his work ethic and principles.

Gearhart says, "He covered it all, worked them hard with practice sessions, and lectured them when they needed it, and they all loved him."

Eddie Day also has had three girls in the program and says they never had any problems. "Hop was always great to all the parents, and he treated the girls so well. Our girls thought the world of him."

Tony Mays' daughters, Amy and Lori, played for Hop and said, "we got along fine and the girls all loved him. Nobody has done more for sports around here." He knew Hop's love for sports because they grew up playing sports together, even tried some hockey with sticks and crushed cans when Tygarts Creek froze over, Mays remembered. "I dreaded facing him in baseball in Little League, though, he was a great pitcher as well as a good hitter."

David Tabor was a principal at Upper Tygart during Hop's brief stay there and his daughter, Michelle, starred for the Lady Comets. "Hop never had anything bad to say about anyone." Tabor says he was real patient with the girls and there was improvement in the teams every year, and "I think the girls always knew how much he cared for them."

Parents agreed there was no favoritism in coaching his own daughters, as Hop would get on them just like the others and everyone was treated fairly.

Hop always tried to keep lines of communication open between himself and the girls with the help of Von and Dana. The breaking of team rules was never a real problem in any year. Most of the rules centered around preventing illness. The coaches wanted to make sure the girls didn't catch colds, got plenty of rest, did their homework, and made it to practice and games on time. Hop wanted them to eat right, wash their hands, put a coat on when they went outside and stay healthy. The curfew was up to parents during the school year, but during tournaments, a curfew was imposed. He simply worried about his girls constantly.

A part of Hop's program of gaining respectability for girls basketball was the dress and actions of both him and his team. His goal was always to make West Carter a truly "class act"–to do things right. He always wore a coat and tie to games, often putting the coat on the back of the seat, but shirt pressed and neat, with ties that some might call "unique." He expected equally appropriate dress from his assistants and the players. This was a rare sight in girls basketball where many of the male coaches and even the women opted for more casual attire, even at games. That was never allowed at West Carter, and the girls were expected to match their quality dress with polite and courteous actions toward everyone, to win and lose with dignity.

Hop wanted nothing that resembled "trash talk" from his girls. He kept his language clean and his words about others positive and he expected the same from them.

In the lean years of West Carter girls basketball, the parents made up the bulk of the fans, but since the late-1980s and the winning tradition solidly established, the Lady Comets have been the darling of the Olive Hill community. Sales of Lady Comet t-shirts and paraphernalia are huge and are worn by young and old, in astonishing numbers. Tickets sales at games have risen steadily and during the regional championship runs of the late-'90s and after the 2000 State championship, the girls outdrew the boys in attendance at games.

Many rival battles, like the East game, guaranteed a full house, something unheard of in girls basketball in most parts of Kentucky. School officials were amazed at the folks who began following girls basketball religiously and kept track of Lady Comet action on the radio and in the newspaper faithfully.

Gene Cline, local merchant, sold sportswear and said anything maroon with West Carter on it, was a great seller, "and it was not just the students, it was the parents and the general public, you'd be amazed." He said, "The team meant a lot to this small town."

Hop Brown's colorful style and personality, which he, along with others, would describe, as 'extrovert' made him popular with fans and respected and loved by other coaches and officials not just at home, but around the state.

Fans throughout the area had admiration and affection for Hop and the Lady Comets, even if they weren't from Olive Hill. Charles Ramey of Ashland, wrote letters to the staff, filled with insightful and complimentary observations about the team and the coach. He believed Hop Brown had set "the high water mark" in the state when it came to coaching girls. "Coach Brown started those girls in the right direction of always trying to do right in all they did and with whatever they encountered." He said that Coach Brown had certainly touched his heart and soul and that of so many fans, and was worthy of the honors he was receiving. "He was a man who could make you laugh, for sure, but you also admired his truthfulness and integrity."

The fans, like himself, especially reveled in the way the team handled themselves in the big 2000 State championship run, but also had shared the sorrow, concern and prayers when the Region learned of Hop's illness. Ramey said, "those girls knew, though, that a winner wasn't defined just on the scoreboard, or on getting another piece of wood or metal, but in giving all you had to give and that was Hop Brown, always fighting to win."

Gayle Rose, UK basketball star and local businessman, always loved Hop in high school and thought he could have been a Division I player. "He gave everything he had when he played and when he coached. He loved his job. His teams were fabulous and he was one in a million."

Suzanne Steele, librarian at West Middle School, was a fan with a special connection. While she didn't have kids playing, her father was Coach Jack Fultz and she grew up watching the Comets, including Hop Brown, play ball for Olive Hill. She remembers her mother washing the uniforms after each game and her job was to press and fold each one.

She got involved with the Lady Comets when fellow faculty members Sharon Brown and Dana Smith, would come talk to her about the team. "It was in my blood, of course, so they just got me started again." She fed the team during tournament times, and gave each girl a special gift and note of encouragement during the District, Region and State, before every game. "I love it," she said, " it just sort of feels like I'm continuing with what my dad did and it is close to my heart."

And when the girls won the State Tournament, "I couldn't have been happier for any group of girls in my life. I told them, when they would ask why I was crying, that you'll understand someday, exactly what you have accomplished." She added, "words just can't describe what Hop and these girls mean to me and to the community."

Debbie Brown had a daughter on the team for nine consecutive years, with Charity and then Ginger. Like so many parents in the small town, she had known Hop since childhood and graduated with him in 1969. She had called him "Hoppy" until they started working together at West Carter High and in the cafeteria one day, he told her he really didn't like that name, just "Hop." She has called him by John Carl, ever since. She has witnessed him "mellow" over the years as a coach. "He used to dance jigs, and run after referees when he didn't like calls." She remembered one game he was so upset with the way the girls played, he didn't go to the locker room at halftime, just letting them think to themselves. She said her daughter, Charity, sort of took over in his absence.

She believed the trip to the State in 1988 was the most memorable because it was the first time, but obviously bringing home the 2000 title and putting Olive Hill on the map was a dream come true. She will miss John Carl on the sidelines, "he's a great person and coach. We will all miss him down there shouting out plays as the Lady Comets continue to make history."

Without a doubt, Mickey Grills of Olive Hill, gets the designation as the number one West Carter basketball fan, with an incredible record of missing only a couple of boys games in forty years, home or away! He followed the team faithfully and started also attending the girls games when the level of play increased in the late-1980s and has gone to the girls games ever since. He loves basketball and said what the Lady Comets have done is "just totally amazing, because they play all year and dedicate themselves with such hard work. In the old days, the boys dropped the ball at the end of March and didn't pick it up again until fall."

Grills has missed very few girls games and cheers for them just like the boys, because "it's West and the team has really been exciting." He said, "the girls have had some really special players and Hop Brown is such a great coach and so knowledgeable of the game." He attended Olive Hill High with Hop and called him the "best player I have ever seen, especially when it came to ball handling. He could keep the ball away from anyone."

Tex English, Hop's neighbor and friend, says more people really became fans of girls basketball after the big years in '88 and '89. "Hop was a real worrier when it came to the players and to everyone for that matter.

'You know you should' was one of his favorite phrases. He wanted to make you feel better, though, a real encourager."

Hop said Tex was always ready to offer his help and his opinion. "Tex puts me in my place, Tex keeps me humble," Hop joked.

Hop's relationship with referees has not always been amicable. His temper coupled with the intense desire to succeed, in the infancy years of his coaching, led to several technical fouls, but because he had no assistants, he was always careful not to get tossed from the game.

"I know the referees were always thinking about ways to try to calm me down," Hop remembered, "they even gave me their *Best Bencher* award for most cooperative coach one year (1981) when I didn't deserve it, I think, just to see if that would settle me some."

He later received the award from the officials association many times for the right reasons. As he became established on the basketball scene, Hop realized he needed to become better acquainted with the referees and calm his bench demeanor. He began talking more with refs from around the state and even developing some friendships as he concentrated on coaching and not refereeing.

Nobody in the Comet organization can now remember the last time Hop Brown ever received a technical foul, but scorebooks seem to indicate it was in a regional tournament game of 1982–83, making it 20 years without a "T." Hop points out that his wife, Sharon, did get one, though, in 2000, while sitting at the end of the bench in the Lady of the South Tournament!

In the early days of girls basketball, coaches often had to round up the officials themselves, and one of Hop's favorite crews became two guys from the Grayson area, Walter "Budge" Johnson and Robert Jackson. "Budge" officiated for 33 years in the region and says he can't recall Hop with a technical. "He would ask you questions and sometimes state his case, but he never was abusive," Johnson says. The two developed a good friendship and went to state tournaments together at times. He recalls one game in which Hop had informed him that a previous call had been one of the worst he'd seen. On the next trip down the floor, Hop asked Jackson what he thought of Budge's call and he replied, "You were right, Hop, it was the worst call!"

Johnson said, "I knew Hop when he played ball and when he coached. I have always thought he was the best coach in the state of Kentucky."

Bobby Hall began officiating in the 16th Region in 1992 and has been invited to call the Kentucky State Tournament three times. He said, "Hop

Brown brought the region to a new level of play in girls ball." Hall admired Hop's ability to teach the game and the way the girls could shoot free throws. "You knew he was going to work hard at coaching and you just wanted to work hard at your job of officiating. You never heard him bashing the refs in the press or leaving the floor irate. He was always your friend and supported our association and all our banquets and activities."

Like most observers of the basketball scene, Hall believed Hop Brown helped to put the 16th Region girls program on the map in Kentucky. "I've traveled a lot and I have never heard anybody say anything negative about Hop Brown," Hall reflected. "We are going to miss him so much on the court, but his spirit, I think, will always be there."

Another veteran official, considered one of the best in the state, Bobby Craft agreed, "Hop Brown was the kind of coach you wanted to work for every night out, the best coach I've ever dealt with. He let you do your job and he did his." Craft credits Hop with really bringing 16th Region girls basketball to the attention of the rest of the state. Craft recalls "Hop was not one always griping, so if he ever did have a question, the officials certainly would listen." His admiration continued for the way he coached the girls. "Having Von there on the bench was a great asset in helping with the girls, and Hop knew how to be firm with them and get on them, but he knew how to pat 'em on the back and give out praise, too, he was just such a great coach."

As much as he came to love his team and girls basketball, Hop Brown admits that he often still had a longing to try his hand with the boys, as he had always dreamed. In fact, after his state title accomplishment, when a change was contemplated in the boys program at West, he wanted the job.

However, he didn't want to give up the Lady Comets. Yes, he actually proposed that he make a little history and coach both teams at the same time. He had principal Jim Webb convinced he could do it and to support the idea. Sharon was against such a wild plan but began to warm up to the idea some, when Hop said he would find real good assistants for the boys like he had for the girls, and just sort of supervise both. Of course, it would mean a game almost every night.

He dropped the notion, though, when he thought more deeply on it and decided it would offend some people and make him appear a bit overzealous.

He had also considered moving up the ranks into college coaching and pondered some overtures in that direction. His love for the area and family roots, though, was a deterrent and the Morehead State job was probably the only one he would have ever seriously considered.

On building the Lady Comet dynasty, Hop Brown smiled and said, "It's not easy sometimes being the big winner, because you know everyone works extremely hard to beat you, they want to win against you, really bad. I know all about that, because we used to be that way in the earlier years, always working to beat the big dog."

Without a doubt, the strong teams of West Carter sent a challenge to the teams around the region and eastern Kentucky to improve their game and for players to aspire to be the best.

Hop Brown wanted to leave his girls with more than a knowledge of offense and defense, but also wanted to make them a better person for having played basketball as a Lady Comet. One poster in the locker room reminds: "What is popular is not always right and what is right is not always popular."

Every girl seemed to carry away a principle that would have some lasting effect on the way they conducted their life.

 Hop Brown became one of the most well-liked coaches in Kentucky girls basketball during his 25-year tenure and one of the reasons was not only respect for his ability, but his genuine interest in other people.

He was known for always speaking to all the coaches and even writing or calling them with encouragement. Hop Brown truly liked people and loved working with young people.

The only coach to work in basketball longer in the region than Hop, was Charles Baker, East Carter boys coach for 26 years, and a good friend of Coach Brown. Baker retired in 2002 and turned the reins over to his son Brandon.

Coach Baker recalled how impressed he was with the way Hop carried himself as a player at Olive Hill. The two had the distinction of having Jack Fultz give them both their first pair of basketball shoes, as Baker spent a short time at Olive Hill in elementary school, before playing his ball in Grayson for Prichard High School in the late-1960s, and then starring at Rio Grande College.

"Hop was a person so easy to get to know. He cared about people, and just had the natural ability of relating to people and talking to them and that is so important in coaching. He had a good insight into how kids work and act and tried to treat them right, never robbing a player of his dignity." Baker said he tried to practice the same principles of fairness and discipline himself to get a better feel for the kids perspective, as a coach, something he and Hop talked about often.

They both agreed that the key to their longevity in a volatile profession was that they both loved what they did, of course, but also learning to listen to advice and adapt.

Baker also admired Brown's integrity. "He was always trying to do and support what was right." Baker's East Carter team in 1986 was the only other basketball team in the county to make it to a state tournament, after consolidation. He recalls Hop got some opposition from the west end of the county, when he told everyone he was going to go to Lexington and root for the East Raiders, and they should come along as well.

Baker summarized it, "Hop Brown is an Andy Griffith kind of coach—approachable and plenty of good common sense."

Coach Baker noted that he and Brown were both lucky in getting to coach their kids and having the loyalty of good assistants through their long years as coaches—Brown with coaches Perry and Smith, and Baker with coaches Hager Easterling and Jack Calhoun. The assistants had played for them, so it was easy to pick their brains about what they liked and didn't like when they were players.

Easterling had been assistant to Coach Baker of the East boys for 16 years before accepting the girls head coaching job in 1996 and taking the Lady Raiders to challenge the best in the region, including West.

Hop would also develop a strong friendship with Easterling, the coach who broke West's district and conference winning streaks. Easterling said, "We didn't have any personal rivalry, we just relished playing against each other because of the big crowds and all the excitement." The two exchanged scouting reports, never had a cross word, and rooted for each other, when they weren't opponents. He says without a doubt that Hop Brown made every coach in the region work harder. "He just raised the level of play and expectations and people starting taking girls basketball seriously. You knew you weren't going to outcoach him, so you just had to get your kids to play hard."

When Easterling took the East girls job, it became part of a growing trend in the state of male coaches involved with the boys willing to take on the girls job without fear of appearing to step down.

Easterling described his experiences with the girls very much like Hop had warned him. He had to learn to deal with different emotions and adjust his techniques after being on the boys staff for so many years. As his

Lady Raider teams got better, he says, "that just pushed Hop even more, and as a result, Carter County became the true "hotbed" of quality girls basketball. They both admit that the East-West rivalry could get a little nasty at times, with the fans, but it was certainly not like that for them.

Claudia Hicks, long-time successful coach for Rowan Co. in Hop's early years, remembers that Hop's emphasis on defense and pressing caused other teams to make adjustments then. She said that as West started getting better athletes, Hop started playing the girls earlier, giving them more varsity experience. "A coach can really take a kicking for using the younger players over those seniors, but Hop built his program that way, and you have to if you want to be a winner."

Hicks and Brown were fierce competitors in those early years, yet good friends and she holds him in high regard as the first male coach in the region to really build a winning program. They shared the great desire to make girls basketball respectable. Hicks believed that the West program certainly set the standard for that respectability in the 1990s, even as her teams had done in the 1980s and helped make the 16th Region as good as any in the state.

While the goal of the early West teams was to beat Rowan Co., the fans were interested in the East-West games. The West girls had beaten East only once before Coach Brown arrived on the scene. His overall record against the county-rival was 60 wins and 21 losses. East dominated the early years, but owned only seven victories over West in Hop's last seventeen years.

Kevin and Vicky Young coached East Carter girls for 12 years in Coach Brown's first years at West and had a winning record against him. They developed a strong friendship that all have cherished. Kevin also played many years of softball against Hop.

Vicky Young says without a doubt, Hop brought stability and enthusiasm to West girls because he was such a positive individual. She said, "he is a high-energy person, so well-grounded and what a sense of humor, he never met a stranger. He always felt the team was like his family and that relationship with the players made the difference."

Von Perry did her student teaching at East Carter and Young noted how much she complemented the program when she signed up to help at West, because Hop enabled her and all his staff to grow and share in the goals and beliefs of the program.

Another East Carter coach Hop Brown befriended was Brian Buck, who coached the girls from 1986–1992, during the time of the Lady

Comets surge to prominence. Buck said he could see it coming when the young players developed in Olive Hill, and knew the Lady Comets were going to be tough for a long time.

Buck first remembered Hop Brown after watching him play independent basketball and loved his passes and jump shots and tried to mimic those "things of beauty," in his own game during high school.

Buck recalls the first impact of Brown's coaching came in 1979, when the team his future wife, Jessica James, was playing on at East Carter met West. That Raider team seemed destined to win the region and had been ranked in the top ten in the state, when they were upset by the Lady Comets in the first game of the District.

Buck says that knack for coming up with a unique plan in the big games was one of Brown's great abilities and he would experience that when he took over as East girls coach. In his first season, 1986–87, he had beaten West Carter and appeared headed for a great post-season when Hop upset his team to take the District championship, using a 1–3–1 half court defense, Buck said he hadn't seen him use all season.

"It was then I learned that Hop never showed his full hand in regular season but worked hard on the games that counted the most," Buck confessed.

Buck remembers that Hop was always there to pump you up. "He called me up after big wins to congratulate me, and we always tried to encourage each other's players. I had predicted he would win the region in 1988 and when the girls won it again in '89, then lost in the State to Southern, I told them the back-to-back wins were so special and probably something nobody would ever accomplish again. I was trying to comfort them, but boy was I wrong," Buck admitted, after years later witnessing West's five consecutive titles and a State championship.

Hop always respected Buck's coaching ability and felt he was one of the toughest coaches to go up against. He asked him to be his assistant in the first Ky-Ohio All-Star game that he was selected to coach. Buck still sees that as one of his most cherished honors, coming from his long-time pal. Buck and Brown were golfing buddies and knowing Brown's superstitions, Buck sent a lucky ball marker to Hop right before the 2000 Sweet Sixteen, and he carried it in his pocket through that big ride to the title.

As West Carter got more competitive, Hop Brown sought to take his girls to higher levels of competition by trying to schedule teams outside the region. He developed good relationships with other coaches, including one of Kentucky's most successful girls coaches of all time, John High.

High invited West to play in his Whitesburg tournament in the late-1980s, and developed a strong friendship with Hop through the years, socializing with each other at events, and High admitted, "had a lot of fun together." Hop is such a great person, a real talker, and of course, a wonderful coach. It was such a nice honor when they named the court after him." High coached at Whitesburg, Breathitt Co. and Montgomery Co.

Greg Todd, coach at Lexington Catholic, became another good friend, and loved playing against Hop. "He always had his teams ready and was able to get the most out of his girls."

Anna Chaffins, was head coach at Russell High for ten years and in 1994, handed West their first loss in a region title game. She remembers that game as a real battle as you had to have your girls prepared to play any West Carter team. She also retired in 2003 and said she has always seen Hop Brown as sort of a mentor, as he was there to help her and other coaches, too. "When I had a really down year, he wrote me a full-page letter to encourage me. That meant so much. He always had nice things to say about people."

"With Hop Brown," Chaffin said, "it wasn't just about his team, it was about everyone in the region and doing good by them." Chaffin viewed him with respect, "Many fans think with his success that we looked at them as the big enemy, but nothing could be further from the truth, we were always great friends. His presence on the court will really be missed."

Indeed with Hop Brown it was more than only about his team, as he was often talking to and encouraging the players on the other teams he played. He and his players often developed good friendships with them.

Andrea Kelley, East Carter star in the mid-1990s, who went on to play at Cumberland and Alice Lloyd College, remembers that it was Hop Brown who sent her a card, congratulating her and wishing her well in her college career. She had to sit out her junior year in high school, 1997, with a torn ACL in her knee and Hop told her he was glad she was fully healed and ready to play. Andrea said, "In warm-ups he was always talking with the players, kidding with them, and wishing them luck and telling them to play their best and to have fun."

Deborah Bondurant, of the Lady Raiders, remembers that the day after she scored her 1,000 career point, Coach Brown sent her a balloon and note of congratulations on her accomplishment. "He was always really nice to all the players and talking and wishing us well." Bondurant said he was an incredible coach as she was on the team he directed in the 2001 Ky-Ohio All-

Star game which Kentucky won. She went on to play on a national championship team at Kentucky Christian. Sarah Click, former Boyd Co. star, recalled that Hop Brown was one of the first to check up on her when she had knee surgery in college.

Roy "Doc" Murphy, long-time Hitchins High and then East Carter's first boys coach, coached when Hop played for Olive Hill in high school and has observed the basketball scene in the area for forty years. He said, "no man has meant more to girls 16th Region basketball. It was always his demand for excellence that made it so wonderful."

Hop's old coach, Jack Fultz, continued to work for the Carter School Central office, after retiring. He also served as commissioner of the Eastern Kentucky Conference for thirty years, and kept close to the program and to his former players through the annual Comet reunion.

The Comet reunion was unique in that it brought back all the players from the Olive Hill teams yearly to talk over old times and have a couple of days of fun. It also showed the kind of attachment players had to the Comet tradition.

The accomplishments of the girls teams at West have made him proud of Hop and for Olive Hill. Fultz's boys' teams had some great players and came close but never gained that State championship. "it's such a difficult accomplishment for a small school to win the whole thing," Fultz said. "That 2000 team seemed destined to be champs as they had everything it takes—-team players, right attitude, right kind of parents, good coaching, and stayed healthy and got some breaks. He also had the advantage of two special ladies who loved the game and wanted to help him win it all, in Von and Dana."

He said that Hop ran an excellent program because "he had the ability to organize and deal with people, players and parents better than anyone. He was just a superior coach who had his players attack and not quit until they won."

Fultz, a member of the Dawahares Kentucky High School Athletic Association's Hall of Fame, believes Hop Brown is destined to be there with him. Jim Webb agreed and when he realized Hop's 25th season would be his last and his very life was under a cancer death sentence, he appealed to the KHSAA in the Spring of 2002 to induct Coach Brown, at the conclusion of his career the following March, which would mean they would have to make an exception to their rule, of no coach being eligible until three years after his retirement from the game.

In a letter from Commissioner Brigid DeVries, the appeal was denied. DeVries stated that everyone on the Board was familiar with Coach Brown's great accomplishments and his fine example as a representative of girls basketball. However, she stated to Mr. Webb that the KHSAA had worked extensively to standardize the Hall of Fame selection process to ensure every nominee met the standards so that "exceptions" are eliminated.

Commissioner DeVries stated that there was no doubt in anyone's mind that Coach John Hop Brown will become a member of the Hall of Fame.

Jim Webb was obviously disappointed with the decision and after the 2003 season, when Hop had officially retired, appealed to the KHSAA again to make an exception to the rule, citing the coach's deteriorating physical condition and Webb's desire to see Hop, his family and the community see and celebrate "what we all consider to be the crowning achievement in high school sports."

Again the appeal was turned down, and Webb was left with the feeling that it was a sad injustice that the Hall of Fame presentation could be posthumously. It was stated to Webb that Hop's nomination would be considered with the 2005 class.

Jim Webb reflecting of the Brown era, "It's been wonderful for the school, of course." He said that Hop Brown loved basketball and they talked about the boys and girls program often, "He became a master at watching and exploiting the weakness of other teams, and his structured practices and routines were really good for the girls."

In his own coaching career, Webb had come close to taking a West team to the State when he finished a region runner-up in 1984 and then he stepped aside after 1989 to watch son Jeremy play for the Comets.

He admits the boys coaches felt a "tinge of jealousy" when the girls built big winners that the boys couldn't do, but "you felt good for Hop."

Boys' coach Grady Lowe agreed that the celebrations made you feel like you wanted your players to be a part of it and it was hard on the guys, but you had to feel good because "the girls were deserving and Hop is a great guy."

For Webb and the boys parents, it was hard during those years from '96–'02 when the girls were always winning the Region and the boys had opportunities to succeed but just couldn't get a big win. It was especially tough on those parents, but Webb said, "I think everyone handled it well, for the most part."

Jim Webb has been a staunch supporter of athletics and on February 28, 2002, he was presented the "Mr. Comet" award by the school for all his work, through the years.

Ron Arnett, who has coached the womens team at Kentucky Christian College in Grayson since 1991 and has won six national titles, has been friends with Hop Brown for 30 years and played basketball against him in the independent leagues. Ron says that Hop Brown's shot was smooth as silk and he was able to pass on shooting hints to his players. "His two favorite subjects were kids and basketball." Arnett had the privilege of having his daughter, Aimee, help him coach a team to the National championship.

Arnett said, "After West won the State and we were talking in his office," Hop looked at me and said, "Ron, why didn't you tell me, winning it all was so much fun? We both agreed it was much better than losing."

Morehead State's womens coach, Laura Litter, who recruited two of Hop's players, Kandi Brown and Megen Gearhart said those girls were "examples of what athletes with determination, good work and ethics can accomplish. They, like Hop, are winners." She said she considered Hop Brown as a "giant" in the development of girls basketball and set the foundation that will last a long time in eastern Kentucky. "He had a way to make working and mastering the fundamentals of the game seem like fun."

Hop Brown's coaching comrades appreciated his interest in them, congratulating them, encouraging them, promoting the game, and truly wishing success for them, except, of course, when they were playing West Carter.

If Kentucky girls basketball had ever chosen an "ambassador of good will," John Hop Brown, would have won the election in a landslide.

CHAPTER 11

THE MAN

Family, friends, players, and coaches are in agreement in describing Coach Hop Brown as one of the most competitive people anyone would ever meet, yet one of the most caring. Add a dash of wit, love of laughing, and organization skills, and you have a recipe for a successful coach and a person loved by all.

You have to include as well, though, a penchant for superstitions, and a slight neatness compulsion if you want a total description of this coach as a man.

Coach Hop Brown simply hated to lose. The intense desire to be a winner started in his early years and never relented. He would find ways to punish himself for a loss. When he lost a game in high school, he mourned to the point of not even allowing himself to be driven home after the game. He would walk back, the nearly two miles, to his home at Clark Hill regardless of the weather. It didn't matter how well he personally had played, but winning was the key.

That desire to win was true of basketball, baseball, softball. . . . any game he engaged in—he wanted to win. It was not a win at any price, however, as Hop always believed in playing by the rules. He wanted to do it right, but if he didn't win, he was angry. He admits he had a real temper, too, when it came to that desire to win.

His attraction to all sports began at an early age and he just loved to participate. Baseball was his real first love, and the Cincinnati Reds his favorite team. His childhood hero was Vada Pinson, Reds outfielder. When Hop saw Pinson was a left-handed hitter, he determined to teach himself to bat left-handed, and he did.

His power hitting was well known in high school and later on the local softball circuit. When he returned home from the army and couldn't find anybody wanting to play baseball, Hop and friends turned to softball and with the help of his neighbor, Tex English, who had the local oil distributorship, and friend Moe Crawford, formed the Texaco Sluggers team. Hop played softball until his mid-40s, and the team had over an 80% winning record including finishing as high as fourth in the state. One of their chief rivals was a Grayson team, the Shake Shoppe. Everyone who watched Hop play marveled at his ability to crush the ball, and always with a distinctive "grunting sound" when he would swing for the fences.

With Hop, though, winning was paramount. Moe Crawford tells the story of losing a game in a state tournament, where Hop had hit four homers and each one earned him a lunch at a local restaurant. "He tore up those certificates and wouldn't use them, because we had lost the game." Crawford and others say that losing just destroyed Hop and he would often throw away or smash those runner-up trophies.

Also on the team were friends like Jim Webb, Grady Lowe, Max Hammond, David Tabor and Hop's brother, Gary, and the camaraderie was a pleasant memory for Hop. He also played for teams in Ashland and in Elliott County.

Hop satisfied his desire for basketball, by playing in the local independent league during the 1970s, with an Olive Hill team that included many of his softball buddies and brother Gary. Again, it was the Grayson guys that were the big rival. The Grayson Vets team featured players like Charles Baker, Terry Marshall, Rick Adams and other former high school players like Kelly Newland and John Buck, whose daughters would grow up to play for East Carter.

Many people say some of the best basketball games ever played in the county were between those teams, in the old Prichard gym. The battles

The Texaco Sluggers softball team, with Hop and friends

between two great guards and coaches, Charles Baker and Hop Brown, were especially memorable.

The old Olive Hill High did not have a football team, so Hop never had the opportunity to play that sport in organized fashion, but he loved the game as well and became one of the most high-profile Cleveland Browns fans in the area. Every year he and his friends made one or two trips to Cleveland to see a game. If not seen in a Lady Comet shirt and jacket, he likely would be sporting something promoting the Browns. Brown's paraphernalia adorned his office and home. But Hop said, he had learned to be careful about wearing all that garb while attending the Browns-Bengals games at Cincinnati!

As he did in his youth, he continued to admire great sports figures, especially those who seemed to really work hard to excel. He spoke often of stars like Bernie Kosar and Tim Couch, and his favorite basketball stars, Larry Bird and Kyle Macy.

Hunting and fishing were also passions, two past-times, though, that he had little time for since taking up coaching. One game he never had an interest in and even mocked those who played, was golf.

Finally, though, Tex English and some buddies talked him into coming to Carter Caves and playing a round. Swinging hard at the ball, left-handed, like softball, Hop took a par 4 on the first hole he played at the Caves. He declared the game simple, only to post a 13 on the second hole and a 15 on the par 3, third hole, drop his clubs and head home in anger over the silly game. When he got home, though, he was disgusted with himself over his action and determined that no game would beat him. He returned to his buddies at the course, became a regular, often playing 36 holes a day and practicing until he could reach his goal, which, at first, was to beat his neighbor, Tex English.

He determined to break 50 for the nine-hole Caves course, then 40, and finally was able to shoot par and even the low-30s. At one Comet reunion tournament, he carded an eight-under par, 62 for 18 holes. He played a lot in the local golf league and with fellow coaches including Grady Lowe and Brian Buck, whom he said helped him a lot. Buck was a good golfer and continued to teach Hop as he worked so hard to improve at a game he once despised. Buck said, "He could really hit it a long way, but what helped Hop score well, was that he was such an awesome putter."

His career at golf, not taking it up until his mid-30s, is certainly a story of his determination and competitive spirit that characterized most everything Hop Brown did in life.

Hop later even coached the West Carter golf team for three years, starting in 1999, while Buck was coaching the East team. In fact, they both admit that they actually coached both teams together. Buck credits Hop with promoting him to other coaches for Coach of the Year honors. They played a lot together and after hearing of Hop's surgery, Buck dedicated his victory, a few weeks later, in the Grayson Chamber of Commerce golf tournament to his friend. The news of Hop's cancer created quite a sad and ironic feeling for Buck, since Hop had always nicknamed him "Piccolo" after Chicago Bears running back, Gayle Sayers' best friend Brian Piccolo, whose battle with cancer was portrayed in the movie *Brian's Song*.

Whether it was his attachment to sports and the routines and rituals involved or other reasons, Hop is not sure how he developed his famous "superstitions," but he followed his rituals religiously.

For example, every game was started with the girls in a circle reciting the Lords Prayer together, and every position was to be maintained exactly as it was at the first game of the season. It wasn't as if he rubbed a rabbit's foot constantly, but game day followed regular, pre-planned routines that he didn't want to change. He was always the last one to get on the bus and the first one off, sitting in the same seat. He wanted the fifth seat on the bench each game, as he considered "5" his lucky number, although he wasn't real sure why. He wanted to have two sticks of gum in his pocket before each game for use during the game.

Part of his mode of operation was also to create a regular and familiar routine for the girls, which he thought was important in their feeling of security and belonging. Many team members would pick up on the superstitions and develop little "lucky" routines of their own.

Hop was a true collector, as he kept every souvenir, plaque or gift given him. He didn't throw anything away. He was not a disorganized junkmeister, though, he kept every memento in its proper place and didn't want it moved. His office was clearly a museum of West Carter girls basketball, with plaques, gifts and pictures given by players, coaches, or fans. Posters, pictures, mottoes and clippings lined the walls of the locker room. The championship teams were all properly recognized with pictures in the gym lobby. Candy and pop in the refrigerator all had to be well-stocked and in order. The girls all say he knew exactly when something was out of place or missing!

The same orderliness was what Hop expected at home as well and the family room at the Brown household was likewise adorned with reminders of sports, family, friends and events, including the trophies of all the Brown daughters. He admitted that besides liking things neat, he "can't stand dirt . . . I take a lot of showers."

Hop could be seen on weekends cleaning up around the gym and parking lot, and almost daily took care weeding and raking around the big State Champion sign in front of the gym.

Despite his great love for sports, Hop hoped he would be remembered first for his love for family, students and friends, for they were truly most important to him. "I truly like people." And friends and family say he would try to do anything for you.

He came to cherish working with young people, and took a special interest in the troubled students, the underprivileged, or ones that seemed stuck on dead-end trails. The guys were often addressed as "big cat" and the girls were simply "honey" as he asked about what was going on in their lives and how they needed to hang in there. He would often joke with the guys that they had better get their act together or he'd "give them a black eye." Dozens of students point to the encouraging word, received from Hop Brown, as a incentive to do better.

While family life at the Brown household for 25 years centered almost exclusively on West girls basketball since everyone was involved, Hop made room for other family matters including watching after his aging mother who lived alone, still on Clark Hill in the home where he grew up.

He would drive by or drop in twice each day to check on her and take care of any needs, always stopping after ball practice before heading home. It was obvious from conversations that Hop loved his mother dearly, and she felt he was "just a good, honest, and very humble boy." She said, "you know, he was never any trouble for me. He was always working, doing something for family or other people. I just love him and pray for him every day." She said she was proud of his accomplishments, and equally happy that all Hop's girls "got a good education."

While she had no interest at all in sports, she always wanted to know about how the family was doing and constantly concerned about Hop's work schedule and his health. When he learned of his brain cancer, the family made a concentrated effort to keep the news from her and try to continue as normal. She did wonder why Hop had stayed away for so long, when he was in the hospital and in recuperation. One of Hop's first concerns when he was sick for three weeks after the surgery, was what his mother was being told.

This was especially hard, too, when Hop began to lose his hair and went with the shaved head look. But his mom simply thought it was a fad when brothers, Gary and David, showed up with the same style, after they had cut theirs in support of Hop. Betty Brown, at age 92, moved to be with daughter, Maxine, in Dayton, early in 2003.

Hop loved all his brothers and sisters, with Gary and David, living in Olive Hill and close in age, occupying a special place in his heart and the feeling was mutual.

It was Gary who gave John "Hop" Brown, his other nickname that the public may not be aware of, because it was used only by family members and some close friends. To them, he is actually "Bucky" after the Bucky beaver cartoon character.

The three brothers did a lot of things together and the cancer was tough on them. Hop had a great deal of respect for the military, remembering his days in the Service. He often ended his radio interviews with "remember to pray for our troops." He was proud of his brother David, "he was a heck of a soldier." David was a medal winner of the Vietnam war, and was often called on to deliver patriotic messages and could do what Hop called, "the most beautiful tribute you have ever heard for military funerals."

Hop lived in a house with five females for a good deal of his life, his mother-in-law, Eunice James, who he cared for dearly, passing away in 1991. She was what people called a fanatic Lady Comet supporter.

The daughters all said, that despite basketball being such a huge part of their lives, it was not always the big topic at home. "We didn't spend time rehashing everything at the house." The girls recalled. "We didn't travel too much on vacations, either, because Dad couldn't sit still that long to go very far. He always had to be on the move."

Kim says, "Dad, was the mediator, mostly. You could get into trouble with Mom, but if Dad was mad, that was big-time trouble." He could be a disciplinarian as well, Karla remembers, and they had specific bedtimes and rules to follow.

As to the question of all his one-liners, Kim responded that "Dad was always quipping something or quoting." Hop said he never really sat and thought about one-liners, but they often seemed to pop into his head, and he probably got most of them by listening or reading.

Like Hop, the daughters all had nicknames, . . . Kimberly was "Kimbo"; Karla was "KarKar"; and the youngest, Kandi, was "Punkin" or "Kandi Jo." Kandi's real name was actually Kandice Jordan using Sharon's mother's name. When she became a basketball fan, she wondered why she couldn't just change it to Micah or Michala Jordan!

The Brown daughters say they mostly got along well, with the usual sister feuds. With the bigger age difference between Karla and Kandi, Karla says "little sis used to be a thorn in my side, because I had to play with her." They all agree that they became very close as they grew older.

Certainly it was quite a shock when Sharon informed the family that she was pregnant, "a 40th birthday surprise," she said, and gave birth to Kyle in 1994. They had planned a family meeting to break the news to the girls, Kim, Karla and Kandi, but the schedules didn't work out and it mostly got passed around by phone to a delighted trio of daughters. Kim said it was great that "Dad finally had the boy he wanted, in the household."

Kyle became a special treasure to the family, and he grew to became the same sports nut like his dad. Hop had been amazed at his son's love for every kind of ball and his ability to play them,—every sport from fishing to golf, basketball, football, baseball and even soccer, a sport Hop had never tried. The girls, naturally, made him the center of attention and affection, and with all the sisters grown up, he had plenty of "mothers."

Sharon remembers the difficulty though in having a baby at such a late age, and while the girls were pretty healthy, Kyle had what seemed like a lot of early illness.

The first grandchild that came into the Brown family was also a boy, Dalton Michael, born to Karla, August 20, 1998. When Karla became pregnant, she was struck with fear about telling her father of an out-of-wedlock birth. "This is not something you want to break to your dad, I thought he'd kill me," she remembers. But she recalled he handled it pretty well, and didn't shun her and "loved Dalton so much." Being a single mom was not easy, but she had plenty of family support. She received her degree from Morehead State and is working on a Masters, while teaching at West Carter in her father's old classroom.

Tim Johnson became the family's first son-in-law when he married Kim in July of 1994, and he recalled Hop graciously welcoming him into the family when he asked for Kim's hand in marriage. Johnson, a teacher and principal, had played basketball for East Carter in the early 1980s. He said, the "East-West issue" never impacted his relationship with Hop, whom he said loved him like a son. In fact, one day after he had heard Hop on the phone with Brian Buck, Hop remarked to him that he had more friends in Grayson than Olive Hill. Tim thought maybe it was because he had made some folks mad in Olive Hill with the coaching, but Hop responded that, "he loved each and every person in Carter County and there were just more people in Grayson, than Olive Hill."

Hop rooted for all the county, but that wasn't true of the rest of the family as their loyalties were with West Carter, and wouldn't want to be caught rooting for East.

Johnson said he and Hop had many conversations and while people might see him only in light of his coaching ability, he was a very all-around intelligent person.

A second grandchild was born in July of 1999, when Kim and Tim had their first, another boy, Jonathan Thomas, who became quickly known as "J.T." A little girl came into the Johnson household in July, two years later, when Kelsey Jordan was born, and Hop and Sharon had their first granddaughter. Kim received her degree from Rowan Co. Vocational School in respiratory therapy but after being on the job for awhile in that field, decided to go to work for the school system and eventually made it back to her old school, West Carter, as an administrative assistant.

Sharon said that life with Hop has had its ups and downs for sure, especially in the early days. She missed maybe, just two games in all the years, and "when we weren't at our game, we were watching somebody else play. Hop couldn't get enough basketball."

"By the end of the season, we'd be so tired, but then it would only take a couple of weeks to recuperate and it would be boring, and we'd be ready to go again."

One of Hop's special times was when the season had ended and he could relax for a few days. He would always treat the family and the families of the coaches at his favorite restaurant, *Red Lobster.*

Sharon believes Hop has taught her many lessons about life, but she has often had her input into changes for him, as well. It was obvious that they both passed on their strong work ethic and love for life and sports to their children.

But the toughest days have been dealing with the cancer. Folks have been fantastic in their compassion and care. Fund-raisers such as a benefit concert, organized by Delbert Crank and the American Legion post, and motorcycle poker runs, put together by ball parents, Jeff and Sheila Shelton, have been held in his honor, to help with medical expenses. There seemed nothing that people wouldn't do to lend a hand.

Gerad Parker of Louisa became Kandi's boyfriend when they started dating in 2000 after graduation from high school. Both have relied on their Christian faith to help them through the difficult year of Hop's illness. Gerad says, "Kandi is such a sweet person, always with good things to say about people, and she has been so strong." The family has really embraced Gerad, an All-State athlete himself in basketball and football and playing football at the University of Kentucky. He came to love Hop like his own father and enjoying the fact that he was so much fun to be around.

Hop relived his playing days a lot with friends and often spoke of Bert Greene's pure shooting ability, and stories of Coach Fultz, and how his friend, Moe Crawford, was the "all-time leading scorer of halftime games." In those days, the coach, only took a few players to the locker room at the half, it was so small.

You could often hear Moe, Hop, his brothers, David and Gary, along with Skip Christensen and Pud Fisher get into arguments over sports, with George Hogg serving as the peacemaker and Owen Fielding, the man Hop called the walking sports trivia book, usually settling the matter. Son-in-law, Tim Johnson, became privy to some of those cold winter day conversations and said the experience was amazing to just sit back and listen to those guys, who obviously loved each other, but had their own ideas about which players were the greatest.

For Hop's buddies, the sight of someone they loved suffering with the ravages of brain cancer was hard to bear and while they came around to be with him, they didn't know what to say to offer much comfort. They just wanted to let him know they were with him in the fight.

For his neighbors, Tex and Sarah English, it was particularly heartbreaking, they were so close, "he kind of lost the sparkle in his eye," Tex said, "and to see the cancer drag him down was really tough."

The realization of his own mortality, caused Hop to take a closer look at his life and priorities. He dealt with fears and thoughts of an abbreviated future on this earth. Every moment with family became precious and he prayed for both strength and time. With the same preciseness he conducted his life, he remembered his struggle with the pain of the cancer. He would say, "I was sick for 32 straight days," or "I've felt good for 18 days now." It was truly a battle of victories and then set-backs, but each time he had bad spells, he bounced back.

He tended to rely heavily on Sharon. Hop said, "She was so strong and I needed her so much. She does so much for me and everyone." Sharon had been dealing with physical problems of her own, with two surgeries on a leg, injured in a May 2001 auto accident, that didn't want to heal and had left her with a constant limp and periodic pain.

Hop's dream was to be around to see his son grow up and play ball. "I want Kyle to have his dad around, because he likes his dad to play with him and sometimes doesn't understand the illness has really slowed me down." Hop lost his own father at the age of six. He knew Kyle may not be understanding the full seriousness of the illness and Hop tried to keep

Hop and Sharon enjoy some private moments during their island vacation

up the fighting spirit and make everything as normal as possible. Karla sought to find ways to make it easier, as the social-worker in her came out. The girls knew it was hard on their mom, who also tried to keep up appearances. "It's not easy seeing Mom get upset and sad," the girls remarked.

Kandi said that when everything is going so well, you think cancer is " something that affects others, but when it hits home, it really hurts. But we just have to pray and allow the Lord to work whatever His plan is."

Reflecting on his life, Hop said, "I have been blessed to have so many wonderful friends and family, and grandchildren, and to coach my three daughters has just been special."

Hop had never been much of a church-goer as an adult, although his family attended with his mother-in-law at the Methodist church, and his girls had been active in youth groups especially at First Christian in Olive Hill. He considered himself a believer and had been attending some in the months before his cancer was detected.

He admitted the usual questions about "why me, Lord" when the illness struck, but determined to try to beat the odds while everyone was praying for a miracle.

After the brain surgery, he decided to make his commitment to the Lord and asked the man who had married him, Dick Damron, who was now minister at Oak Grove Church of Christ and professor at Kentucky Christian College, to baptize him into Jesus Christ. That took place June 11, 2002 in the Brown's backyard pool and family and friends watching called the joy on the faces greater than a million state championships.

Dick and Hop shared a love for basketball as Damron had coached the Kentucky Christian mens team for 20 years and to four National championships. They had played golf together some, both lefties, and Hop's daughter, Kim, with Tim and the kids attended at Oak Grove in Grayson.

Hop wanted to identify with the church in Olive Hill, though, and began attending at First Christian, where Dave Shanklin had been minister for many years. He enjoyed Shanklin's messages and said it was special when his preacher attended the Lady Comet games.

All the girls admit they broke down, during the days following their dad's surgery and just wished things could be normal again. Karla said, 'It's just so hard, we love him so much, there is just nobody as special as our dad."

For Kim, he was the "glue that kept the family together and made everyone laugh." Kandi Brown declared, "Our dad would have been known as a great man, even if he had never coached."

He was a man with a big heart and brave confidence who had conquered many tough opponents on the court, but faced a devilish physical opponent that threatened a life he loved dearly.

Carter Co. Supt. of Schools, and a former coach himself, Larry Prichard, believes, "folks with leadership like Hop Brown, don't come along very often, maybe once in a lifetime."

Von Perry said, "he has influenced so many lives, and the way this community feels about this man is overwhelming."

His friend, Skip Christensen, felt Hop was one of the great humanitarians, and not a braggart at all, a totally humble man. "I am proud to call him friend." William Waddell, Olive Hill businessman, said, "No one could have a better friend."

If a man's wealth is judged by the number of people who called him "friend" the richest man in the world lived at 120 *Champion Lane* in Olive Hill, Ky.

CHAPTER 12

THE POST-GAME

The post-game coaches interview is the job sportscasters and sports-writers know must be done as they attempt to summarize the game for fans. Coach John Hop Brown was always a willing partner with the media to get the message out and was without a doubt an all-time favorite among those on the basketball beat.

Tim Carper, a long-time East Carter public address announcer starting working sports for WUGO Radio in 2000 and remembered the first phone call he got was from Hop Brown to congratulate him on being named sports director and reminding him, now that he would be on the air, "you can't be rooting for the Raiders."

In one of his first post-game interviews, Tim said, he was talking with Hop about Penny Gearhart fouling out of the game and said his opinion was that a couple of the calls were questionable and she didn't deserve to foul out of the game.

To which, Hop replied, "Well, Tim, I don't deserve these hemorrhoids I have, either, but that's the way life is sometimes. Sometimes you're in a game and sometimes you gotta sit, and sometimes it's hard to sit."

Tim said he took a thirty-second laugh break after that one. Another memorable interview came during the pre-game after Hop had been named to coach the Ky-Indiana All-Star team."That must be quite a thrill, coach" Tim queried.

"Well, Timbo, Hop replied, "there are three things I have always wanted to be in . . . the girls State tournament finals, the coaching box at the Ky-Indiana All-Star game and Bill Gates' will. Two out of three ain't bad and if I ever get that third one, you and I will be walking in high cotton, brother." Carper noted, "Hop Brown has influenced my career for the better through laughter."

Mark Maynard is sports editor of *The Independent* newspaper in Ashland, and has covered Hop Brown through his career. He wrote this tribute:

Go radio team covers Lady Comet Action, Tom, KJ and Tim

Mark Maynard, The Independent sports editor, getting the news from the witty coach.

It is said that you can't be a hero in your hometown. John Brown, the man affectionately known as "Hop" throughout the state, never believed it.

Hop's legacy, in fact, is all about his hometown and the area where he lived. There was no better place to rear a family–or coach a girls basketball team—than Olive Hill. That was always the belief of Hop Brown, a man with the talent and skills that other bigger schools and bigger communities would have loved.

But Hop had a home here. He never quit dreaming of the improbable, some may have even said impossible, in this small community. Hop Brown wanted to win a state championship not for him, not even for his girls, but for the community he loved.

There has been no better ambassador for 16th Region basketball than Hop Brown. And there's no bigger fan of this area, either. It didn't have to just be West Carter. Many, many times Hop would call me at work and we'd talk for an hour about boys basketball in the region. Believe me, he was very much up on what was happening there, too. He always wanted to coach boys basketball and, had he not taken ill, may have tried to pull off being the boys and girls head coach at West Carter, if the administration would have let him.

Late in his career, Hop was approached about coaching an area boys team. He called me to ask what I thought about it. My advice to him was to stay where he was. He appreciated the honesty and he knew I was going to give him a straight answer. We talked about the pros and cons and it just didn't add up for him to leave the wonderful program he built at West Carter. I'm glad he stayed.

He kept up with all the goings-on throughout the area because he loved it so much. When you have a passion for something, you eat, sleep and breathe it. Such was the case of one John Hop Brown when it came to high school basketball.

Hop became West Carter's girls basketball head coach about the time I was getting into the journalism profession. And maybe because of that, we have such respect for each other. I watched him mature as a coach and he watched me mature as a writer. I have never felt uncomfortable around Hop Brown, because he wouldn't let you. I have been with him during many great victories. Of course, it's easy when you're winning. But I've also been with him through some devastating defeats; some that you could tell bothered him a great deal. But, you see, one thing that made Hop Brown such a great coach was that he is such a great competitor. Losing should hurt and it did him. But even during some of those difficult losses, Hop Brown always talked candidly and cleverly. Sometimes, we'd go back in his office and sit for an hour. We'd walk away laughing, joking, kidding. You never felt uncomfortable there.

Hop's office, for those who have never seen it, is a basketball shrine. It's wall-to-wall memorabilia of West Carter accomplishments. Forget wallpaper or paint for that office. It's clippings, and honors, plaques and pictures. I always felt honored when I looked around and saw a story on the wall that I had written.

Hop Brown was a sports writer's dream. His quick wit and wisdom made covering West Carter girls basketball a joy and not a job. You would come back from an interview with Hop, a happy man because of all the great quotes. There were no cliches to be found. They were the kind of quotes that made you laugh out loud. He put a smile on stories.

I've told him more than once that in my nearly 30 years of covering sports in the area that the 2000 Girls State Tournament, when West Carter won the title, was my favorite event. That's saying a lot. I was in Philadelphia when Duke beat Kentucky with the Christian Laettner shot. I covered Final Fours, including UK's titles in 1997 and '98. But the 2000 State Tournament was better, for a lot of reasons. Some of it was the excitement of an area team winning a basketball championship (it was the first one since the 1961 Ashland Tomcats and I was only three years old at the time of that title.) Most of it was because of Hop Brown, a man I had come to admire, respect and love throughout the years. This was his time.

He didn't just play up West Carter on the statewide stage either. He made sure the Lady Comets' victory was not just for Olive Hill, but for the 16th Region. Of course, he was especially happy for Olive Hill for people like Jack Fultz and Bert Greene and so many others. Hop Brown never forgot where he was from. Home is where his heart was.

Mike Fields, veteran sports columnist for the *Lexington Herald-Leader* penned these words:

In his heyday, Hop Brown was the most quotable coach in Kentucky. When he talked his black mustache would rise and fall with every rapid-fire syllable. As fast as he talked, Brown's mustache was nothing more than a dark blur most of the time.

There was a moment at the end of the 2000 season, however, when Brown gave his upper lip a rest. His West Carter Lady Comets had just beaten Shelby County for the State title at EKU's McBrayer Arena and Brown was silent. Brown let out a deep breath with a heave of his shoulders, took off his glasses, wiped his eyes and stood speechless.

The indefatigable coach, who had been running on about two hours of sleep over the previous three days, was exhausted. Oh, but what sweet exhaustion.

Not only had West Carter captured the first state basketball championship for his beloved hometown of Olive Hill, the Lady

Comets had done it with a special group of young ladies that included Brown's youngest daughter, Kandi, the tournament MVP.

Brown wiped tears from his eyes and exchanged hugs with his wife, Sharon, the team's scorekeeper and oldest daughter, Kim.

He then took a moment to introduce his 5-year old son, John Kyle Cleveland Brown. Yes, that's the boy's real name. His dad is a huge Cleveland Browns fan from way back, so why not?

That's John Hop Brown in a nutshell. Never has a more entertaining, fun-loving coach won a state championship. Brown was a favorite of the media because he was the best quote this side of Bartlett's.

Some of my favorites-

After West Carter freshmen, Megen Gearhart turned in a dazzling performance in the State semi-final win over Manual, Brown had this to say about his 14-year old point guard: "Gosh, I've got underwear older than she is."

When asked once if the stress of coaching basketball ever wears on him, Brown's response: "You gotta remember, I teach driver's ed!"

And when talking about daughter Kandi's many-splendored basketball talents, Brown said he "wouldn't trade her for any player in the state and two Babe Ruth rookie cards."

The coach had a knack for making people feel good. "He could always put a smile on people's faces, daughter Kim said.

A man couldn't ask for a better tribute than that.

Another radio broadcaster, Jim Forrest of Morehead's 106 FM has been calling Rowan Co. basketball since 1982 and also did Lady Eagle basketball for MSU. He says, "of all the high school and college games I have covered and of all the coaches I have interviewed, Hop is the best, always professional, always friendly, and always the best one-liners. High school basketball will not be the same without Hop Brown. He will always be my favorite sports interview and one of my favorite people."

Ivan Ralls worked the WMST, Mt. Sterling girls games and their state tourney network. He said he admired Hop because he was able to keep his sense of humor even when on the biggest stages. He remembers the first game of the 2001 State Tournament coming in as the defending champion and asking Hop how this team compared to last year. "Ivan," he said, "we are like Heinz ketchup, we are pretty good, the problem is we are just slow getting there."

Montgomery County was a yearly opponent for the Lady Comets and Ralls said their sports crew always pulled for Hop, Sharon and West, when they weren't playing Montgomery.

Doug Ormay, the Kentucky Network sports director, called State tournament games for the Sweet Sixteen Network and has seen Hop's team since the early '90s.

He called Brown, "a great promoter of the sports and certainly girls basketball needed people like him. He was a promoter but not because he necessarily made a conscious effort at it, it was just him. He was a fabulous guy, who loved his players and who obviously truly loved him back and you could always sense that closeness."

Ormay noted that Hop always had time for the media and was so cooperative. He remembered being on the floor with a mike after the State Championship victory in the delirious mob and Hop calling him and all the crew by name and addressing them as his "friends." Ormay said the media is not used to hearing that kind of personal touch that Hop gave to you and it was a memorable moment. "Hop was a true character and I say that with great affection, because we need more coaches like him."

Chuck Mraz, sports director at Morehead's public radio, WMKY, has covered area basketball since the late-1980s and also broadcasts Morehead State University games.

He said that when he thinks of Hop Brown, he not only thinks of a legendary coach that produced an extraordinary list of accomplishments, but the legendary person he was. "I relished the opportunity to interview him, because it was always a lot of fun. Hop and I not only shared a conversation, but always a few laughs, as well."

He remembered that, "just spending a few minutes with him on the phone could actually turn a bad day into a much better one. For that, I will always be grateful to Hop. He was a great coach . . . but even a better man."

Tom Gemeinhart was a part of the Go radio-WUGO sports team for over three decades and Hop often consulted with him on statistics. "Mr. G" said that Hop Brown always conducted himself as a gentleman and a model for other coaches to emulate. "To win a game was important to Coach Brown, but not by resorting to unsportsmanlike behavior. At times when a player was not performing to her ability or not following instructions, he removed her from the game to hear a few choice words, but never to degrade her."

Tom remembered Hop's habit of simply throwing up his arms and walking away if he voiced his disapproval of an official's call but maybe didn't get a suitable response. Post-game interviews were always interesting, often funny, and sometimes took a moment to decipher. One incident Tom recalled was while listening to KJ's interview through his headphones, Hop had said he wanted his players to go "belly up." He got a funny picture in his mind of a dead fish floating belly up on the surface. Of course, he had misunderstood Hop's intention, in that he wanted the girls to play tight defense–belly to belly. He said, "Hop and I often exchanged barbs after the games since I was a Steelers fan and he, a big Browns supporter. Those post-game shows will be sadly missed."

The long-time voice of Ashland high school sports is Dicky Martin, who has referred to Hop Brown as a broadcaster's dream. "He was always one of the great interviews with kind words about his opponents or players. He always had a good joke to share." Martin declared that his experiences with Coach Brown have been "some of my most enjoyable in the radio business."

Denver Brown, has been sportswriter for the Morehead News Group that includes the *Olive Hill Times,* since the late 1990s. He takes a lot of joking from folks who thinks he and Hop are related, but they are not. He said, however, "There's nothing better than someone assuming you're a relative of Hop Brown, because he's an incredible person. It's the best compliment I can receive, being associated with that wild and wonderful Brown clan of Olive Hill."

Brown says you know from walking into the West gym and the banners hanging there about the "blood, sweat and yes, even tears" that Hop has put into building the West Carter girl's program.

He said he has relished the many wonderful talks he and Hop have had and not just about hoops, but about fishing, especially. He remembered one winter coming into the gym with a sunburn from being in Florida deep sea fishing. Hop had found out from his parents where he was and they immediately started talking about fishing. Hop told him he ought to write a story about Florida fishing for the paper. So with Hop's endorsement of the idea, he did.

"Hop Brown is the single most outstanding coach and motivator of young people that I know, and he has given this two-bit community sportswriter years of practices, games, and shoot-arounds to cover, but more than that, he has given me memories to last a lifetime."

Chip Cosby, a sportswriter for the *Herald-Leader* in Lexington has covered every coach who has passed through the state in the past decade, including Tubby Smith, Rick Pitino, Rich Brooks, Hal Mumme, Denny Crum. He wrote:

> If you ask me who my favorite coach of all-time is, it's without question, Hop Brown and it's not even close. I was a young reporter just out of college when I started at the *Herald-Leader,* and Hop was

the first coach that I really felt comfortable around. He made our jobs so easy. He was friendly; he was approachable, he was hilarious. And the thing most writers loved about Hop was that he always remembered your name, no matter who you were or what paper you wrote for.

Girls basketball really started to take off in the mid-to-late 1990s, and there's no question Hop played as big of a role as anybody in that. He gave the sport personality; he was the kind of pied piper that you need in order to make the game grow. I don't know of anybody who represented his community better than Hop Brown.

But for everything I could say about Hop as a basketball coach, it doesn't begin to measure up to how I feel about him as a person. They say the true measure of a man is his family, and when you get to know Hop's wonderful wife and children, that tells you all you need to know.

Jody Demling, veteran sportswriter for the *Louisville Courier-Journal,* said he had built a great deal of lasting impressions, through the years.

"I remember the first game I covered. I remember the first angry parent who called me a jerk, and I remember the first time I met most of the folks with whom I have had contact."

He came to the conclusion that he would never have a better lasting impression like the one of Hop Brown. While he had heard of Hop Brown and his funny ways and had met him on a few occasions, he had not had a lot of dealings with him until the State Tournament of 1998, He remembered:

> It was that year he made me laugh and smile and I've never been the same. You see, Hop was in the interview room and talking about the game that his team had just won in the opening round.
>
> He had just made that point that he had underwear older than Megen Gearhart and also that some people had said his team would have a long year, "I guess they were right, because we're still playing here in March." Hop said.
>
> I still to this day haven't been in a news conference where the entire place was almost on the floor crying because they laughed so hard. It was a treat.
>
> And it was also the start of a great friendship. Hop Brown is one of those folks in life that I truly admire and feel special to call my friend. It's the little things like the way to make everyone laugh in the media room, his way to smile, even after his team had lost a Sweet 16 game, and his way to call me during the season and just chat about basketball and life.
>
> Hop Brown is not only the best girls' basketball coach in the history of the state of Kentucky but he's a true friend and one you can't ever replace.

Each sportswriter and broadcaster carries a special memory of working with Coach Hop Brown. For 25 years, he provided the information, quotes, and comments they sought for reporting on the game. Their comments, in the post-game of Coach Brown's career, provide a fitting tribute to his work, his love for people, and dedication to that game he fondly called "roundball."

CHAPTER 13

THE STATS

John Hop Brown was the dean of 16th Region girls basketball coaches, working 25 straight years for the same team. He led his West Carter girls to the State championship, as well as 8 Region championships, 18 District titles, 10 Eastern Kentucky Conference championships and 12 EKC tournament titles. The accomplishments include a string of ten straight 62nd District titles, five consecutive 16th Region titles, ten consecutive years of EKC tourney champs and eight consecutive EKC regular season, first-place finishes. West was one of seven teams in the state to win five or more region crowns in a row.

His number of region titles ties boys legendary coach, Letcher Norton of Clark Co. in the late-1940s to mid-50s, and is one more than Roger Zornes, Boyd Co. boys coach.

His 514 victories is fourth on the all-time state list, (KHSAA as of 5/9/03) but the second best percentage of any coach at the same school for his career -71.7%. Howard Beth, who has coached at Marshall Co. 23 seasons, has an 85.9 winning percentage. Brown's eight appearances at the Sweet Sixteen is also among the top five. No other girls 16th Region coach has more than four region wins-(Claudia Hicks and Connie Greene)

Hop was selected Ky-Indiana All-Star coach in 2002, Mountain Shoot-Out Coach in 1989, Ky-Ohio All-Star Coach, four times. The MVP trophy for the Eastern Ky. Junior All-Star Girls Classic is named in his honor.

He has been EKC Coach of the Year, seven times, All-Area (*Independent* newspaper) Coach of the Year, eight times, State Coach of the Year, twice. He has received the Best Bencher award in the region from officials, seven times. KABC (Ky. Association of Basketball Coaches) Award in the region, eight times. He was Sportsman of the Year, 2001 in the *Independent* newspaper, Ashland.

West Carter Lady Comets-STATE CHAMPIONS 2000

West Carter Lady Comets 62nd District Champs—1979, 1980, 1984, 1987, 1988, 1989, 1990, 1991, 1992, 1993, 1994, 1995, 1996, 1998, 1999, 2000, 2002, 2003.

West Carter Lady Comets 16th Region Champs—1988, 1989, 1996, 1998, 1999, 2000, 2001, 2002

West Carter Lady Comets . . . EKC Tournament Champs—1988, 1989, 1993, 1994, 1995, 1996, 1997, 1998, 1999, 2000, 2001, 2002

West Carter Lady Comets . . . EKC Season Champs—1983, 1989, 1995, 1996, 1997, 1998, 1999, 2000, 2001, 2002

16th Region Runner-Up-1994, 2003

All-A 16th Region Champs-2002, 2003

All-A State Runner-Up-2002

Hop Brown's teams won 514 games and lost 203 in his 25 years of coaching for a 71.7% winning percentage. He was 41–8 in 62nd District Tournament play, 34–15 in 16th Region Tournament games, and 5–7 at the Kentucky Sweet 16.

Season ending records of Coach Brown

1979–13–7	1991–11–17
1980–15–7	1992–16–14
1981–16–8	1993–20–8
1982–14–10	1994–23–7
1983–18–8	1995–25–4
1984–8–16	1996–31–3
1985–2–15	1997–26–5
1986–7–15	1998–27–8
1987–19–9	1999–29–4
1988–26–7	2000–38–1
1989–29–5	2001–25–4
1990–19–11	2002–31–3
	2003–26–7

Three seasons of 30 wins or more, thirteen, 20–win seasons, and only four seasons, below .500

Best Record-38–1 '00; 31–3 '02; 31–3 '96; 29–4 '99;

West Carter in the State KHSAA Record Books

2000–01 3rd All-time in consecutive wins with 37

2000 Lady Comets hold the record for most Field Goals attempted in a season (2,270)

2000 Lady Comets hold the record for most Field Goals made in a season (1, 097)

2000 Lady Comets are 3rd all-time for most 3–point field goals attempted in a season-755

2000 Lady Comets hold the record for most 3–point field goals made in a season-301

1998 Lady Comets hold the record for most consecutive Free-Throws made-29

Kandi Brown is 3rd all-time in most 3–pointers made in a career-381 and in attempts -917

Mandy Sterling is 4th on 3–pointers attempted in a career-870

Mandy is 6th in 3–pointers made in a season at 109 and Kandi 8th with 105, both in the 2000 season.

Mandy Sterling is 9th in career field-goal attempts-2,048

Megen Gearhart is 4th in career assists -850 and Kandi Brown is 9th all-time in career assists-640.

Kandi Brown holds the state record for highest Free-throw Percentage-career 84.4% and Megen Gearhart is 4th at 82.3 % in her career

Megen Gearhart has the 2nd highest season Free-throw Percentage '02–90.1% and 4th for the '01 season at 87.2% and is 4th in consecutive free-throws made with 33.

Kayla Jones is 3rd highest season Free-throw Percentage '02–89% and is 5th in consecutive free throws with 30.

Megen Gearhart is 4th in career assists with 850.

State Tournament records-
Kim Brown, most 3–pointers 7, 1988 vs. Clark Co.
Kandi Brown, most 3–pointers made, all tournaments, 20

In the modern era, only one team, Laurel Co., with five, has won more than two State championships in Kentucky

The Lady Comets 2000 record of 38–1 is the best all-time season mark, but it is not deemed official by the KHSAA because of the post-season sanction of too many regular season games.

LADY COMET RECORD HIGHLIGHTS

POINTS-SEASON
Megen Gearhart 707 (02–03)
Kandi Brown 681 (99–00)
Marla Gearhart 644 (95–96)
Kandi Brown 616 (98–99)
Megen Gearhart 585 (01–02)

POINTS-SEASON TEAM
2908 (99–00)
2373 (95–96)
2170 (02–03)
2159 (01–02)
2127 (88–89)

FIELD GOAL % 2'S–SEASON
SEASON
Jennifer Justice 63% (95–96)
Kayla Jones 60% (00–01)
Kayla Jones 60% (99–00)
Kandi Brown 57% (99–00)
Stefanie Rose 57% (92–93)

FIELD GOAL % 2'S–CAREER
Jennifer Justice 56%
Kayla Jones 54%
Marla Gearhart 51%
Jessi Jones 51%
Amy Tackett 50%
Megen Gearhart 50%

FIELD GOALS % 3'S-CAREER
Kandi Brown 42%
Kim Brown 39%
Mandy Sterling 38%
Mira Gearhart 38%
Megen Gearhart 35%
Michelle Tabor 35%

POINTS-CAREER–1000 pts
Megen Gearhart 2711
Kandi Brown 2599
Mandy Sterling 2377
Marla Gearhart 2264
Meghan Hillman 1722
Mira Gearhart 1683
Kayla Jones 1527
Michelle Tabor 1470
Sheila Porter 1250
Pam Biggs 1224
Brenda English 1154
Gina Taylor 1016
Annette Messer 1000

FIELD GOAL % 2'S TEAM-

53% (99–00)
51% (00–01)
51% (95–96)
48% (02–03)
46% (01–02)

FIELD GOAL % 3'S-SEASON
Kandi Brown 49% (99–00)
Mandy Sterling 45% (99–00)
Kandi Brown 45% (98–99)
Kandi Brown 45% (97–98)
Stephanie Hall 43% (00–01)

FIELD GOALS-3's CAREER
Kandi Brown 381
Mandy Sterling 333
Megen Gearhart 283
Michelle Tabor 257
Mira Gearhart 230
Kim Brown 141

FIELD GOAL % 3'S-SEASON
40% (99–00)
37% ('03,'02,'99 '98 '97)
MOST 3'S IN A SEASON
301–(99–00)
209–(02–03)
206–(95–96)
203–(01–02)

MOST 3's IN SEASON
Michelle Tabor 115 (93–94)
Mandy Sterling 107 (99–00)
Kandi Brown 105 (99–00)
Stephanie Hall 96 (02–03)
Kim Brown 89 (88–89)
Madonna Tackett 84 (89–90)
115 by Tabor was State record
   that year
89 by Brown was State record
   that year

MOST 3'S IN A GAME
Mandy Sterling 8 (99–00)
Steph Hall, Kandi Brown
Michelle Tabor,
Kim Brown 7

FREE THROW %-SEASON
Megen Gearhart 90% (01–02)
Kayla Jones 89% (01–02)
Michelle Tabor 88% (93–94)
Megen Gearhart 87% (00–01)
Kandi Brown 86% (99–00)

FREE THROW % -CAREER
Kandi Brown 84%
Megen Gearhart 82%
Amy Tackett 80%
Michelle Tabor 79%
Mira Gearhart 77%

Gearhart's 87% in '01 and 90% in '02 were State records for that year.

West Carter was 1st in the State in Free Throw Shooting Team-Season in '02–81% '03–76% '01–76% '99–73% '96–71%

They shot 70% in '98 and '00

Megen Gearhart hit 33 consecutive Free Throws in 02–03, Kayla Jones hit 30 in 01–02 and Kandi Brown hit 29 straight in 98–99.

REBOUNDS-SEASON
Kandi Brown 313 (97–98)
Meghan Hillman 297 (99–00)
Sheila Porter 277 (87–88)
Tammie McGlone 271 (89–90)

REBOUNDS TEAM-SEASON
1249 (99–00)
1139 (88–89)
1115 (97–98)
1106 (87–88)

REBOUNDS-CAREER
Meghan Hillman 1289
Kayla Jones 1086
Kandi Brown 1077
Sheila Porter 850
Stefanie Rose 788

DEFLECTIONS-CAREER
Kandi Brown 787
Megen Gearhart 769
Kayla Jones 531
Cathy Day 482
Meghan Hillman 391

BLOCKS-SEASON
Meghan Hillman 89 (00–01)
Meghan Hillman 84 (01–02)
Kandi Brown 73 (99–00)

STEALS-SEASON
Kandi Brown 149 (99–00)
Brenda English 139 (87–88)
Mandy Sterling 133 (99–00)
Marla Gearhart 123 (95–96)
Megen Gearhart 106 (99–00)

STEALS-TEAM-SEASON
625 (99–00)
498 (93–94)
495 (94–95)

ASSISTS-SEASON
Megen Gearhart 203 (99–00)
Kandi Brown 177 (99–00)
Megen Gearhart 172 (00–01)
Kandi Brown 172 (97–98)
Marla Gearhart 165 (93–94)

DEFLECTIONS-SEASON
Kandi Brown 273 (99–00)
Kandi Brown 229 (97–98)
Mandy Sterling 180 (99–00)
Megen Gearhart 172 (99–00)
Megen Gearhart 164 (02–03)
Cathy Day 164 (99–00)

DEFLECTIONS-TEAM
1127 (99–00)
758 (97–98)
647 (02–03)

BLOCKS-CAREER
Meghan Hillman 263
Kandi Brown 140

STEALS-CAREER
Megen Gearhart 481
Marla Gearhart 464
Kandi Brown 449
Mandy Sterling 414
Kayla Jones 330

ASSISTS-CAREER
Megen Gearhart 850
Marla Gearhart 674
Kandi Brown 640
Mira Gearhart 486
Mandy Sterling 443

HOP'S GIRLS . . . THRU THE YEARS

1978–79–Julia Sparks, Angie Messer, Brenda Reynolds, Charla Bauers, Elizabeth Dalenberg, Annette Messer, Kathy Kitchen, Larae Kiser, Kim Stafford, Lisa Messer, Nici Raybourn, Lori James

1979–80–Charla Bauers, Elizabeth Dalenberg, Annette Messer, Kathy Kitchen, Lisa Messer, Nici Raybourn, Connie Baker, Diana Bradley, Pam Biggs, Brenda Carpenter, Cheryl Nolen, Jill Vincent

1980–81–Annette Messer, Kathy Kitchen, Nici Raybourn, Lisa Messer, Brenda Carpenter, Cheryl Nolen, Pam Biggs, Connie Baker, Lisa Jones, Lenore Sparks, Dana Smith, Linda McGlone

1981–82–Brenda Carpenter, Pam Biggs, Lenore Sparks, Nici Raybourn, Cheryl Nolan, Lisa Messer, Linda McGlone, Dana Smith, Connie Baker, Lisa Jones, Falissa Greenhill, Shawna Keener

1982–83–Cheryl Nolan, Connie Baker, Lisa Jones, Pam Biggs, Dana Smith, Lenore Sparks, Tammy Crank, Linda McGlone, Falissa Greenhill, Pam Skaggs, Melissa Elliott, Cindy Piper

1983–84–Dana Smith, Lenore Sparks, Tammy Crank, Falissa Greenhill, Cindy Piper, Candie Baker, Rena Bond, Candie Messer, Shannon Minor, Sue Lynn Stiles, Lisa Waggoner, Annie Douglas, Janena Greenhill

1984–85–Cindy Piper, Candie Baker, Candie Messer, Rachael Henderson, Suzi Layne, Jana Jones, Samantha Layne, Elizabeth Tomlin, Karla McDowell, Sheila Porter, Becky Middleton,

1985–86–Sheila Porter, Carolyn Reynolds, Rena Bond, Candie Baker, Rachael Henderson, Gina Taylor, Suzi Layne, Jana Jones, Wendy Tackett, Kim Brown, Brenda English, Karla McDowell

1986–87–Rachel Henderson, Suzi Layne, Sheila Kay Porter, Jana Jones, Samantha Layne, Karla McDowell, Kim Brown, Brenda English, Gina Taylor, Missy Greenhill, Amy Mays, Carolee Barker

1987–88–Samantha Layne, Karla McDowell, Sheila Kay Porter, Kim Brown, Brenda English, Melissa Greenhill, Gina Taylor, Carolee Barker, Amy Mays, Tammie McGlone, Stephanie Rayburn, Madonna Tackett

1988–89–Kim Brown, Brenda English, Missy Greenhill, Gina Taylor, Carolee Barker, Donna Gilliam, Tammie McGlone, Malissa Minor, Stephanie Rayburn, Madonna Tackett, Nancy Birchfield.

1989–90–Carolee Barker, B.J. Hogg, Tammie McGlone, Malissa Minor, Stephanie Rayburn, Madonna Tackett, Nancy Birchfield, Charity Brown, Chelle Gilliam, April Knipp, Lori Mays, Lauri Sparks

1990–91–Nancy Birchfield, Charity Brown, Chelle Gilliam, Lori Mays, Laurie Sparks, Missy Taylor, Charissa Barker, Karla Brown, Michele Garvin, Stephanie Kiser, Stacy Piper, Stefanie Rose, Michelle Tabor

1991–92–Lori Mays, Laurie Sparks, Melissa Taylor, Ute Halbritter, Betsy Bailey, Charissa Barker, Karla Brown, Michele Garvin, Stacy Piper, Tracy Piper, Stefanie Rose, Michelle Tabor

1992–93–Stefanie Rose, Karla Brown, Amy Tackett, Marla Gearhart, Kimber Rayburn, Michelle Tabor, Betsy Bailey, Charissa Barker, Jennifer Justice, Tracy Piper, Tara Duncan, Michele Garvin, Stacey Carter, Ginger Brown

1993–94–Michelle Tabor, Amy Tackett, Stefanie Rose, Candy Boggs, Tara Duncan, Stacey Carter, Ginger Brown, Marla Gearhart, Shonda Goodan, Jennifer Justice, Kimber Rayburn, Jessica Jones, Summer Whitton, Mira Gearhart

1994–95–Tara Duncan, Stacey Carter, Candy Boggs, Jessi Jones, Summer Whitton, Mira Gearhart, Marla Gearhart, Amy Branham, Kimber Rayburn, Shonda Goodan, Wanda Dean, Jennifer Justice, Ginger Brown, Carrie Jones

1995–96–Ginger Brown, Marla Gearhart, Jennifer Justice, Kimber Rayburn, Amy Branham, Becky Collingsworth, Carrie Jones, Jessi Jones, Wanda Dean, Mira Gearhart, Jennifer Faulkner, Kandi Brown

1996–97–Amy Branham, Becky Collingsworth, Carrie Jones, Jessi Jones, Summer Whitton, Beth Baker, Wanda Dean, Mira Gearhart, Leigh Pendlum, Jennifer Faulkner, Stephanie Lyons, Kandi Brown

1997–98–Mira Gearhart, Wanda Dean, Beth Baker, Leigh Pendlum, Kerri Day, Kandi Brown, Shanna Shelton, Cathy Day, Chelsa Hamilton, Kayla Jones, Meghan Hillman, Megen Gearhart

1998–99–Kandi Brown, Kayla Jones, Meghan Hillman, Cathy Day, Megen Gearhart, Chelsa Hamilton, Kerri Day, Shanna Shelton, Nicki Burchett, Wendy DeBord, Cassondra Glover, Leah Frasier

1999–2000 STATE CHAMPIONS
41 Kandi Brown 5'11 Sr.
42 Shanna Shelton 5'4 Sr.
34 Mandy Sterling 5'9 Sr.
45 Nicki Burchett 5'6 Jr.
40 Cathy Day 5'5 Jr.
30 Leah Frasier 5'3 Jr.
32 Cassondra Glover 5'6 Jr.
55 Robin Butler 5'7 So.
31 Chelsa Hamilton 5'4 So.
43 Kayla Jones 5'9 So.
50 Meghan Hillman 6'1 So.
35 Megen Gearhart 5'5 Fr.
33 Jenise James 5'10 Fr.
44 Brooke Mullis 5'9 Fr.

2000–01–Cathy Day, Megen Gearhart, Meghan Hillman, Kayla Jones, Cassondra Glover, Brooke Mullis, Jenise James, Stephanie Hall, Kelli Issacs, Nicki Burchett, Leah Frasier, Robin Butler, Chelsa Hamilton, Brandi Rayburn

2001–02–Kayla Jones, Meghan Hillman, Megen Gearhart, Brooke Mullis, Steph Hall, Brandi Rayburn, Jenise James, Chelsa Hamilton, Robin Butler, Leigh Audra Perry, Courtney Duncan, Kelly Barker, Shawnte Minor, Sarah Barker

2002–03–Megen Gearhart, Steph Hall, Jenise James, Brooke Mullis, Brandi Rayburn, Leigh Audra Perry, Kelly Barker, Sydnie Cox, Kelly Shelton, Ashley Shelton, Kristin Burchett, Charla Burchett

LADY COMETS—Early Years

1973–74–Jody Burchett, Shirley Rice, Sandy Wilburn, Patricia Viars, Fredia Clark, Carla Rice, Brenda Gearhart, Suzanne Burchett, Tammy Vanlandingham, Cheryl King, Janet Sparks. Mike Barker, coach

1974–75–Sue Ann Burchett, Ellen Abrams, Garnet Messer, Marcella Logan, Tammy Vanlandingham, Julie Sparks, Debbie Maddix, Joe Ann Edison, Freida Clark, Angie Messer, Brenda Leadingham, Sandi Wilburn, Kathy Gee, Shirley Rice, Mike Barker, coach

1975–76–Linda Dunaway, Kathy Erwin, Maggie Damron, Angie Messer, Patty Fultz, Brenda Cooper, Marsha Terry, Tammy Wilson, Brenda Reynolds, Jenny Lowe, Ingrid Camron, Ellen Hicks, Sherry Blevins, Marcella Logan, Julia Sparks, Natalie Camron, Garnet Von Messer. Kathleen Lewis Mullins, coach

1976–77–Julia Sparks, Garnet Von Messer, Glenda Rimer, Kim Stafford, Elita Duvall, Marcella Logan, Annette Messer, Brenda Reynolds, Charla Bauers, Angie Messer, Lisa Messer, Benita Molton. Bette Greenhill, coach

1977–78–Nici Raybourn, Marcia Miller, Kathy Kitchen, Donna Shoemaker, Pam Biggs, Larae Kiser, Brenda Reynolds, Lori James, Garnet Von Messer, Annette Messer, Elita Duvall, Julia Sparks, Angie Messer, Charla Bauers, Lisa Messer. Kathleen Lewis Mullins, coach

THE THINGS THAT A GREAT TEAM DOES

WORKS TOWARD A COMMON GOAL
DEVELOPS ITS MEMBERS SKILLS
EFFICIENTLY USES ITS TIME AND TALENTS
EMBRACES THE DIVERSITY OF ITS MEMBERS
COMMITTED TO CONTINUOUS IMPROVEMENT
BUILDS MORALE INTERNALLY
PERFORMS EFFECTIVELY AND PRODUCES RESULTS
ACCEPTS CRITICISM AND PRAISE
COOPERATES WITH OTHERS RATHER THAN COMPETE
MAINTAINS A POSITIVE ATTITUDE TOWARD EVERYONE'S IDEAS
STAYS ON TASKS
USES ITS RESOURCES WISELY
COMMUNICATES OPENLY
TEACHES AND LEARNS FROM ONE ANOTHER
RESOLVES CONFLICTS EFFECTIVELY
WELCOMES CHALLENGES
SHARES PRIDE IN ITS ACCOMPLISHMENTS
CELEBRATES SUCCESS

THE EPILOGUE

ON August 27 2003, at 4 a.m. JOHN HOP BROWN died at his home in Olive Hill. The community heard the news on the radio that morning, and while expected, his death cast a veil of sadness over the school and community. Locally, it was front-page headline news. Coach Brown had lost his battle with brain cancer, but everyone knew he had won in the game of life.

He was 53 years old, and was survived by his wife of 33 years, Sharon, his daughters, Kim Johnson, Karla Brown, Kandi Brown, and son, Kyle. He had three grandchildren, Dalton, J.T. and Kelsey, and was survived by his mother, Betty, by three brothers, Clell, Gary and David and three sisters, Janie, Nancy Sue and Maxine.

Tributes from all over the state were heard on radio, TV and seen in newspapers, as the media hailed the accomplishments of one of Kentucky's most colorful and loved high school coaches. Fellow coaches and players spoke of Hop's great influence on them and the game of girls basketball.

The school issued a statement saying they had lost one of their most loyal faculty members. "Coach Brown was not only a shining example to follow at school; he was a compassionate friend, mentor, and positive role model for everyone. His unique sense of humor and always positive comments made people realize what a joy he was to be around. Coach Brown's passing leaves an emptiness in the Comet community that will never go away."

The coaching staff declared, "we have lost the best friend we ever had and not just a friend but a brother. The one thing we will always remember about Coach Brown is his positive attitude and how he expected us to be the same way. Not only is this a loss to the community but to girls basketball as well."

Stephanie Hall, will be a senior on the first team without Coach Brown, "In my eyes Coach was more than special, he was a gift from God. He touched many lives and he changed my life completely. He took my hand and heart when I was young and showed me how to live, how to care and love, and make the best out of my life, I could. He just wanted to see people happy and enjoy life, enjoy it as he did."

It was the biggest funeral the small town of Olive Hill had ever witnessed as family, friends, coaches, players, and fans came to the Hop Brown Court at West Carter gym to pay their respects on Saturday, August 30th. A place that had resounded with many cheers now saw tears flowing freely because the physical presence of a person of such caliber would be missed, yet remembered forever. Former players gathered to offer comfort to each other as they mourned the loss of a man who was more than a coach to them, but a friend and father-figure.

The program was highlighted by the message from Dick Damron, the eulogy read by George Steele, prayer and comments from Dave Shanklin and poem from Tim Carper.

Damron characterized Hop Brown as a successful coach, good husband and father and a true friend. He quoted the great football coach Ara Parasheghian who wrote: "A good coach will make his players see what they can be rather than what they are." Damron said Coach Brown did this and that his life was spent building relationships, truly a big key to success.

Using the Scriptural references of I Corinthians 3:10-15, Damron concluded that Hop Brown had built his life, not of hay or stubble, but with the best materials possible. "A life of commitment to do and be the best he possibly could, whether it was loving his wife, rearing his children, or coaching his girls. This man was a success."

But Damron noted, that his commitment to his Lord and Maker capped all these and truly made him great.

The day was called a celebration of Hop Brown's special life and music was provided by the group New Creation, Gerad and Alicia Parker, and Philip Stephans. Thirty pallbearers served including rival coaches. The scoreboard at the gym was set at 58-50, the final score of the 2000 State title game, with four fouls listed on number 41, Kandi Brown, the way it was when the final horn sounded on the greatest moment of Lady Comet history.

The service ended with an audio tribute to the coach that had aired on GO radio, the day after his death. It included excerpts from interviews, and special events with the final words from Hop:

"I love each and every one of you…..good night!"

The family expressed their heartfelt thanks to the hundreds of people who had been with them through the difficult final eighteen months. "We know there is no way that we could thank everyone who has been there for us because words could never express our gratitude for your thoughts and prayers."

John Hop Brown was laid to rest in the Garvin Ridge Cemetery near his boyhood homeplace on Clark Hill.

The final horn had sounded for Hop Brown and he went to receive that ultimate trophy on the court of heaven. (II Tim.4:7-8)

 John Hop Brown 1950-2003

"Winning isn't everything,
but wanting to is"

A LIFE GIVEN TO THE LOVE OF "ROUNDBALL"

Lessons for Basketball and Life from Coach Brown

STAY POSITIVE.....HELP SOMEONE TODAY.....WORK HARDER THAN YOUR OPPONENT.....SHOOT THE LONG ONE.....PLAY AS A TEAM.....DRESS WITH CLASS.....SAY SOMETHING GOOD ABOUT OTHERS.....LAUGH A LITTLE TODAY.....KEEP ON WANTING TO WIN.....NEVER GIVE UP.....

"We'll see you later, brother"
-- Hop Brown, 8/26/03

Olive Hill, Ky.